**WRITE LIKE YOU TEACH**

# Chicago Guides to Writing, Editing, and Publishing

*Writing for Social Scientists: How to Start and Finish Your Thesis, Book, or Article, Third Edition*
Howard S. Becker

*Writing Your Journal Article in Twelve Weeks: A Guide to Academic Publishing Success, Second Edition*
Wendy Laura Belcher

*Writing Fiction: A Guide to Narrative Craft, Tenth Edition*
Janet Burroway, with Elizabeth Stuckey-French and Ned Stuckey-French

*Writing Abroad: A Guide for Travelers*
Peter Chilson and Joanne B. Mulcahy

*The Architecture of Story: A Technical Guide for the Dramatic Writer*
Will Dunne

*The Business of Being a Writer, Second Edition*
Jane Friedman

*From Dissertation to Book, Second Edition*
William Germano

*Getting It Published: A Guide for Scholars and Anyone Else Serious about Serious Books, Third Edition*
William Germano

*On Revision: The Only Writing That Counts*
William Germano

*From Notes to Narrative: Writing Ethnographies That Everyone Can Read*
Kristen Ghodsee

*Storycraft: The Complete Guide to Writing Narrative Nonfiction, Second Edition*
Jack Hart

*Thinking Like a Political Scientist: A Practical Guide to Research Methods*
Christopher Howard

*Write No Matter What: Advice for Academics*
Joli Jensen

*Economical Writing: Thirty-Five Rules for Clear and Persuasive Prose, Third Edition*
Deirdre Nansen McCloskey

*Developmental Editing: A Handbook for Freelancers, Authors, and Publishers, Second Edition*
Scott Norton

*The Writer's Diet: A Guide to Fit Prose*
Helen Sword

*Write Your Way In: Crafting an Unforgettable College Admissions Essay*
Rachel Toor

A complete list of series titles is available on the University of Chicago Press website.

# WRITE LIKE YOU TEACH

## TAKING YOUR CLASSROOM SKILLS TO A BIGGER AUDIENCE

### JAMES M. LANG

The University of Chicago Press  *Chicago and London*

The University of Chicago Press, Chicago 60637
The University of Chicago Press, Ltd., London
© 2025 by The University of Chicago
All rights reserved. No part of this book may be used or reproduced in any manner whatsoever without written permission, except in the case of brief quotations in critical articles and reviews. For more information, contact the University of Chicago Press, 1427 E. 60th St., Chicago, IL 60637.
Published 2025
Printed in the United States of America

34  33  32  31  30  29  28  27  26  25      1  2  3  4  5

ISBN-13: 978-0-226-82325-6 (cloth)
ISBN-13: 978-0-226-83967-7 (paper)
ISBN-13: 978-0-226-83966-0 (e-book)
DOI: https://doi.org/10.7208/chicago/9780226839660.001.0001

Library of Congress Cataloging-in-Publication Data

Names: Lang, James M., author.
Title: Write like you teach : taking your classroom skills to a bigger audience / James M. Lang.
Other titles: Chicago guides to writing, editing, and publishing.
Description: Chicago ; London : The University of Chicago Press, 2025. | Series: Chicago guides to writing, editing, and publishing | Includes bibliographical references and index. | Audience term: Teachers
Identifiers: LCCN 2024047448 | ISBN 9780226823256 (cloth) | ISBN 9780226839677 (paperback) | ISBN 9780226839660 (ebook)
Subjects: LCSH: Authorship. | Rhetoric.
Classification: LCC PN147.L323 2025 | DDC 808.0024/3711—dc23/eng/20241030
LC record available at https://lccn.loc.gov/2024047448

♾ This paper meets the requirements of ANSI/NISO Z39.48-1992 (Permanence of Paper).

# CONTENTS

*Prologue* ix

| | | |
|---|---|---|
| **INTRODUCTION: WRITE LIKE YOU TEACH** | | **1** |
| Expanding Your Audience | | 5 |
| The Benefits of Writing for the Public | | 7 |
| From Product to Platform | | 9 |
| A Sort of Book Overview | | 11 |
| Final Gift | | 14 |

| | | |
|---|---|---|
| **1** | **INTRIGUING QUESTIONS** | **16** |
| | Identifying Questions | 19 |
| | Creating Better Ideas | 23 |
| | From Idea to Action | 28 |
| | Why Do Readers Need Your Great Ideas *Right Now*? | 31 |
| | Strategies: Questions, Answers, Actions, Timeliness | 35 |
| | Final Question | 36 |

## 2 WRITING DESIGN — 39
Choosing Structures — 42
Setting the Pace — 53
Maintaining the Throughline — 56
Strategies: Structures, Pacing,
    Throughlines — 61
Final Possibilities — 62

## 3 USING EVIDENCE — 65
Varying Evidence — 68
Streamlining Evidence — 72
Contextualizing Evidence — 75
Telling Great Stories — 81
Strategies: Varying, Streamlining,
    Contextualizing, and Storytelling — 85
Final Confession — 86

## 4 CULTIVATING READER ATTENTION — 89
Openings — 91
Text Divisions — 95
Small Attention Tools — 100
Closings — 108
Strategies: Openings, Text Divisions,
    Small Attention Tools, and Closings — 112
Final Enthusiasm — 114

| **5** | **INVITATIONAL LANGUAGE** | **116** |
|---|---|---|
| | Words, Sentences, Paragraphs | 119 |
| | Invitations to Think | 130 |
| | Being Good Company | 137 |
| | The Readers in the Room | 142 |
| | Strategies: Words, Sentences, Paragraphs; Invitations to Think; Being Good Company; and the Readers in the Room | 145 |
| | Final Imperative | 146 |
| **6** | **REVISING AND EDITING** | **149** |
| | Moving | 151 |
| | Adding | 157 |
| | Cutting | 160 |
| | Listening | 163 |
| | Strategies: Moving, Adding, Cutting, Listening | 167 |
| | Final Injunction | 168 |
| | **A FINAL WORD** | **171** |

Appendix: Submitting, Publishing, and Promoting a Book: A Syllabus  173

Acknowledgments  217

Notes  221   Bibliography  229   Index  233

# PROLOGUE

In the spring of 2021, in the wake of some middle-aged deliberations about the purpose of my life, I decided that I would step away from my twenty-year career as a professor of English at a small liberal arts college to devote more of my time to writing. I accepted a retirement package offered by the college and shifted from full-time teaching and part-time writing to an even split between the two. I accepted an adjunct position in my former department to teach a course in British literature in the fall, and I launched a series of writing projects designed to keep me busy for the foreseeable future.

Seven weeks into the fall semester, five months after my early retirement, an infection attacked my heart, landing me in the hospital, where I stayed for the next three months. The cardiology team tried everything to save my heart, but the inflammation caused by the initial infection had done irreversible damage. But we live in an age of wonders, and in late December, I received a heart transplant. I returned home in early January 2022 with a donor's heart beating in my chest. Everyone who receives a heart transplant will spend the rest of their life taking medicines that suppress their immune system to prevent rejection of the donated organ. The doses of those live-saving medications are gradually reduced over the course of one's first year, but in the early months after transplant, patients are especially vulnerable to infections and illnesses. I was cautioned to stay at home for the first month or two post-transplant and leave the house only for medical appointments.

In late February, two months after my transplant, my wife and I spent a weekend on Cape Cod in Massachusetts. I had determined that this weekend would mark my first outing in a public building, and I had already scouted the location. Cape Cod can be a lonely place in February, a far cry from the madding crowds that swarm there every summer. I could have gone into dozens of stores and been the only customer. But this English professor made an obvious choice for his first outing: a used bookstore. I had visited there the previous summer and found a bibliophile's dream in an old house stuffed with ancient volumes tottering over uneven shelves.[1]

My wife dropped me off and went to run some errands. I set foot inside the store and inhaled a grateful breath of learned dust motes. Like any good used bookstore, the layout was a maze of narrow corridors and unexpected nooks opening from seeming dead ends. Over the course of my wanderings, I noticed a shelf or two devoted to classical studies, and I paused there; I had recently been reading a novel that referenced Homer's *Odyssey*, which had made me want to reread the Greek classic. On a high shelf I spied a battered old copy of Homer's epic—a little too battered for my taste—but a different book caught my eye instead: *The Greek Way*, by Edith Hamilton, a semischolarly series of reflections on the flowering of Greek civilization in the fifth century BC. I bought *The Greek Way*, which was first published in 1930 by W. W. Norton, and in the coming days I read it with great pleasure.[2]

While Hamilton's scholarly reflections on the ancient world pleased this onetime student of Greek and Latin, I found even more fascinating the origins of the book in Hamilton's life story.[3] In 1867, she was born in Germany to American parents, who returned shortly afterward to the United States. Her father, who had degrees from Harvard and Princeton, kindled in his oldest daughter an interest in the language and literature of the classic world.

She attended Bryn Mawr College as an undergraduate and then spent a year in Germany continuing her study in the languages and literature of Greece and Rome. She had intended to pursue graduate studies, earning a doctorate in classics, but the field of education came calling instead. In 1896, after she had returned to the United States, she was invited to join the staff at a college preparatory school for women, the Bryn Mawr School in Baltimore. She became the first female head in the school's history and spent the next twenty-six years in that position. She retired in 1922, in part because of some health issues, at the age of fifty-two.

And then her story takes a fascinating turn.

In her retirement Hamilton began writing scholarly articles for academic journals, drawing on her lifetime study of classical authors. She eventually crafted a fuller summary of what she saw as the achievements of the ancient Greeks in philosophy, politics, literature, and art. Her choice of thinkers and artists to profile has its quirks—Plato has a featured role; Aristotle hides in the shadows—but it covers enough territory for her to establish large themes and track them through diverse areas of Hellenistic life. The book straddles a delicate line between academic audiences and the more generally well-educated reader. Hamilton titled it *The Greek Way*, and it was published in 1930, after she turned sixty-two.

Strange to think of it now, in an era more focused on lionizing books from the latest business mogul or lifestyle influencer, Hamilton's semischolarly analysis of Greek culture was selected as a Book of the Month Club title, found a wide audience, and went through many printings. Spurred on by the success of *The Greek Way*, Hamilton went on to write many more books on ancient civilizations of the West, as well as several translations of Greek dramas. Her work was feted by scholars and the public alike. She received honorary doctorates from the University of Pennsylvania and Yale University. She continued writing throughout her eighties; at the age of ninety she visited Greece to great acclaim, where King Paul of Greece honored her accomplishments and she was made an honorary citizen of Athens.

The trajectory of Edith Hamilton's life, and the late success she achieved as a writer, gave me the first glimpse of the core argument that animates this book: the skills we develop as teachers enable us to become great writers. When I read her elegant prose, which has continued to enchant me since I encountered *The Greek Way*, I see the mind of a teacher at work. I recognize the familiar moves that great teachers make as she grabs the attention of her readers, guides them through complex material, and crafts sentences and images that stick in the mind. Like any good teacher, she tells fascinating stories about her subject matter, but she doesn't shy away from the hard work of analytic thinking. She reminds readers frequently why they should read these ancient authors and how their stories and texts remain ever current to modern readers. She doesn't cheerlead or canonize, but the reader can feel her passion and devotion to her subject.

Reflecting on Edith Hamilton's life transition, from teacher to writer, not only inspired the approach that I develop in this book but also continues to inspire me as a teacher, a writer, and—once again, much to my surprise—a professor. Six months after I came home from the hospital—at the age of fifty-two, the same age in which Edith Hamilton began her second life—I began giving workshops and presentations on teaching and writing, speaking about my previous books and developing the ideas you will find in these pages. One of those presentations inspired a teaching center at a research university to offer me a position as a professor of practice. When the director asked me what I could contribute to the many existing programs they were already offering for faculty, my response was immediate: I was writing a book about the connection between writing and teaching, and I wanted to offer a seminar for faculty who wish to expand their audiences through public forms of writing. In January 2024, when I finally met my class of aspiring faculty writers, I felt myself closing a long and circuitous loop.

On the first day of that seminar, I showed my faculty-students an image of Edith Hamilton and explained how she had opened my eyes to the ways in which the teaching and writing vocations inform each other. I promised that we would engage with ideas and examples from great writers and educators, and draw from their own experiences and convictions as teachers, to create new audiences for their writing. By the time they finished the seminar, I said, I hoped they would have written something new—something that would challenge them, give them new opportunities in their lives, and maybe even quicken their pulses with energy and excitement. I shared a little bit of Hamilton's story, and some of my own. Then we began our journey together.

I'm grateful for the privilege of launching it again now, with you, in the pages that follow.

# INTRODUCTION

*Write Like You Teach*

This book has a simple thesis: if you want to write great nonfiction, *write like you teach*. Nonfiction writers create learning experiences for their readers, just as teachers create learning experiences for their students. Instead of guiding students through learning activities in the classroom, nonfiction writers practice their pedagogy with readers on the page. They inform their audiences about new discoveries in science, encourage readers to step back from the present and learn from history and biography, teach them to develop new skills and habits, or convince them to conceive their lives and societies in fresh and unusual ways. They leaven their research with story and example, capture and sustain the attention of their audiences, and provoke them to think, discuss, and respond.

Unfortunately, the great educators who work in the classroom don't always perceive how their work can translate to the page. A couple of years ago I consulted with a business professor who wanted to write a book about how small-business owners could better understand and manage the commodities in their industries. At that time I had been doing some freelance editing for an organization that helped graduate students and faculty achieve their writing goals, and this faculty member reached out to me after attending one of my workshops. In our initial meeting, he expressed his desire to write a book that would help regular people navigate the complex economics of commodities. I prompted him to share his vision for the project. He described how he could support his ideas with spreadsheets, formulae, and screenshots of relevant data from his years of academic research. He explained the premises of his arguments, and they were couched firmly in the technical language of his discipline. I shrank slowly into my chair, in part because even the dumbed-down explanations of his subject he was offering were flying over my head. He had come to me because he was stuck, and I wasn't sure I could help him.

Then he stepped back and mentioned, almost as an afterthought, that this topic mattered to him because he had grown up on a farm in another country, and his father struggled his whole life to understand how to deal with the fluctuations of the agricultural market. He remembered how one year his father got lucky, sold his produce at the right time, and piled presents under the family Christmas tree that year. Other years the children received almost nothing. This story had me sitting up a little straighter in my chair. I asked him to explain how his potential book could have helped someone like his father. He launched immediately into a brief and layperson-friendly explanation of how commodities work. The transformation from academic researcher to teacher was instantaneous, and marvelous to see. Could you write a book, I asked him, that would teach small-business owners like your father, who might not have formal business education, to understand your solutions and apply them? He looked thoughtful. "I suppose so," he said, stroking his beard. And to do that, would they need all the data from the spreadsheets and formulae and screenshots he was telling me about? He paused. "Not really." With those dominoes fallen, the pathway opened up in his brain. To achieve his writing goals, he just needed to teach. He had been doing that for his entire career.

I intend for this book to serve as the bridge between classroom practices and writing practice, because too many academics either don't see that bridge or fear to cross it. Many academics experience the writing process as an intimidating or even paralyzing one. Reframing writing as an act of teaching can prove immediately enabling, as it did for that business professor.

Having accepted this book's core thesis only starts the process, though. The challenge of writing like you teach will play out in the many choices you will make as you put words on the page. The same holds true in the classroom. Great teachers don't have static approaches; they experiment with new techniques, improve existing ones, and respond to the specific learners in the room. A group of teachers in a pedagogy workshop might all agree on the value of a new teaching strategy they have learned but walk out and implement it the next day in varied ways in their classrooms. Most of the chapters in this book will thus review research-based or innovative teaching strategies, offer examples of how great teachers implement them in their classrooms, and then give you specific ways you can translate those practices into your writing.

Note my use of the word *great* in that last sentence. That's an essential modifier to the notion that you should write like you teach. You can certainly compose a nonfiction book in the same way that a poor lecturer anesthetizes an audience: launch immediately into dense theories, cram content into every moment of the hour, monologue long after students have packed up their things and exited the room. Instead, in this book we will follow the lead of teachers who care about their students, have an interest in how students learn, and love to explore, discover, and invent in the classroom. We will consider the questions that great teachers ask themselves before a learning journey gets underway: How do I make these students curious about the subject? What stories or examples will illustrate the more difficult concepts or theories in the course? When will I pause in the class and give their brains a break from hard thinking? What will I do at the end of the class to remind them about its key messages, and leave them wanting to learn more about my fascinating subject matter?

Although I make no claims to be a great teacher, I have spent much of my career studying great teachers. Teaching was not my first subject; twentieth-century British literature was. I spent twenty years as an English professor at a liberal arts college. But back in graduate school I had become fascinated by research about how people learn and what that research implied for how I should teach my own courses. This fascination turned me into a serial experimenter as a teacher, always searching for new ideas to implement in my literature and writing courses. A dozen years into my professorial career I founded a Center for Teaching Excellence on my campus and directed it for the next eight years, observing and talking with great teachers at my institution and beyond. I launched my own writing career by becoming a participant-observer in the higher education classroom, writing essays and books about my experiences and reflections. In this book I will continue to draw from that lifelong engagement with teaching and learning in higher education to help you adapt the practices of great educators.

I hope that my experiences as a teacher and a studier of great teachers will resonate with the teachers who are reading this book. But two other parts of my professional life will inform the recommendations that you find here. Although a very small number of my publications have appeared in traditional academic outlets, most of them have been written for more public audiences. Early in my writing life I decided that I wanted to engage with readers outside my specialized academic discipline. It took many painful editorial rejections and much painstaking writing practice to learn how to draft prose that would appeal to readers (and editors) who had backgrounds and interests that differed from mine. As I learned to deploy the writing techniques you will learn about in this book, I saw the fruits of my craftwork ripen. You will read a few of my own publication stories, and the lessons I have learned from them, in the chapters that follow. But more frequently I will also provide examples of great nonfiction from many authors, such as Edith Hamilton, who model what it looks like to help a reader learn.

The second pillar of support for the ideas I will pass along comes from my work as an editor. In 2013 I cofounded a trade book series at the West Virginia University Press and shepherded fifteen titles from a hopeful author's query email to a finished book. Some of those titles have wildly exceeded the expectations of their authors, this editor, and the press. The best-selling titles in the series have sold several thousand copies or more, and several have gone well beyond that figure. The authors of those titles have become in-demand speakers on college campuses around the world. All of them were college and university faculty members who applied their pedagogical expertise to the business of educating readers. I have learned much from observing the author journeys of these writers, and what I have learned from them I hope to pass along to you.[1]

## EXPANDING YOUR AUDIENCES

I will teach these lessons with a particular goal in mind: not only to help you become a better nonfiction writer but also to *expand the readership* for your research and ideas. Not all scholars who produce great writing have ambitions to broadcast their writing beyond the purview of the practitioners of their discipline. Their scholarship may occupy a rich and important place in their professional lives by securing jobs, supporting tenure and promotion cases, or chasing after grants and fellowships—and that's enough for them. If you fall into that category, I still hope you will find the lessons from this book useful as you continue to develop your skills as an academic writer.

But while I assume that your research and writing matter on their own terms, I also assume that your work has broader implications that you'd like to convey to a wider set of readers. Suppose, for example, that you research shell morphology in deep-sea snails, but you want nonacademic readers to learn from these fascinating creatures how we are slowly poisoning the world's oceans. To reach those readers, you will have to make different decisions about the shape of your specific pieces of work. Essays composed for academic journals look different from ones published in *Slate* or the *New York Times*. Traditional works of academic scholarship from a specialized university press look different from ones published by Basic Books or Norton. And books that appeal to the colleagues in your department might not appeal to your neighbors. At the heart of those differences will be the writer's awareness of their audience: their interests, their prior knowledge, their reading habits.

Such awareness will be familiar to any teacher. In teaching as in writing, we don't project prepackaged content into the void. We attune our strategies to the minds in the room, considering their interests and prior education. If my department chair asks me to teach a new course in British literature, I won't start the course design process until I know the nature of my audience. Am I teaching a survey course for incoming first-year students to fulfill a general education requirement, or a senior seminar for English majors? The answer to that question will condition every major decision I make about the course: amount of content, the nature of the assignments, the classroom strategies I deploy on a daily basis. The first-year students need more background information before they can fully engage in the discipline's core questions, which might translate to a few more lectures than I might give in the senior seminar. The first-year students, familiar with the constraints of high school writing, will receive a limited choice of possible topics for a traditional essay as a way to transition them into higher education; the seniors can peruse a menu of possibilities to demonstrate their learning at the end of the semester, from traditional essays to podcasts and video productions. Even if both courses essentially center on the same content area and have similar goals, my awareness of the audience will create distinctive learning experiences.

Whether you realize it or not, you have a lifetime of practice in modifying your writing in the same way: tuning and retuning it in service to particular audiences. Perhaps you discovered in high school that your biology teacher only wanted the facts, while your English teacher welcomed your personal stories. You learned to adjust your writing strategies accordingly. In graduate school you might have observed two faculty members on your thesis committee argue about some issue in your writing; you had to find a way to make them both happy. As you acquired your degrees, you had to further develop your writing skills as you began authoring essays and books for peers in your field. You tailored your written submissions to different journals, different editors, different conferences. And even in your daily correspondence or committee work, which might take up much of your time these days, you continue to write like a chameleon: composing an email to the provost in one register, and the next one to your best friend on campus in another; drafting an assignment sheet for students and then turning to the committee report you are coauthoring for the board of trustees.

Awareness of audience drives both good teaching and good writing. The writing strategies in this book should help you jump the gap between composing sentences and paragraphs for one set of learners—your disciplinary colleagues and fellow experts—to communicating those ideas in writing to readers who don't share your deep background knowledge and your lifetime devotion to your subject. Long after you have finished this book, I hope you will continue to remind yourself of the special skill you have in shaping your expertise in response to specific learners, whether they live on your campus or pay occasional visits to the classrooms of your prose.

## THE BENEFITS OF WRITING FOR THE PUBLIC

No doubt, teaching the widest possible audience of readers—the equivalent of teaching students who are fulfilling a general education requirement—can be a challenge for academic writers. The most successful nonfiction writers, the ones you find on bestseller lists, have spent years honing the craft of writing for the public in blogs, essays for news and culture outlets, and even on social media. They have run the gauntlet of agents and editors and critics, perhaps many times before they achieved success.

Is it worth it?

My own experience has led me to believe the answer is an enthusiastic yes. The rewards that you can reap from expanding your audiences can come in many forms: new career opportunities, both at your home institution and elsewhere; easier access to publications in which you can share your research, such as the op-ed pages of national publications; financial boons from book advances and royalties; honoraria for lectures and consulting; and—my favorite—the opportunity to travel and share your ideas in places with people you might otherwise never have encountered. I have experienced many of these rewards myself and have observed them make a positive impact in the lives of other authors.

But however many of these benefits might accrue to you personally, it's equally important to remember that expanding your audience can make a positive difference to the world. As William Germano argues in his book *Getting It Published: A Guide for Scholars and Anyone Else Serious about Serious Books*:

> Serious nonfiction permits writers to share reflections with our not very reflective society. One could mount the argument that academics have a social obligation to publish—not because many have jobs that taxpayers support, but because the scholar's pledge to the advancement of learning must be a *public* advancement. And publishing, down to its etymological roots, is about making ideas public.[2]

Our research and ideas can play a role in human and planetary flourishing, whether we are studying the root systems of trees to reveal new discoveries about biological communities or extracting new insights about religious belief from the worship ceremonies of ancient peoples. Scholars who can lose themselves in the minutiae of their field sometimes need to remind themselves of the thread that connects their object of study to advances in our understanding of medical science, vaccine safety, mental health treatments, the environment, ancient history, art, religion, government, and all the many other things that contribute to a good human life.

Suzanne Simard is a professor of forest ecology at the University of British Columbia whose research focuses on the ways that trees can communicate with each other through fungal networks in the soil. She poured three decades of research into her book *Finding the Mother Tree: Discovering the Wisdom of the Forest*, published by Vintage Books in May 2021. The book received glowing reviews in the *New York Times* and the *Wall Street Journal*. Then by some strange pathway, her book leaped into an even more public view. In October of that year, she began to receive texts from friends who let her know that her research had been mentioned by a character on the popular TV comedy show *Ted Lasso*.

She had never heard of the show, and she had hardly been seeking that kind of pop publicity for her work. "I mean, I'm a scientist, right?" she said in an interview with the Canadian Broadcasting Company. "I'm used to having my head down and writing and publishing journal articles and being out doing experiments and teaching." But then she realized that this dissemination of her work could help her advance causes that she had deeply cared about. "This is what we need," she said, "this kind of publicity over science. And so I'm happy about that."[3] The newfound awareness of her work strengthened her ability to promote research-based forest renewal practices to a range of audiences, and she continues to educate the public about her life's passions.

No amount of work you put into building your platform (a process described in the next section) will guarantee that you and your research get mentioned on an Emmy-winning television show, but that only happened to Suzanne Simard because she decided that she wanted to educate a broader public about her work. Had her work stayed in the pages of academic journals, it seems much less likely that she would have received that unexpected attention from *Ted Lasso*—and that attention enabled her to further educate the public about how we care for our forests.

## FROM PRODUCT TO PLATFORM

As a reader of a successful book like Simard's, I might be understandably focused on the final product: her finished book. But the reason her book was able to make a splash in the world is because a lot of other kinds of labor went into getting it the hands of readers—every piece of which would have tested her ability to translate her research into terms that were accessible to a variety of new audiences.

Those demands would have been placed on her throughout the entire process, from drafting her initial ideas to promoting the book after it was published. That work likely started when Simard reached out to an agent with an email inquiry: an audience of a single person. Then she would have been asked to craft a book proposal, which would then have been reviewed by an editor and then by an editorial board. Then she would have drafted the book with the help of other audiences along the way: perhaps some trusted reader friends, or a writers group; an editor who provided feedback on the manuscript; an editorial committee or board for final approval. Even after she submitted the final draft, that work wasn't finished. A copy editor would go through the manuscript one more time, and Simard would still be offering language and ideas to the marketing and promotion people at the publisher.

When the book was published, an entirely new set of audience-based demands was then placed on her. Simard would have been asked to promote her work on podcasts and interviews, including one conducted at the Hay Literary Festival in Wales. She wrote short essays based on the book for popular publications. She participated in the filming of a documentary on her work. She gave multiple talks and lectures presenting her research and ideas to the public. She maintains a website and social media accounts focused on her research. Her book sits at the center of all this activity, but it extends out from it in many directions. All of them contribute to her awareness about how to write to a variety of audiences as well as to communicate with them via many channels.[4]

*Building a platform* is a common way to describe all of this extra-textual labor. Visualize it by combining the notion of an audience with the image of a platform. If you are standing on the ground in a corner of a room, you can reach an audience of perhaps a dozen. If you are standing on a large stage in a large auditorium, you have now multiplied your audience several times over. But such raised platforms do not appear by magic. You have to build them, plank by plank. Every podcast, every op-ed, every social media post sets another plank in place.

Building your platform is part of the long game of being a successful writer in the twenty-first century. Focus on producing great books and essays, yes, as your primary task. Those pieces of writing deserve your full attention and skill. But every new reader you reach with *this* specific piece of writing might become part of the audience for your *next* piece of writing. As your audience slowly grows from each new piece of writing and promotion, you are establishing your presence as an expert in your field. And when you are ready to submit a query or a proposal or a manuscript to the potential buyer of your work—editor or agent—you will make the strongest case for yourself if you can stand on a platform that faces a packed auditorium of readers, all of whom are waiting for your next project. Thus while the primary focus of this book remains largely on creating a nonfiction book or essay, I will make occasional references to platform building opportunities and challenges, and the book's appendix—which takes the form of a syllabus on how to submit your ideas to editors, guide a manuscript through the editorial process, and promote your published work—will offer specific strategies to succeed in that work.

### A SORT OF BOOK OVERVIEW

Here we are, nearing the final pages of this introduction, and you might have noticed that I have not given you a detailed layout of the book's plan. Such overviews are commonplace in academic books, as the writer provides a blow-by-blow account of each chapter. As a reader, I find such detailed overviews stultifying. I like to get the main idea of the book in its introduction, and maybe a sense of its main arc. But my eyes glaze over when I am staring down ten paragraphs intended to describe content I will be reading in short order anyway.

Thinking like a teacher, I would argue that the nonfiction reading experience, like a classroom experience, should include an element of suspense. My favorite moments in the semester are the class periods when I walk into the classroom and say, "We're going to try something a little unusual today." Students quickly learn that those days are ones in which I have designed something to create a little fun. I want the same thing for my readers. I want you to learn from this book, but I also want it to give you reading pleasure. As mystery writers have long taught us, we all enjoy a little bit of suspense. You should have the book's destination in view by now—using pedagogical thinking to expand the readership for your writing—but our exact route will be revealed chapter by chapter. (As any experienced reader might recognize, you can always give yourself a very aerial view of this book's territory by checking the table of contents to get a sense of the teaching-writing connections I will make.)

But I do want to mention two features that will appear throughout the book, both of which are designed to inject some (optional) active learning into the reading experience. First, at the end of each chapter you will find writing prompts connected to one or more of the chapter's core recommendations. Although I hope individual readers will find these exercises useful, I really intend them as a resource for teachers and writers who gather in groups over the course of a few days, weeks, or months and support one another as they read the book's chapters, engage with the exercises, and develop and hone their writing skills in the service of manuscripts in progress.

A second active learning feature encourages you to engage with a writing and editing tool that deserves the attention of any writer in the third decade of the twenty-first century: generative artificial intelligence (AI) programs (such as ChatGPT, Copilot, Claude, and whatever new names they have invented for themselves by the time you are reading this). I would not have written this book, and continued to write books of my own, if I did not believe that outputs from large language models should not replace writers. The books that have educated me have reflected the mind of a unique human tackling difficult questions, inspiring me with their passion for their subject, beguiling me with beautiful sentences, or coining striking phrases that opened new pathways in my brain. I relish the prospect of encountering the strange machinations of another person's thinking and seeing how it can modify my own. When I want basic information, I am happy to consult a technical manual or an instructional video or an artificial intelligence tool, whether that's a search bar on the internet or prompt box in a generative AI program. When I want a deep engagement with a subject, I turn to a human. I don't want to play the role of a futurist, but I don't foresee the demise of our desire to meet and learn from both teachers and nonfiction writers.

At the same time, most of us in higher education have recognized that learning-supporting machines can help us do our work more effectively. We rely on learning management systems, digital engagement tools, or platforms upon which students can complete assignments. We can take the same approach to generative artificial intelligence (GenAI) in supporting writing. It can serve as a research assistant, an always-available editor, or an intellectual sparring partner. I have thus inserted "GenAI Callouts" within most of the book's chapters. Those brief sections explain how GenAI tools can model, intensify, or support the book's recommended writing strategies—but never replace them. The callouts contain suggestions for prompts that could benefit nonfiction writers.

But I remain neutral about whether you should use AI tools to support your writing. I leave that decision up to you. If you prefer to write your manuscripts by hand or draw your inspiration from walks in the woods, by all means ignore those callouts. If you have a phone filled with personal productivity apps and your courses are delivered with the latest digital pedagogies, I hope they will strengthen your ability to expand the audiences for your research.

**FINAL GIFT**

If you flip quickly through the book, you will notice that the titles of each chapter's concluding sections follow a set pattern: they pair the adjective *final* with a noun: "Final Recommendation," "Final Example," "Final Caveat." The chapters thus finish not so much with standard restatements of the chapter's main ideas but instead with an invitation to reconsider the content of the chapter in a new way. I like to think about these concluding sections as each chapter's final gift. This might seem like a presumptuous metaphor, but the idea of authorial gift-giving was suggested to me by Robin Bernstein, a professor of cultural history at Harvard and the author of *Racial Innocence: Performing American Childhood from Slavery to Civil Rights*.

Since Bernstein's book was published in 2011, she has increasingly been writing for wider audiences, inside and outside the academy, including op-eds for the *New York Times*. She has written about the challenges that she encountered while working on her book, including confronting discouraging metaphors that convinced her that writing a book was like climbing a mountain or jumping over a high hurdle. While she was struggling with these thoughts, a friend told her that she needed to think about the task in front of her another way. "Your book in progress is a gift," her friend said, "not a test. It's a gift you will give the world." This metaphor struck a chord in Bernstein's mind, and that turn of phrase eventually helped her change her approach to her writing.[5]

That friend's metaphor reminds us that the specific gift that academic writers are prepared to offer to readers is the same one that we offer as teachers to our students: learning. In our classes, as in the pages of our writing, we are offering people (in Bernstein's words) "the gift of discovering or understanding something new."[6] The research and thinking you have done in your field have made you especially qualified to give the gift of learning. The world needs the unique gift that only you can offer, whatever it might be. When we use our writing to build bridges from our disciplines to public audiences, we are performing a service to the cause of human flourishing.

I hope that my final gift to readers of this book, in addition to the specific writing lessons it offers, will be confidence. Right now you are facing down the daunting challenge of writing for new audiences.

You can meet those challenges by drawing from the tools you already possess.

You are a teacher. You help people learn.

Write like it.

**CHAPTER ONE**

# INTRIGUING QUESTIONS

I once attended a teaching workshop in which the facilitator encouraged us to review and revise our course descriptions—the brief overviews of our courses that appear at the top of our syllabi.[1] Those few sentences or paragraphs, usually couched in benign and abstract prose, might not seem like they deserve much attention. They can read like afterthoughts to the real work of creating a syllabus: laying out the course topics, learning objectives, assignments, and materials. But that workshop facilitator convinced us (and I have remained convinced ever since) that course descriptions can spur teachers to think deeply about the purpose and shape of their courses. Which is why it's such a shame, and a wasted opportunity to inspire learning, when students start reading the syllabus and meet a course overview that reads like this:

> CHEM:1070 provides students with an introduction to chemistry and is designed for students who have not had an advanced chemistry course in high school or for student [*sic*] who plan to take only one year of chemistry. Students will develop concepts and learn specific chemical information that will be applied within the context of chemistry related problems and applications. Through participation in course activities, each student should expect to

improve his/her knowledge of chemistry, to develop improved qualitative and quantitative problem-solving skills, and to learn the attitudes and practices of scientific investigators. The course comprises three 50-minute lectures or two 75-minute lectures (faculty instructors) and a 50- minute discussion session (TA). The course requires a significant time commitment (an average of 4 hours in-class and 6-9 hours out of class per week). Grades are based on exams (three 1.5-hour exams and a 2-hour final exam), homework/quizzes, and completion of lecture/discussion activities.[2]

To be sure, there is important information in here: the audience for the course, its requirements, and some descriptions of the topics and skills that will be addressed. But if you are not a chemist, who would be able to recognize the importance and fascinating nature of this material, I'm guessing you probably didn't jump out of your seat and yell, "YEAH, CHEMISTRY! LET'S GO!" Whatever the course and professor will *actually* be like, what this course overview implies is that students are going to sit in a chair for fifty minutes, three times per week, and have complicated things explained to them.

Course overviews, on their own, might not have a major influence on student learning or motivation in a college course. But great teachers have thought deeply about what makes their course material so interesting, fascinating, mysterious, useful, and more. The course description gives teachers a formal space where they can put their creative thinking about the course into words. Course descriptions invite students to take on a learning journey that will lead them to unexpected places in their thinking or even their lives—as James Egan of Brown University does in this course description:

> Can you be confident that the person sitting next to you on the bus is really a human rather than some remarkable replica conjured up by a mad scientist or, perhaps, an alien from another planet? What evidence is needed to conclude that the person casually looking

at her mobile device is human? . . . How have we constructed the conceptual boundary between what we qualify as human and what we categorize as robotic, animal, android, or alien? What, in the end, makes the human "human"?[3]

This brilliantly constructed series of questions starts with one grounded in a concrete scenario, and then grows in scope into big, philosophical queries. While these questions should make us think and wonder, this course description also suggests that this course has been designed with curiosity and questioning in mind and will not be a content dump by a lecture bot.

Your first task as an author looking to expand your audience is to think like James Egan does in his course description, articulating what will make your Big Idea so intriguing to learners, whether they are editors or potential readers. Too many books, proposals, and articles written by academics falter on the shoal of "Providing Content," instead of recognizing that our first task as writers is to excite the curiosity of a reader. You might have a great idea, or a sweeping view of some facet of the human condition, or a useful skill you can teach to your readers. But unless you spend time thinking and writing about what will bring people to the table—including editors—your great idea won't get the readership it deserves.

Your research and your teaching have given you expertise in a specific area, and you probably already have topics and ideas in mind for a book. The first three sections of this chapter provide a blueprint for shaping your existing ideas into book topics that will entice readers into a transformative learning experience. The first step in that process is to brainstorm the **questions** that will pique the curiosity of a potential reader and provide the impetus for your project. From your questions will arise your potential answers—the heart of your book. But while you might have a good answer in mind already, I'll suggest that most answers improve when they are put in **dialogue with other answers**. With your questions and answer in view, you can then ask yourself a key question: What do you want readers to do/think/value when they have finished reading? Essentially: How will your project **change your audience**?

The first three sections of the chapter provide guidance for shaping your idea; the last one speaks to its framing. Most nonfiction writing connects itself to the concerns of the **present moment**, but writers have considerable leeway in how they define the present moment: this week, this year, this century, this millennium. Even if we are debating eternal truths, we should consider how we can offer current pathways into those perennial dialogues.

## IDENTIFYING QUESTIONS

One of my favorite examples of a successful book written by an academic author illustrates the power of questions to drive the presentation of academic research to a public audience. Robert Sapolsky is a primatologist at Stanford University and the author of a book that has now sold more than 200,000 copies since its first publication by Macmillan in 1994. It has been through three editions and has more than two thousand reviews on Amazon, with an average score of 4.5 out of 5 stars. Here are the title and subtitle of the first edition:

> *Why Zebras Don't Get Ulcers: A Guide to Stress, Stress-Related Diseases, and Coping*

The main title poses a very specific question, one that almost sounds like a riddle or setup for a joke. (OK, I'll bite, why don't zebras get ulcers?) But when you combine the main title and the subtitle, you realize the deeper implications of the book's question: Why do humans suffer from the effects of stress, while most animals don't? Most wild animals live a precarious existence in which they are subject to predation by other animals (including humans). They spend most of their time hunting for food and water and responding to shifts in their environments. In the face of all of this, why don't animals consult therapists, take benzodiazepines, or slowly worry themselves to death? What's the difference between animals and humans when it comes to stress? What can we learn from the animal kingdom that would help us understand stress?

The subtitle offers a promised answer to this question. This is a very common strategy in book titling: the work's main title raises the question, and the subtitle gives a hint of the answer we'll find if we open the book and start reading. In the subtitle the key word is *guide*, which tells readers not only that they will receive information about the questions posed in the previous paragraph but also that they will receive advice about how they can reduce or manage the stress in their own lives. You'll see many variations of that important little word. Two of my works include the word *lessons* in the subtitle, which imply that I am going to give you some advice. You'll find no shortage of book subtitles using words like *tips*, *advice*, and *guidance*. In most cases, the advice represents the author's answer to the question raised by the main title.

But your project doesn't have to give advice or guidance or tips; instead you might be looking to spark discussion, provoke reflection, or make arguments about your subject matter. All of these are promised in Beverly Daniel Tatum's now classic work, *"Why Are All the Black Kids Sitting Together in the Cafeteria?" And Other Conversations about Race*. Note first the intriguing question raised in the title. I remember being taken aback by the title when the book came out, and feeling vaguely uncomfortable about it: are we supposed to ask questions like that? But that was exactly the point of the book, which Tatum encapsulates in the word *conversations* in the subtitle. Frank conversations about race are missing in the education of our children, she argues, because so many educators are afraid of saying or doing the wrong things. She draws on her work as a psychologist, educator, and parent to make the case that we should "embrace the conversations," as she explained in an interview on the publication of a twentieth-anniversary edition of the book in 2017.[4]

You might scan your nonfiction bookshelves and notice plenty of books in which the question doesn't jump out from the title. But if you want to become adept at raising questions yourself, get in the habit of sleuthing out the main question of nonfiction books and essays you are reading. *How We Read Now: Strategic Choices for Print, Screen, and Audio*, an Oxford University Press title from linguist Naomi Baron, does not broadcast its question in its title. But within the first few pages she articulates it clearly: Given the different ways in which we *can* read, she asks, which form of reading (print, screen, or audio) seems to produce better learning? She hints at the book's content in a phrase from the subtitle: "strategic choices." (The answer to this question, as with every complex issue in the world, is that it depends. Print definitely has a general advantage when we are reading for learning, but there are times when the other two choices might serve our specific needs better.) Hence even titles or book premises that don't raise questions explicitly will still have an intriguing question embedded in their skeletal structure.

If this book were a writing workshop, this would be the point at which I would ask you to stop and articulate the question for your writing project. But since I have done exactly that with many faculty writing groups, I have learned that many first-time authors approach that task by reverse engineering a question that will allow them to deliver a preprepared lecture about their subject. An environmental scientist might start with: *How do lawn fertilizers impact the local environment?* Academics love *how* questions, because the responses to them require an explanation from an expert like you. They do the same work as plant questions given in advance to a friend in the audience at a lecture. ("Good question: In fact, I happen to have some relevant slides for that . . .") But for both you and your reader, the real questions are lurking underneath the grass: *Most people are aware of the damage that lawn fertilizers can do to local waterways. Why do they still keep using them? Why do people like lawns so much that they are willing to endanger the wildlife or water quality in their own backyards? Why and when did we start valuing crisply manicured patches of grass on our properties? Have we always behaved like this? How do other societies curate their outdoor spaces?*

Such questions might push you further than you intended to go in your writing project. Uncharted territories loom ahead—and that can be scary. But if you aren't challenged and puzzled by your own questions, neither will your reader be. At whatever point you might be in your writing project, now would be a great time to pause and write out your driving question. Then push yourself further. What are the harder, more unanswerable questions beneath that question? What are the deepest *why* questions in your subject? What bodies of research would those questions demand you consult—including ones that might draw you far afield from your expertise? Think about this process as offering yourself a new challenge in your scholarly and writing life. Get excited about the possibility of reading different kinds of books, collecting new data or field notes, discovering new people whom you can consult or interview.

If you find yourself stuck in terms of developing a really challenging question, think about the questions that drive the great nonfiction books you have read or that have been prominent in your field. What are their *why* questions? One of the best pieces of advice I ever received as a young and aspiring writer has stayed with me for a couple of decades now, and I still follow it when I am thinking about writing a book in a specific area. Go to a good bookstore or the nearest library, find the bookcases or shelves dedicated to your subject area, and start pulling down titles. The person who gave me this advice wasn't thinking about finding questions inside of books; he was advising me on how to ensure that I would have something new to say and not simply repeat what others had written. But follow this same practice with the goal of identifying the deep questions of as many books as you can pull off the shelf.

You don't have to go to a bookstore or library to scan books for their questions. You can read the first few pages of many nonfiction books by using the "Read Sample" feature on the virtual book purveyor that dominates our landscape today. Nor do you have to limit your research to books. Great articles in periodicals such as the *Atlantic*, *Aeon*, or even major newspapers will also spring from intriguing and baffling questions. But the advice I received about visiting bookstores has made a positive difference in my writing career, so I'm passing a slightly revised version of it along to you. Set aside a little time to visit the nearest bookstore or library, park yourself amid the bookshelves dedicated to your discipline, and look for great questions.

## CREATING BETTER IDEAS

So now you've come home from your trip to the library, taken a walk, and landed upon your driving question. The answer you eventually develop in response to that question will be your Big Idea. When you first present your work to an editor who acquires manuscripts for a publisher, you should have mastered a quick description of both your Question and your Big Idea. You have spotted a gap in the traditional models of your field, or you have come to believe that something important in your discipline needs to find space in the public consciousness. Ideally you have discovered something new in your laboratory, collected pioneering survey data, or realized that the traditional interpreters of a literary or historical event have been getting it wrong for decades now.

But in my work as both teacher and writer, I have come to believe that Big Ideas expand and improve when they rub against other Big Ideas. Before you jump into your chair and start writing, spend some time testing your idea in dialogue with others and see what emerges. We often use this strategy when we are designing upper-level or graduate courses in our discipline, especially when we are trying to attract students into the seats. I can design a course entitled "The Post-1945 British Novel" and rehearse to students the themes that I first began studying in graduate school. But the course will engage students more deeply, and challenge me as a thinker, if I marry that content area with an intriguing question: In the face of the waves of immigrants who came to the United Kingdom in the wake of the Second World War, how do the writers of those small islands conceive—and even shape—what it means to be "British"? Conversely, a political scientist could design a course around a fundamental question about British national identity but then create a fascinating interdisciplinary course in which students apply abstract political theories to the work of British novelists. Both the question and the content area on their own can teach people things, but the hybrid created by putting them in dialogue has the potential to generate unexpected learning, thinking, or writing.

I recognized the power of idea hybridity on the page during my long nonfiction-writing apprenticeship. Since the fall of 1999, I have been producing 1,500-word essays for the *Chronicle of Higher Education* every month or two. The *Chronicle* has published more than two hundred of them as of this writing. The challenge with a monthly column is to come up with new ideas to write about every month. Over time I have learned that seeds of column ideas come to me all the time, just by virtue of the fact that I am regularly teaching, parenting children (including a few college-aged kids), and reading essays and books about teaching and learning. Because I have written so many columns at this point in my career, I can quickly germinate the seed of an idea into a focused look at something that will resonate with my audience: a review of a pedagogy book, a description of an interesting teaching technique, an experience from my classroom. These kinds of columns tend to have a simple point or practical takeaway, without making too much fuss about the writing. These are serviceable-idea columns.

But the best columns I have written, the ones that have generated the most responses and of which I am especially proud, come from another place. These are the columns in which I start with a good idea, and then—either inspired by the muse or just by the randomness of human experience—put that idea in dialogue with a completely different one. Forging a new connection between two disparate areas of thought and then creating a synthesis of them has been the most reliable pathway to Big Ideas for me. Once I started to become deliberate about using this strategy, and saw its positive effects in my own writing, I began to teach it to my students. In my creative nonfiction courses, I would ask students to write three or four short paragraphs, each of which focuses on a different essay topic—and then surprise them by asking them to take two of these discrete topics and intertwine them into a single essay. This technique doesn't always work, but when it does, it regularly yields the best essays in the course.

Good ideas, described well and supported with the kind of research that academics love, can lead to jobs and promotions and the admiration of your disciplinary peers. But if you are looking to reach a wider audience for your writing—not to mention inject some new creativity into your thinking and your life—you need to push those good ideas into new, interesting places. They have to find new dance partners to inspire some new choreography. The great ideas that emerge from those dances are the ones that will catch the eyes of editors. Remember that *good* ideas are pitched to editors every day; *great* ideas must stand out.

When the coronavirus pandemic hit in the spring of 2020, many of us had to learn in a hurry how to teach online. A host of potential writers who were already online teaching experts had the same idea: people need guidance for connecting with students and building a sense of community in an online course. Many of us did indeed need guidance on this issue (I sure did), and for my book series with West Virginia University Press we accepted a couple of proposals in this area. But as the pandemic continued ad nauseum, the proposals on this topic just kept coming. They were all perfectly serviceable proposals or manuscripts, solid ideas, but they pretty much started to look exactly the same. Eventually when an email popped into my inbox that used the words *online* and some variation of *community*, I knew exactly what was coming, and I took an almost immediate pass.

Aspiring authors would have needed to develop a new synthesis of ideas to break through that conceptual logjam. For example, what if an online learning specialist studied communities that

### GenAI Callout

I have come to relish the act of combining disparate ideas when I am undertaking a new writing project. It satisfies my creative urges more than anything else in the development of an essay or book. When an unexpected pairing of ideas or texts or fields suddenly opens a new writing pathway, it lights my remaining hairs on fire. But if that brainstorming process doesn't yield immediate results for you, you can turn to generative artificial intelligence (GenAI) for some inspiration. As Ethan Mollick argues, in his popular Substack feature on GenAI, these tools have a special facility for this work:

> In the real world, most new ideas do not come from the ether; they are based on combinations of existing concepts, which is why innovation scholars have long pointed to the importance of recombination in generating ideas. And LLMs [large language models] are very good at this, acting as connection machines between unexpected concepts. They are trained by generating relationships between tokens that may seem unrelated to humans but represent some deeper connections.*

You can prompt GenAI in two ways to create combination models for you to emulate or explore further. First, you can play with it by asking to combine and recombine random areas of your own expertise or interest, as in this prompt that combines literature and pedagogy: "What works of recent British literature could illustrate the challenges of teaching neurodivergent learners?" (As always, you will need your expertise or some additional research to evaluate the quality of the bot's results; two of the novels that ChatGPT recommended were by American authors.) If you come to the prompt box with some vague sense that a connection exists between two fields or ideas but you are struggling to determine whether that the connection will lead anywhere productive, you can feed it a different prompt: "What can teachers in higher education learn about neurodiversity from *The Curious Incident of the Dog in the Night-Time* by Mark Haddon?" As you evaluate the results of such prompts—in this case, ChatGPT offered seven possible connections—you might realize that your vague idea doesn't have much traction, or that it merits an essay instead of a book, or that it sparks enough of your own curiosity to pursue the connection into a larger project. Ideally, your experiences creating such prompts and evaluating the outputs will lay the foundation for shifting the locus of this creative work from your digital device to your creative and unique brain—the traditional source of the world's best Big Ideas.

*Ethan Mollick, "Automating Creativity," in *One Useful Thing*, Substack, August 13, 2023. https://www.oneusefulthing.org/p/automating-creativity?utm_source=profile &utm_medium=reader2.

existed *outside* higher education and analyzed their community-building practices—and experimented with applying those strategies to online courses? How do people bond in multiplayer games? How does a yoga studio build community among its participants? What makes religious believers feel connected to their pastors and their fellow parishioners? Perhaps such idea breeding might have led nowhere—or it might have inspired that author to discover something new that would help struggling online teachers. Not every idea we develop has to be developed in synthesis with one or more ideas, but it will never hurt to spend a little time thinking about your first idea, whatever it might be, in dialogue with others and see what might emerge.

## FROM IDEA TO ACTION

Consider the final class period of your favorite course to teach. You have survived another semester. You see winter break or summer on the horizon. You are feeling philosophical about your life's work, reflective about the experience of the course, a little nostalgic for the months you have spent with this group of students. As you stand before them on the final day, you intend to remind them about the Big Idea of the class. But you want more than this. You want your course to have made a positive change in the lives of your students. You want them to understand why that Big Idea *matters*. What should they *do* with what they have learned? Maybe you articulate this in your send-off speech, or with some final activity on the last day of the semester, or in an email sent out before the final exam.

In a writing project, you should pose a parallel question to yourself: When a reader has closed the final page of your book, how will they have been changed by the experience? Instead of just cramming a response into your final paragraphs or pages, let it shape the book as a whole. BJ Fogg is the founding director of the Behavior Design Lab at Stanford University and the author of *Tiny Habits: The Small Changes That Change Everything*. The premise of the book is pretty well encapsulated in its title. He presents research and guidance for how people can develop and sustain new habits in their lives. Fogg builds his argument from research in psychology, experiments from his own research lab, and the many dozens of stories he tells about people who have used his habit-forming system to make sustained changes in their lives. One running example he uses throughout the book is the case of someone who wishes to improve their health by adding daily push-ups to their routine. Fogg uses his behavioral system to argue that if you want to build up this habit, start *very* small. Start your coffee brewing, do just two push-ups, and then reward yourself with the taste of your freshly brewed coffee. Tie your habit to an anchor (coffee brewing), start small (two push-ups), and then reward yourself (delicious coffee).

From its opening to its closing pages, Fogg keeps the purpose of the book directly in front of the reader's face. Adopt his system, he argues, and you'll be happier in life.

Your great idea likewise might be oriented toward improving the daily lives of your readers. But maybe you have a different outcome for your Big Idea. Johann Hari is not an academic, but he conducts pretty extensive research both through reading and through interviewing academic experts. His book *Stolen Focus: Why You Can't Pay Attention—And How to Think Deeply Again* (2022) is a disturbing dissection of the ways in which tech and social media giants are arrayed against us all and our desire to stop feeling distracted all the time. We can't battle such powerful forces as individuals, he argues; instead, we need a grassroots movement to fight back against the tech giants that are destroying our focus for their financial gain. He lionizes a few tech rebels from within the industry and urges readers to follow their example: "We all need to decide—are we going to join them and put up a fight? Or are we going to let the invasive technologies win by default?"[5] He encourages his readers to support industries, companies, and activities that will allow us to reclaim our attention in the face of constant technological creep, from the use of internet blockers to a return to reading physical books. But ultimately, he wants to start a revolution.

So what do you want readers to do when they put down your book, or swipe to the next thing on their laptop or smartphone screen? Consider the possibilities:

- Make changes to their daily habits.
- Find greater fulfillment in their work or leisure lives.
- Embark on a new adventure, see someplace new, take up a new passion.
- Perform their jobs or life tasks more effectively, such as parenting or time management.
- Educate themselves further about your subject—and then educate others about it.

- Join (or start) a movement—environmental, political, social, antitechnological.
- Engage in service of some sort, such as volunteering at poll stations or feeding the poor.
- Adopt a new mindset toward a commonly misunderstood problem or challenge in life.

Gain clarity on your project's purpose by considering it in light of your audience. If you want to start a revolution, who would be best positioned to launch or join it? Write with those readers in mind. In this book I am writing to college faculty who feel baffled or intimidated by the prospect of writing for nonacademic audiences. That purpose led me to include writing prompts and exercises, as well as boiled-down summaries of writing strategies at the end of each chapter.

As a way to push writers to articulate the purpose of their projects, author Joli Jensen argues that essays and books benefit from a mission statement, like the ones that are created for universities or other organizations. In *Write No Matter What: Advice for Academics*, Jensen proposes that writers "summarize the purpose of your project clearly and concisely on a 3×5 card."[6] Giving yourself a very small space to articulate that statement, like a 3-by-5-inch index card, ensures that you are drilling down the most fundamental purpose of your work. Get an index card in front of you and force yourself to answer this question in one or two sentences: How will my intended audience be changed when they have finished reading my work?

As one final way to encourage your thinking in this area, you could always think of whatever you write on that card as the *learning objectives* of your book. Most of us are familiar with the task of describing the goals of our courses in bullet points and putting them on the syllabus. If you were to create a syllabus based entirely on your essay or book, what would those learning objectives look like? At the end of the reading experience, what do you want your readers to *understand, know*, or *become*? As an experiment, review the learning objectives for the course that you teach that connects most closely to the content of your project. Test a couple of them as potential learning objectives for your writing project. Using the kind of active verbs that are common to learning objectives, craft another one or two that would cover the new territories that your book will explore. Write them all on the back of your index card and keep it in view as you research, think, and write.

## WHY DO READERS NEED YOUR GREAT IDEAS *RIGHT NOW*?

While I was first working on this chapter in early June 2022, I took a break from my writing to check my email. My inbox included a daily summary from the Conversation, an online news source that publishes articles by academics for the public. One of the highlighted stories on that summer day was authored by Kristine Nolin, a professor of chemistry at the University of Richmond, and included an enticing question in the title: "What Makes Smoky, Charred Barbecue Taste So Good? The Chemistry of Cooking over an Open Flame."[7] My writing desk happens to look over the back patio, where I keep our grill. The weather was warm, and suddenly I was hungry. I clicked through and read the article—which was exactly what the smart editor who commissioned or accepted this essay was hoping would happen.

Why did this story appear on the Conversation or in my inbox during the first week of June? Because editors, both of short-form publications and books, are looking for written work that has a timely appeal. When I saw the title of Nolin's article, summertime had arrived in the Northern Hemisphere, people were lounging on patios and decks, and the smoke of grilled food was wafting through the air. You're not going to see news stories about grilling published in Vermont's *Burlington Free Press* in January. The science of barbecue is not earth-shaking news, but the principle that led the Conversation to publish this story on June 6 is one that all aspiring public authors need to think about. You have an interesting question, a Big Idea, and a clear purpose—but you have to ask yourself a final question: Why does the world need this great idea *right now*?

The principle of making your project timely is one that applies to most writing projects you are pitching to a broad audience, although it will look a little different for articles and books. Obviously, articles can be timed more easily to line up with current events, seasons and cycles, anniversaries, and celebrations or holidays. One of the times my work made it into the national media occurred shortly after my book *Cheating Lessons* was published, when I began seeing new stories about a major cheating scandal at Harvard University. I quickly wrote up a thousand-word essay based on the book and submitted it to *Time* magazine. *Time* accepted it quickly and published it under the ironic title of "News Flash . . . Harvard Students Cheat Too."[8] That experience made me much more alert to scanning the news and becoming more aware of the possibilities of timing submissions to get the most readers for my articles.

Although my learning objectives for you in these pages focus on writing nonfiction books, every author of a nonfiction book should also keep their eyes peeled for opportunities to publish timely essays on the subject of their books, both before and after publication. Every essay you publish might catch the welcome attention of an acquisitions editor or a book-buying reader. Create for yourself more publishing opportunities by attending to the following places where your subject matter meets the present moment:

- **CURRENT EVENTS.** In the wake of a mass shooting, the public needs the expertise of a sociologist who can help delineate the relationship between gun laws and shootings. A new galaxy is discovered which has potential Earthlike planets; an astronomer can help us explain whether the aliens are gathering above the atmosphere.

- **SEASONS AND CYCLES.** In early October, a plant biologist educates readers about the fascinating science behind the turning of the leaves. The calendar page flips to the month of December, and a historian of American culture gets the opportunity to publish a lighthearted history of the Christmas tree.
- **CELEBRATIONS AND ANNIVERSARIES.** On the exact date on which I was revising this chapter in 2024, the *New York Times* published an essay on why we should still read the poetry of Lord Byron, Romanticism's most neglected poet, on the two hundredth anniversary of his death.[9] Five days later, the *Chronicle of Higher Education* featured an essay about the German philosopher Immanuel Kant on his three hundredth birthday.[10] Birth and death days of famous people in your field provide a natural tie-in. Then there are holidays: think Earth Day for environmental scientists, Valentine's Day for psychologists, Constitution Day for political scientists ... you get the idea.
- **DISCIPLINARY DISCOVERIES.** Many of us have Google alerts or customized newsfeeds that let us know when something radical happens in our discipline. A trove of new letters from Ernest Hemingway comes to light; cultural editors from major newspapers might be on the watch for pitches from scholars of American literature. Artificial intelligence learns to write; room has opened up for writing teachers, pedagogy scholars, and academic integrity researchers to ply their trade in more public forums.

These are not the only ways to make article submissions timely, but once you start turning your brain in this direction, you'll find these are four reliable pathways for op-eds and short-form essays. Because there are so many news and opinion sources available to us today, you can almost always find timely ways to connect your ideas to the present moment if you look hard enough.

Timeliness is much more difficult to gauge with books. Keep in mind the longer cycle of book production, even in the digital era. If you hand your publisher a finished manuscript on June 1, the earliest you might see it in print would be the spring of next year. Your readers might encounter it *years* after that: I noted a few paragraphs ago that I first drafted this chapter in June 2022; you are reading these words in 2025 at the earliest. You can certainly play a long game of planning a book publication by seeing some far-off date and writing your book with it in mind. For instance, you might be aware of an upcoming major anniversary of something important to your work. If in 2025 you begin drafting your book on modern medicine, the hundredth anniversary of the invention of penicillin, in 2028, would be a great projected publication date (which means you should have the book drafted by 2026 or so).

But I certainly don't have those long-game organizational skills. Many successful nonfiction books are ones that are grounded in subjects which are generally topical but not tied to any very specific time frame. The slow melting of the glaciers, for example, will be (unfortunately) relevant for the foreseeable future. Jemma Wadham's *Ice Rivers: A Story of Glaciers, Wilderness, and Humanity* pins its climate activism to recent developments in the ice—but the process of glaciers disappearing will take years to unfold. Likewise, the subject matter of Laurie Kaye Abraham's *Mama Might Be Better Off Dead: The Failure of Health Care in Urban America*, first published in 1993, seems likely to remain topical. To be sure, there is some guesswork in orienting your work to current trends or problems, but there is no shortage of perennial problems like climate change and health care to address.

Does every book (or article) have to be timely, oriented to something in the news? No. If you are writing about the joys of being alive, philosophizing about the challenges of the human condition, praising the work of a neglected author, or describing how animals behave, these topics are still important for us to write and read about, even if they are not timely. In recent years I have developed an interest in Stoic philosophy, especially as it appears in writers from ancient Rome. I've discovered a very large community of people who share my interest in the wisdom of writers like Seneca, Marcus Aurelius, and Epictetus. A community of active readers exists for new books in this area, and that might be true for your field as well.[11] But even if you are writing a book that presents your research and ideas on Stoicism, you are likely still going to be asked by potential editors to make a case about what makes it worthwhile for them to invest a publisher's time and money in bringing it into the world at that specific moment.

## STRATEGIES: QUESTIONS, ANSWERS, ACTIONS, TIMELINESS

- **ARTICULATE THE QUESTIONS OF YOUR PROJECT.** See if you can capture the intriguing, fundamental question in a single phrase or sentence. Then play around with the question and see if you can capture it in a title. You can focus on the *big* question, or you can narrow it down to a specific, more focused question that encapsulates the main focus of your book, as Robert Sapolsky or Beverly Daniels Tatum did. Once you have decided on the big question, write the subtitle that will make a promise to your reader. Will they be getting advice? Information? A glimpse into some hidden world? A prediction about the future?
- **MAKE NEW CONNECTIONS.** Have your good idea make friends with other ideas. Play with possibilities. Perhaps you have, as I have, a collection of half-finished pieces of writing that seemed interesting to me at first but then petered out after a few pages of writing. Sometimes when I am stuck on a project, I will scroll through those files and see whether anything in there could be brought into dialogue with the current project. This is a good reason not to ever give up on previously unfinished projects. They might return and offer you the new perspective you might need to bring your current idea to life.
- **CONSIDER PURPOSE.** What do you hope that readers will *do* when they have finished reading your work? If you have penned an essay for the local newspaper, what do you hope your fellow citizens will do as soon as they read the final sentence? Are you instilling in them a desire to go learn more? Inspiring them to change a

daily habit? Or just giving them something to think about over the course of a day? A book can make more of a sustained impression in a reader's life. Your goal might be to inspire a movement, educate the public about an urgent issue, or give people guidance when it comes to their ethical, spiritual, political, or social lives.

- **MAKE IT TIMELY.** Does your research or idea address a topic that has captured the attention of the public right now, however you might define that public? If so, consider getting your work into the hands of editors and readers of magazines, news sources, websites, and other outlets. In a book, you will have to make the case that while your project does have a timely appeal, it's one that will last beyond the cycle of the book's creation and production. Every book publisher hopes that your title will join its *backlist* (essentially, books that were published in previous years and are kept in print); what will secure its place there?

---

## FINAL QUESTION

We have reached the end of the first chapter, in which I have recommended that you develop a book-driving question, and you might be wondering at this point about the question driving this book. Why didn't I put the book's big question in the title, or highlight it for you in the opening pages?

This is an advice book, and the presence of the question in an advice book will often be muted. Almost every advice book in the world, including this one, responds to some form of the same question: *How do I do it?* Readers of advice books seek specific guidance: they want to write a book, lead a happier life, or beat the stock market. Instead of the author bringing the question to the reader, the readers pose it to the author. Because the readers know what they want already, the author can jump immediately to the answers.

But although you might have brought the *how* question to these pages, a deeper *why* question still has animated their creation. I spent my career at a liberal arts institution that had relatively light standards for publication. I knew many faculty members who were terrific teachers and had incredibly interesting ideas but who didn't publish much. Especially when I was directing the teaching center on campus, I had countless conversations with colleagues who described an innovative teaching strategy they had pioneered or a fascinating discovery they had made in their research, and I would say, "You should write about that!" Some of them would demur: "I'm not much of a writer." Others would say, "Yes, I tried that, I sent a query to an editor, and I never heard back. Then I gave up." These were people who had spent their careers cultivating the skills of explaining complex ideas to nonexperts. What was holding them back from sharing their ideas with a wider audience?

This question niggled around in the back of my mind for years. I wanted to help these folks, but I couldn't figure out how to do it. I don't remember any specific *aha* moment when it occurred to me that what might break their impasse was to convince them that they could transfer their teaching skills into their writing. But once I had put those two bodies of thinking together—teaching and writing—I saw a glimmer of light. I began testing the idea in my interactions with faculty in workshops, pitching it to publishers, and thinking through the nature of my answer. The concept of "write like you teach" lands easily on most teachers' ears, but that doesn't mean the implications follow automatically. It took me two and a half years to work through the connections between the classroom and the written word, with both my *how* and *why* questions dangling in front of my nose.

Writing a book takes many months or years and will challenge your ability to remain interested in a single subject. A writer who is merely filling in the blanks of a prepared outline will write a boring book, just as a teacher who has lost interest in their subject will teach a boring class. A baffling but important question, one that tests your limitations as a thinker, will impart staying power to a writer. The reader needs such questions—and so do you.

## CHAPTER ONE WRITING PROMPTS

- Articulate the deepest question of your book. You can pose it as a question about the reader—Why should readers care about this issue?—or as a question to yourself: Why do I care about this issue? See if you can address both the *why* and the *how* of your project in a single paragraph.
- Craft the learning objectives for your project. What do you hope that your readers/learners will understand, undertake, feel, or believe when they finish your book or essay? See if you can summarize it onto an index card, and keep it handy. (And don't be afraid to revise it as the book progresses.)
- Take a walk, go for a drive, or spend an hour working in your garden—wherever else you do your best creative thinking. As you do so, play with pairing your book's topic with other subject areas you know well, academic or not: including walking, driving, or gardening. Does your idea make friends easily?
- What makes your project timely, whether the frame for timeliness consists of this year, this century, or beyond? You can address this question in the first paragraph or write these sentences as a second paragraph following your why/how paragraph.

**CHAPTER TWO**

# WRITING DESIGN

During my first year on the tenure track, I was assigned a course in English composition, which is standard fare for an English professor at a teaching-focused institution. At that time, we received our room assignments just a couple of days in advance of the semester. Overwhelmed with all the challenges of adjusting to teaching in a new place, I didn't have time to check out the classroom before the first day of the semester. I walked in the first time and saw immediately that it was going to be a tough semester: the room was small, the right size for twenty students and me, but it had a massive square column in the middle of it. No matter where I stood at the front of the room, some students would be blocked from my view. I recollect that course as one of those courses that just never got off the ground; I never felt comfortable in that space, and it rippled into my teaching.

    I learned my lesson from that experience, and in future years I made sure to visit my assigned rooms in advance of each semester. Then I smartened up even further and began to request the classrooms that matched my teaching styles. Faculty members on my campus were encouraged to do so, even if our requests were not always honored. Some of my colleagues preferred rooms with fixed seating; I gravitated toward the small seminar rooms where we could move the desks around if needed. While the layout of the room made the most difference to my room requests, the furnishings also influenced my choices. Some rooms had comfortable chairs and spacious desks, but they were cramped into a small area; others tested the limits of human back support but offered generous whiteboard space or the latest educational technologies. Each semester I learned anew that the design of the room partially conditioned the nature of the semester, both for me and for the students. My teaching strategies, and the student's learning experiences, unfolded within the limits of the room's design.

The physical space of a traditional classroom puts one set of limitations on a teacher; but so does time. Any synchronous class will play out within a period marked out by the institution: fifty minutes, three times per week; seventy-five minutes, twice a week; three hours, once a week, just to name the most common ones. Just as we have to acknowledge and adapt to the physical spaces in which we teach, so we have to acknowledge and adapt to the limitations of these temporal structures. Fifty-minute classes sometimes push teachers into lecture mode, as they feel the pressure of that ticking clock and the weight of their content. Within a seventy-five-minute class, they might feel more breathing room, be more open to digressions or longer discussions. Two courses with the same content, taught by the same teacher, might take different forms because of these distinct structures.

Writers, like teachers, have to put their words within the confines of distinctive structures: a thousand-word op-ed, a long-form essay, a three-hundred-page book. In their academic writing, scholars have the luxury of working within writing structures that have been handed down to them by tradition. Most of us will recognize the basic design of an academic journal article—introduction, literature review, methods, and so on—and know how to move comfortably within that space. Those of us who work in disciplines where books are the coin of the realm also know what usual book structures look like: introduction, theory chapter, a handful of case studies to demonstrate our thesis, conclusion. Once we have come up with our good ideas, we can lock ourselves into the predesigned spaces of academic publications. When it comes to our academic writing, we are lecturers who walk into our assigned room for a fifty-minute class, see a bunch of comfortable chairs in tiered rows, spy a clock on the wall, and breathe a comfortable sigh as we take our place at the podium.

As you shift your writing practices to reach wider audiences, you will find that you have more choices in designing the structures in which you educate your learners. If you are writing a book aiming to educate readers about the basic science of climate change, then you might indeed choose a traditional nonfiction book structure—introduction, theory, applications, conclusion—that offers the writerly equivalent of a well-timed lecture in an auditorium. But maybe you are producing something designed to spark reflection, and you want readers to join you on an intellectual journey. In that case, you might fold your ideas into a memoir mixed with occasional dips into the research: the writerly equivalent of gathering around a table in a seminar. In that space, your readers will welcome a more leisurely pace, more pauses for thinking, the occasional digression.

The primary lesson of this chapter is that we have *choices* when it comes to the design of our writing projects. To be sure, some design decisions will be made in advance by the traditions of the genre, as in academic journals. But when it comes to nonfiction books aimed at wider audiences, you will have considerable leeway in terms of the structures you erect. This freedom can be both liberating and terrifying. It gives us room to experiment and play, but it also challenges us to think hard about whether our design choices make sense with our content. Returning to our pedagogical conceit: Are we teaching in the right classroom? Have we arranged the desks in support of our objectives? Have we acknowledged the time frame that limits the time we spend with our learners?

To address such questions, the three sections that follow will guide you through options and recommendations in three areas of writing project design. The first section will focus on the **structures** that will hold up all the parts of your work, such as questions, ideas, evidence, and stories. To emphasize the idea that you have choices available to you in this area, I'll describe and analyze three common structures for any nonfiction writing project. In the second section I'll recommend that you pay attention to the **pacing** of the work. The decisions you make about pacing might determine whether the reader stops reading after the first few paragraphs or races excitedly to its finale. The third and final section of this chapter addresses what might be the most challenging design issue for academic writers: maintaining your **throughline**. You have something you want your reader to learn from your work, and it's easy to lose sight of that when you are in the deep of the weeds of drafting chapter 7. The throughline keeps writers and readers focused on what matters.

## CHOOSING STRUCTURES

When you first think about possible structures for your essay or book, you might default to a very familiar principle: I am writing something based on my academic expertise, which means it should be structured just like my academic writing. Almost all of us in higher education know the basic framework of an academic article: introduction, review of existing literature, presentation of a new theory or idea, data or experiment or applications, and then discussion or conclusion (or both). These parts and their sequence might look slightly different in different disciplines, but that basic form dominates academic writing. You can certainly use this familiar structure for an essay or book aimed at general readers, and many academic authors do.

But if you are looking to expand your reach as a writer, you should consider some other possibilities, which you can find in a range of nonfiction books, by academic and nonacademic authors. In the three subsections that follow, I offer a quick review of three common structures—quests, narratives, and lists—not because they are the best three but because I hope they will jump-start your own creative thinking about potential structures for your work.

Once you begin to look at the structures of your favorite works of nonfiction with these three examples in mind, you will begin to see how they work in practice—and you will also discover plenty of other possibilities that you can imitate and adapt for yourself.

---

## QUESTS

In chapter 1, I argued for the importance of raising *questions* at the start of your writing projects, and one way to answer those questions is through *quests*. The words *question* and *quest* share a common root: the Latin verb *quaerere*, which means both to *ask* and to *seek*. We ask questions, and then we undertake quests to answer them. Quests can take many forms, but what they have in common is a presentation of an unfolding narrative in which the author makes gradual discoveries, which are then described for the reader. Such discoveries emerge from the author's encounter with data, research, experiences, or ideas.

Their unfolding quality makes quests distinct from the narratives to be discussed in the second subsection. A common framework in quest narratives would describe some initial state of affairs, pause for an overview of how previous thinkers approached the problem, and then present the story of the metaphorical (or literal) travels that led to your conclusions. Most editors of nonfiction books will want to see a presentation of your main ideas in the first few pages of your first chapter (and readers are pretty well-conditioned to expect this move), but once you have done that, you can initiate your quest framework.

You can recognize that you are in the presence of a quest when you might read sentences like these ones:

- "This book is meant as a passionate personal journey into the heart of a mystery. I do not presume to have emerged, on the last page, with anything more than a key to the puzzle. But that key, if I have succeeded, at least fits into the lock." David Roberts, *The Pueblo Revolt: The Secret Rebellion That Drove the Spaniards Out of the Southwest*[1]

- "When I first set out to write a book about the writing habits of successful academics, I had no real idea what I would find—or even what I was trying to find out." Helen Sword, *Air and Light and Time and Space: How Successful Academics Write*[2]
- "Come with me on my quest to document and understand obsessions surrounding turtles and tortoises." Peter Laufer, *Dreaming in Turtle: A Journey Through the Passion, Profit, and Peril of Our Most Coveted Prehistoric Creatures*[3]

In each of these cases, the authors brought curiosity and expertise to their journeys but did not possess detailed maps. Quests typically include dead ends, wrong turns, and obstacles. Discoveries do not come without cost and effort. The quest eschews a clean presentation of conclusions in favor of revealing the stumbling blocks that led to the finish line. Instead of starting with their conclusions—which they do eventually present—authors of quests play the role of tour guides, just a few steps ahead of the reader on the book's journey.

Barbara Ehrenreich's *Nickel and Dimed: On (Not) Getting By in America* takes the form of such a quest narrative. Ehrenreich sought to understand how the poor live, just as earlier writers such as George Orwell once did, by temporarily stripping herself of her economic privilege and scrabbling to support herself without her degrees, work experiences, or writing skills. *Nickel and Dimed* incorporates research about poverty into her memoir of spending a year working low-paying jobs and trying to survive on poverty-inducing wages. In her opening paragraph she describes the conversation she had with her editor in which she formulated her question: "How does anyone live on the wages available to the unskilled?"[4] She almost gives up in the face of the hardships she experiences, but in the end she returns from her quest with an affecting portrait of the challenges faced by low-wage workers in America.

Quests like Ehrenreich's produce some of my favorite books, with their mix of narrative and research. Quest structures demand that you leave the comfort of your office to explore the wider world of your subject: visiting locations, talking to people, experimenting with new kinds of activities. As a specialist in British literature, I might head off on a quest to visit the English houses where the great works of the tradition were composed to discover how places influence literary writing. Classicist Edith Hall traveled to all the places that Aristotle lived in Greece in preparation for writing her book *Aristotle's Way: How Ancient Wisdom Can Change Your Life*, a synthesis of the ancient philosopher's key ideas. In such quests, the presentation of ideas might be laid over a light travel narrative—which might have a special appeal for some writers, as they flex or develop their skills in telling stories or writing descriptive prose.

What I find so appealing about quests is that they present the writer as an intellectually curious person. Questers are seekers. Energetic and ambitious, they encounter obstacles, but they are stubborn enough to keep seeking their treasure. Quests are the stock-in-trade of literature, and we are accustomed to root for the heroes in such stories, from Frodo Baggins in *The Lord of the Rings* to the eponymous hero in Charlotte Brontë's *Jane Eyre*. We are satisfied at the conclusion of a quest. And if the author has done their work well, readers are then inspired to set off on their own quests to discover new ideas for themselves.

## NARRATIVES

Narrative structures are also very common in works of nonfiction by academic authors. Most narratives use basic chronology as their underlying principle; that is, they put their ideas and research in a story that starts at the beginning, proceeds logically through the middle, and finishes at the end. If you are writing a history of organ transplantation, you might begin with nineteenth-century experiments on human corpses, move through the discoveries made in transplant research throughout the twentieth century, and then conclude with the story of a recent transplant surgery you witnessed. Even if your subject is not history, chronological frameworks can be used to introduce ideas and research. An economist, for example, could write a book in which they trace the life of a material good from its birth in a factory in China to its final resting place in an Iowa landfill, introducing their research or advocating for environmental activism along the way.

Chronological narratives can be livened up by experimenting with their time frames. John Lukacs's *Five Days in London, May 1940* is an obvious example of this strategy. His analysis focuses specifically on five crucial days in which Winston Churchill's war cabinet was debating how to deal with Adolf Hitler. Lukacs's book does not limit itself to discussing *only* things that happened during those five days, but such a short framework—or other time limitation—can prove useful when you are tackling a subject that is complex and messy, or that many authors have written about already. A veterinarian could author a popular essay about dogs by describing one day in the life of a dog; an epidemiologist could write an account of the first hundred days of the outbreak of the coronavirus responsible for the COVID-19 pandemic, arguing that those early days set the stage for everything that followed.

You can also base chronological narratives on the calendar year and its seasons, whether those are nature's seasons or seasons of other kinds—such as the seasons of the academic year. My third book, *A Week-by-Week Guide to Your First Semester of College Teaching*, used the seasonal structure of the academic year. Each week gave me the chance to offer a new lesson or idea about a successful start to a teaching career. But you'll see seasonal titles and structures in nonfiction books everywhere: Bill Bryson's *One Summer: America, 1927*; Kenneth C. Davis's *Great Short Books: A Year of Reading—Briefly*; and Rebekah Nathan's *My Freshman Year: What a Professor Learned by Becoming a Student*, which puts a quest story within the limited time frame of twelve months and thereby demonstrates how two structures can be combined in a single book.

When you are contemplating a book project and feel overwhelmed by the largeness of it, marking out five days or a month or a season or a calendar year can be an enabling move for a writer. But yearly and seasonal structures also have symbolic resonances.

New years come and go, which evokes feelings of cyclicality or recurrence. Seasons have common associations: spring evokes new life, while summer conjures up sun and relaxation; autumn and winter are often correlated with aging and death. You can work with these common associations or write deliberately against them—as Rachel Carson famously did in *Silent Spring*, her devastating account of the environmental devastation wrought by a harmful pesticide.

Chronological narratives tap into the linear ways in which our bodies move through time. They are familiar to us in many contexts: planning our schedules, telling our life histories, recounting the rise and fall of empires. But not all narratives use chronology as their structuring principle. Aristotle famously wrote in his *Poetics* that every description of events that unfold over time has a beginning, a middle, and an end—but the events do not have to be presented in that order. For example, many authors of both popular and literary works use the strategy of beginning their tale *in medias res*. This Latin phrase refers to the narrative strategy of opening in the middle of the action, tracking backward in time to explain how we got to the middle, and then finishing out from there. Many mystery and detective stories use this structure: they begin with the moment of the murder and then flash back and forth in time to explain what led to the murder and how the killer is discovered and apprehended.

I won't bore you with all the theories I learned about narrative structure in graduate school, so just keep this primary distinction in mind: a chronology presents events in the order in which they occurred, and a nonchronological narrative reorders the events in service to some other goal. There are many reasons that you might disrupt a chronological narrative and draw from the traditions of literary narrative. But the most common one is the desire to grab the reader's attention by starting your article or book with a dramatic event, and then—once you have them hooked—stepping back to recount what set the stage for that event. A philosopher writing about the current renaissance of Roman stoicism might begin with the publication of Donald Robertson's 2023 graphic novel about the Roman emperor Marcus Aurelius and the postpandemic climate from which it emerged; from there the story jumps back to the life of Aurelius himself, in second-century Rome; it then takes one more step backward to the origins of Stoicism in the pre-Socratic philosophers of ancient Greece—after which, finally, the story locks into a chronological narrative that culminates with a final analysis of Robertson's graphic novel, now with the reader's full awareness of its precedents.

Those of us who teach in the humanities and social sciences often disrupt chronology in our courses in support of student learning. Teachers of survey courses in literature, for example, typically default to a chronological order for the schedule of course readings. But creative teachers experiment with alternatives. In an anthology of essays about innovative approaches to teaching survey courses, Kevin Bourque describes how he tells the story of early British literature with a geographical approach, as he and his students orient all of the texts around the city of London. Space replaces time as the organizational principle. The students still engage with the literary texts in their historical context, but the chronological narratives are subservient to the geographical mapping.[5] Likewise, an anthropologist might teach a course on matrilineal societies, with a half dozen discrete units that narrate the development of each society, but the units themselves don't follow a chronological progression. Instead, the course tackles them according to the distribution of power according to gender.

The easiest way to tell a story is to narrate the events in which they happen. But in nonfiction writing as in teaching, educators have other options.

---

### LISTS

Perhaps the easiest way for writers to walk the reader through the presentation of research and ideas is in the form of a list. BuzzFeed-style articles and listicles have given this approach a bad name, but there's nothing wrong with organizing your ideas into a list, especially one that is hierarchical or organized in some visible way. Although it might seem that articles are more conducive to list structures, many books can take this form. Cognitive psychologist Daniel Willingham has written books both for teachers and for students, including *Outsmart Your Brain: Why Learning Is Hard and How You Can Make It Easy* (2023). Willingham makes no apologies for the book's list structure, which consists of fourteen chapters with similarly phrased titles ("How to Understand a Lecture," "How to Take Lecture Notes," etc.). "You can pick and choose which chapters to read," he writes in the book's introduction, "according to which aspects of learning you want to improve. You don't have to read the chapters in order or read all of them."[6] Advice books like his lend themselves especially well to list structures. If you want to give me advice about how to learn more effectively or live a more fulfilling life, it can be helpful to me as a reader to have your research and thinking distilled into a manageable list that I pick my way through or follow in order. A work of positive psychology, one designed to help readers flourish with help of new research on the field, might lay out its advice in stages: "Change Your Attitude," "Start a New Habit," "Break an Old Habit," "Develop a Gratitude Practice," and so on. Although advice books traffic in list structures, one could argue that many nonfiction works are essentially lists. If you have a theory and apply it to a half dozen cases to test it out (as many of us do in our dissertations), you are using a list structure.

What elevates books with a list structure are effective organizing principles. You can create a grocery list by randomly listing all the items that you want from the store, as I do; or you can organize the list according to where you will find the items in the store, which means you can consult it as you move up and down the aisles, as my wife does. Even if you do choose a list structure, you can identify or develop an organizational principle and let it guide a reader through your book. My book *Small Teaching* is a glorified list; it contains nine chapters, each of which is devoted to a single learning principle. But the nine chapters of *Small Teaching* follow two organizational principles. First, they are divided up into three parts, or categories: knowledge, understanding, and inspiration, with three chapters in each part. Second, the early chapters contain the easiest teaching techniques to apply. Ordering them in this way was designed to seduce the reader with some quick victories in their teaching and then push them deeper into a fuller engagement with the research. List-style structures also lend themselves well to revision and experimentation, which I count as another point in their favor. If you see your project as a list, put the chapter titles on a physical or digital whiteboard, and then move them around and keep probing: What are some of the logics that could govern all the items in your list? Propose, move, erase, and reinscribe until you develop the structure that will lead your reader through your ideas.

Any of the following strategies could be used to order the chapters in a list-style presentation of your research:

- **CATEGORIES.** This strategy encourages logical groupings of your ideas, which would be the basic minimum any book should contain. You can enhance a category-style presentation with an explanation of it in your introduction or via short introductions to the groups: for example, a short introduction to part 1, which contains the first five chapters of the book, and then a short introduction to part 2, which contains the remaining chapters.
- **HIERARCHY.** This strategy presents the most important ideas, principles, or chapters first and then moves on to the ones that deal with the finer details or caveats. You could reverse that order, however, and culminate with your major findings.
- **COMPLEXITY.** This strategy invites the reader into your research with the easiest ideas to comprehend and then pushes the reader slowly to grapple with the more challenging ones—as a teacher will typically do in the design of a course or lesson.

Whatever organizational principle you select, you should make it visible to the reader. Typically authors will use the book's introduction to accomplish that task. But readers can easily lose sight of a principle that they encountered on page 12 when they are on page 200. In the classroom, many of us divide our courses into parts, with each week or class period serving as a "chapter" of our courses. What strategies do you use to help students see the organization of the course's chapters throughout the semester—and how could those strategies apply to your writing project?

If you wish to consider the merits and potential challenges of using a list structure for a writing project, spend a few hours reading through the "Advice" section of the *Chronicle of Higher Education* and the "Career Advice" section of *Inside Higher Ed*, which often take the form of lists. In addition to whatever ideas you might acquire there about lists and their organization, you might also consider the decisions that authors make about the *number* of items on their lists. For example, Brittany K. Robertson's "Black Women Navigating the Workplace: A Few Strategies," which appears in *Inside Higher Ed*, notes in her title that the list will include a small number of items, each of which merits several paragraphs.[7] William McComas's "12 Leadership Lessons Based on 25 Years of Being Led," in the *Chronicle of Higher Education*, goes in the opposite direction: it presents a greater number of items, with less than a full paragraph devoted to each of them.[8] Larger lists might make sense when you wish to offer a menu of ideas and let the reader decide which ones hit home for them. But for both essays and books, fight your impulse to include everything that could be included on your list. Part of your work as an author involves curation, in the same way that museums curate their displays. What we see in museums often represents only a fraction of their actual holdings, many of which languish in some basement or storage area. When you are considering the potential ideas that merit a space in your project, accept that some of them belong in the basement, surface the ones that belong in the gallery, and chart the pathway through the exhibits.

You can design the structure of your work with one of these three options in mind (and of course there are others), but for longer works you can also mix and match them. You might make one decision about the framework of the book as a whole but then another one about the framework of individual chapters. For example, you might organize your book as a traditional academic argument, a structure that should be so familiar to you that I didn't address it in the previous list of potential structures. But even such a traditional structure for the project as a whole might use other structures within the chapters or even sections. An example of a mix-and-match approach appears in *My Stroke of Insight: A Brain Scientist's Personal Journey*, by Jill Bolte Taylor. The author is a neuroanatomist who was working in a research lab at Harvard when she suffered a massive stroke at the age of thirty-seven. Her book about her experience became a bestseller, and her TED Talk has close to thirty million views. *My Stroke of Insight* is segmented into parts, which use distinct structures: a narrative introduction to her prestroke life; two chapters of explanation on the basic science of the brain; a series of chronological narratives marked out by specific time periods during and after the stroke ("Morning of the Stroke," "Day Two: The Morning After"); philosophical reflections on her experience; and, at the end, two short lists of ways in which medical providers and others can help stroke survivors.

Thus, even if you choose a traditional framework for your project, you can still experiment within that structure with frameworks that give the reader a more varied experience.

### GenAI Callout

Because the structure of your book will determine many writing choices that you must make as you draft, I would not recommend asking generative artificial intelligence (GenAI) or other programs to hand you a structure. Developing your structure is as much of the writing process as discovering ideas and composing sentences. Your ideas will benefit from being constrained, expanded, or transformed through the structural choices you make. But in this section of the chapter, and then even more briefly in the conclusion, we have considered a small number of possibilities. Plenty of others exist. Use this prompt in your preferred AI tool to generate a complete list: "I am writing a nonfiction book. I want to consider some alternative structures for the book, instead of a traditional argument. Can you give me some examples of other ways that a nonfiction book could be structured, with examples from published books?" GenAI will present you with more than a dozen possibilities or more; dig deeper into the structures that intrigue you. Be aware, however, that GenAI will draw on *descriptions* of the books, instead of the books themselves, to find its examples. When I performed this exercise, the results it returned to me were mediocre in quality, and I would have chosen different models for many of them. Some of them were just plain inaccurate. But so it goes with GenAI: start with it, and then let your expert brain take over.

## SETTING THE PACE

An editor at a large university press told me once that she had just been reading the first draft of a book that she had acquired and was very excited to publish. The author had done qualitative research that derived from a small number of interviews, and this author was poised to make a new contribution to the field. The book started off well in the first chapter, but then the author paused the storyline and presented a second chapter that consisted entirely of short biographies of all the interview subjects. The energy and excitement that the editor had felt while reading the first chapter deflated while she was reading the second. "This author seems to think," she said to me, "that I should have to do my homework before I get to the more interesting parts of the book."

That editor wanted the author to think harder about the *pacing* of their work. Books especially are long reading experiences, and writers have to be attuned to readers' needs. Our impulse as writers and educators is to lead readers from point of origin to final destination in the most efficient manner, slowly laying down the paving stones that will precede each step of their journey. But readers need rest stops, sights along the way, and the occasional side trip. Without those moments of surprise, readers might never reach the destination. Many college courses resemble the products of a meticulous civil engineer, forcing their learners to rigidly follow the steps laid out for them by the professor. I remember my son, an aspiring artist, calling me during the third week of his first semester of college and telling me how bored he was by an art history course that he had been looking forward to. "We're just reading all of this theory, and it's really hard to understand. When are we going to start to look at *actual* paintings?" he lamented. But by the time the instructor finally got to the paintings, my son had already lost interest in the course. It makes good sense to understand the theory before you analyze the paintings—but it also makes good sense to offer the students early tastes of the visual feasts they will encounter in the second half of the semester.

The structures I presented in the previous section will each have their own implications for the pacing of your project. Quests and narratives are typically designed with brisk pacing in mind. The pace might drag here and there, when the reader has to do a little homework or wrestle with some theory, but well-written quests and narratives never keep the reader too far away from the story. If you prefer the idea of a reader moving more slowly and thoughtfully through your book or article, a more traditional argumentative structure or a list might be the better approach. Perhaps your material is so complex that you expect me, as a reader, to read a chapter or even a few pages at a time, over multiple sittings. Maybe I need time to process each new section of the material, and a list structure encourages that. Each chapter has its own specific point, and I can finish it and return when I'm ready for the next one. In some books you can read chapters out of order and not impair your learning experience much, as Daniel Willingham noted to his readers. You might miss occasional references to previous material, but you should still be able to grasp its major writing recommendations.

Even if you choose a traditional academic or list structure, you still have to be careful about *really* making me slow down and plow through a bunch of difficult material. As much as I loved Jill Bolte Taylor's book, it suffers a little bit from this problem—and she seems to be aware of it, as she makes a plea to her reader that the two science chapters of her book (chapters 2 and 3) are important and readers should not just skip them. (But then she says further that, OK, you can skip them if you want, but I wouldn't recommend it.) She could have addressed this pacing issue instead in the book's design by alternating chapters of her hour-by-hour stroke account with chapters focused on the scientific information that explained exactly what was happening in those moments.[9]

One of the easy ways to think about pacing is to compare it to your experiences in the classroom. Unless you are the greatest teacher in the world, there are moments in even the most well-designed courses when you look at the seats and see students starting to slump in their chairs, sneaking glances at the phone, or staring out the window. Perhaps you're thirty minutes into a lecture, and you know you're losing them. Veteran teachers know that those are the moments when we introduce a change—move to a new activity, pause for a quick discussion, have students respond to something in writing. These strategies are designed to change the pace. Any course period might need moments when you want to slow-walk students into reflection, and other times when they need the energy of a suspenseful story with an unexpected reveal.

Writers have to be just as aware and proficient as teachers are about setting a friendly pace for readers. As you are considering the structure and sequencing of your material, focus less on what you want to write next—perhaps because that's the next logical thing—and more on what *the reader will experience*. Can you disperse the book's homework material (its challenging parts) into small portions strategically placed throughout the text? Prepare your reader for some challenging data by introducing it with a great story or rewarding them for their attention with a finishing anecdote. Likewise, consider where the most interesting parts of your text are located. Can that material be gradually introduced throughout the whole text, instead of covered in one big block? If you have one fascinating case study that you know will capture readers' attention, you could narrate it from start to finish in your introduction—or you could give a quick bare-bones overview in the introduction and then parse the rest of it out throughout the book or essay.

Interludes between the major parts of a learning experience, both in the classroom and in nonfiction books, are a common strategy to support effective pacing. A professor in basic chemistry might set aside a class day after each of the course's major units for the students to meet and interview a chemist working in the field. An astronomer writing a book that presents a new analysis of the origins of the cosmos might occasionally pause the argument to offer biographical sketches of each of the book's scientific pioneers. Such interludes can be incorporated within each chapter—as one might argue I am doing in this book with each chapter's writing prompts—or set off between chapters. Envision such interludes as an opportunity for a learner, whose head has been bent over your book or whose eyes are glued to your slide presentation in the lecture hall, to step outside for a few minutes and observe whatever you are describing in the world around them. They will return to their seat energized by their new perspective, ready to process whatever comes next.

### MAINTAINING THE THROUGHLINE

The final major design issue in nonfiction writing is the *throughline*, and it might be the most important one. When you are reading a work of nonfiction, you are having to keep (at least) two things ever present in your mind: the sentence you are reading right now, and a sense of wherever that sentence fits in the overall picture and purpose of the work. Perhaps you lose yourself sometimes in the great stories the author uses to illustrate their ideas, but at the end of the paragraph or page or chapter, you have to step back and remind yourself that there is a larger point being made by the writer. Switching back and forth between these two parts of the reading process makes for challenging cognitive work for a reader—these big brains of ours are up for the task, but we should not take lightly the intellectual obstacles our readers face. The throughline keeps all the words and sentences and paragraphs connected, reminding both the reader and the writer of the point of it all.

In chapter 1, I encouraged you to think about what your writing project will *do*: change people's minds, start a movement, offer life advice. When you have identified the specific objective of your written work, it should be embodied in your throughline. Keeping a constant eye on that throughline is especially important in longer works, which can contain multiple digressions or turns of direction. In my work as an editor of books, one of my most frequent critiques is that the author has lost the throughline. This happens for at least two reasons. First, authors sometimes get lost in the fascinating examples or stories that connect tangentially to their throughline. The word *fascinating*, though, can shift dramatically in meaning from person to person. Most things about your subject will fascinate you, even the digressions. Authors sometimes spend too much time circling conceptual cul-de-sacs before they return to the main road. Likewise, the personal stories that you tell to illustrate your ideas, even when they are barely relevant, fascinate you because they happened to you. But if the reader doesn't share your deep interest in your subject or yourself, those moments derail the throughline. I also know from my work as an editor that clean throughlines sometimes get messy because authors will start drafting their book manuscript with an eye fixed firmly on their great idea. Then through the process of doing their research and their writing, they realize that their great idea was not as great as it could have been, and they decide to revise it into a slightly different idea halfway through.

Discovering new ideas during the writing process is not necessarily a bad thing—and, to the contrary, it can be wonderful, as I argued in the conclusion of chapter 1. As you follow the winding trails that open up through the writing experience, you should be growing as a thinker, learner, and teacher. Indeed, some books have the opposite problem of a tangled throughline: the author has one idea that they cling to desperately and mention on every page, and that can make for a stultifying reading experience. I don't want to hold up specific books for criticism, but we all have read books and thought afterward, "That should have been an article." That happens when the author has a great idea and then just twists and turns it into new shapes throughout a dozen chapters. Thus I would never counsel writers to lock themselves into an idea cage and never pause to look around at what they might be missing. But after you have written yourself into unexplored territories, you might have to return to the beginning and reshape your map and maybe even rewrite the introduction.

A second trap for academics, when it comes to maintaining throughlines, stems from the fact that we know a lot of stuff, and we are passionate about sharing what we have learned with others. But be wary of cramming everything you know into a single container—a book or article—that was not meant to hold the full contents of an academic brain. Readers need what they need, not everything you have learned in months or years or decades of mastering some specialized body of knowledge. Stick to your throughline as much as possible by regularly asking yourself this question: Does the reader need this in order to understand my Big Idea? You'll be amazed at how many times that question will lead you to cut things that you have drafted but were actually not relevant to the primary purpose.

Two strategies can help support your throughline: one designed to support the reader, and one designed to keep you on track as you write.

First, you can remind readers about the throughline through the use of titles and subtitles (for articles, books, and chapters) and section headings (within the article or chapter). Martha Coven, the author of *Writing on the Job: Best Practices for Communicating in the Digital Age*, spent time working in multiple divisions of the Obama White House, reading and writing documents and reports on a regular basis. When it comes to nonfiction writing, she argues, "Headings are a gift to the reader."[10] The special power of that gift helps the reader who might be struggling step back and ask the question, "Wait, what's the main idea here again?" The titles and headings can contribute answers to that question. Many writers think hard about the main title of their work, sometimes going back and forth with an editor on the precise wording of a book or article's title. But they often don't give the same care to the subtitles and section headings that might be used throughout the work, even though those in-text headings are doing essential reader work for the reader.

Coven offers a short taxonomy of heading types, drawn from the *Federal Plain Language Guidelines*, which were designed to increase communication efficiency between government agencies.[11] I'll add a fourth type to those three, one which you will find in many works of nonfiction:

- **STATEMENT HEADINGS.** These essentially offer a summary of the main idea of that section, such as "Three Techniques for Improving Student Metacognition."
- **QUESTION HEADINGS.** These are a miniature version of the question-based approach presented in chapter 1, as in, "What Does the Research Tell Us about Improving Student Metacognition?"
- **TOPIC HEADINGS.** These are more like what you might see in a very simple outline, just words or phrases; for example, "Improving Student Metacognition" or even "Student Metacognition" alone.
- **CREATIVE HEADINGS.** If you want to entice the reader a little bit or show off your wordplay skills, you can pull something from a story or example from the section and turn it into a heading that hints

at the subject but doesn't reveal too much: "What Three Danish Researchers in a Hot Tub Discovered about Metacognition."

If you are using academic or list structures for your project, you might favor Topic or Statement headings, which can guide the reader through complex material. If you like the suspense that is created by quest or narrative structures, you might choose Question or Creative headings. However you title the distinct sections of your book or essay, ensure that they include pointers back to the throughline—which might be as simple as a single word, as in the four listed examples, all of which contain the word *metacognition*.

Your reader needs help keeping the throughline visible in a text, but you might also need help with maintaining it throughout the writing process. A second strategy for maintaining a focused throughline is developing and regularly updating a running outline of your project. You don't have to begin your project with a detailed outline that you follow to the letter. Start with something simple, like a list of chapter titles. But don't stop there. As you write, continue to update that outline, getting more specific with each new update. This book began with a list of single-word chapter titles: "Questions," "Structures," "Revising." As I drafted chapters, I began to fill out that bare-bones outline with bulleted lists of everything the chapter contained. This process helped me keep track of any repetitions and ensured that I didn't leave out anything essential.

Writing experts discuss two kinds of outlines that can help you keep your throughline intact:

- **SENTENCE OUTLINES.** Instead of just a word or phrase for each section or chapter, write a full sentence or short paragraph explaining what the chapter does and contains. In chapter 1, I recommended Joli Jensen's strategy of creating mission statements for each project, and you can do the same for the parts of your project. You can do this before you start, but you then should continue to revise those sentences as you draft.

- **REVERSE OUTLINES.** If you prefer to just start writing before you plan—which I sometimes do—by all means do so. But once you have created your first draft, go back and make an outline of it. That process will give you an aerial view of what you have done and guide decisions about what to cut and keep, or where you need more or less.

Helen Sword, the author of multiple books on writing for academics, argues that the two strategies discussed here, title/headings and outlines, can actually work together. "Make an outline of your article or book," she explains, "based *only* on its chapter titles or section headings."[12] After you have made that outline, look at it from the perspective of the reader. Does the outline give the reader the information they would need to keep their eye focused on that throughline?

**STRATEGIES: STRUCTURES, PACING, THROUGHLINES**

Designing a learning experience on the page means giving the reader the supports they need to stay focused and remain attuned to the major ideas of the book. These three design elements are essential:

- **STRUCTURES.** The structure of your project connects all of parts. Most academic authors imitate the structure of an academic essay or book, with its focus on argument or information presentation, as do many nonfiction books. But as you move away from the work of academic writers and read nonfiction works by journalists or successful academic authors, you'll find alternatives: quests, narratives, lists, and others. Once you have marked out the topic and scope of your project, entertain at least two possible structures, just to make sure you are making a design choice that accomplishes your goals for your book or essay.
- **PACING.** When it comes to pacing, think like a secondary school teacher who has a bunch of teenagers in their classroom and has

to keep them engaged and focused for an hour or two. How long will any single activity hold their attention? Where will the teacher build pauses and changes into the experience? Consider, then, how you will provide that same level of support in your essay or book. Move the reader along by alternating stories and theories, changing the structures of your chapters, or using interludes.

- **THROUGHLINES.** Imagine your text as a forest of research and ideas, one that's filled with fascinating things that might draw the attention of the reader. You want the reader to pause and enjoy the experience of walking in the woods, but you also need to make sure that they follow the path you have created for them—the one that will lead to a new insight or idea. Post signs along the way that remind the reader where they are and where they are going. Use outlines, not necessarily as a prewriting tool but as a digital map that you can consult and revise as you follow your throughline to the project's final destination.

## FINAL POSSIBILITIES

I argued in this chapter that the three structural possibilities I presented—quests, narratives, and lists—were just examples to jump-start your thinking about the structure of your project and its parts (chapters or sections). If you need a little push to envision other structural possibilities for your nonfiction writing, here are three additional options:

- **GUIDED TOURS.** Quests and arguments point the reader to the destination from the beginning. Guided tours give as much weight to the journey as they do to the destination. A neuroscientist might wish to write an argument in favor of the biological origins of human spirituality, but they might arrive at that destination by walking readers through the regions of the human brain, like a docent in a museum. Whether readers agree with the author's conclusions, they have learned much about the brain at each stop.

- **BRAIDED NARRATIVES.** Maybe you have at least two stories to tell: a personal one and a research one, or two different stories that illustrate two sides of the same issue. Instead of telling first one story and then the other in sequence, alternate them chapter by chapter. Historian Erik Larson has popularized this approach in best-selling books like *The Devil in the White City*. In it, one narrative follows the actions of a serial killer; the other chronicles the world's fair where he committed his crimes, the 1893 World's Columbian Exposition in Chicago.
- **LIFE STORIES.** Memoirs and biographies might seem like the province of specialized nonfiction writers, but many academic authors build their works on the narratives of individual human lives. In *Fermat's Last Theorem*, for example, physicist Simon Singh draws in readers who might have no special interest or knowledge in mathematics with his accounts of historical figures such as Pythagoras, Pierre de Fermat, and Andrew Wiles.

If you are hoping to craft a nonfiction book that deserves attention not only for its ideas but also for the creative quality of its writing, structure represents one of the best places to experiment as a writer. Play with possibilities. Even if you don't end up using an experimental structural form, you might find that exploring those forms might help you develop new skills as a writer, ones that you could deploy in future projects.

I can't close this chapter without referencing my favorite experiment with structure, but it occurs in a work of fiction: Julie Schumacher's *Dear Committee Members*. An academic novel written entirely in the form of letters of recommendation? Yes, and it works. Read it for its humor and very recognizable academic moments, and perhaps it will set your wheels spinning about structure. A dialogue between you and a colleague? A critique of your own dissertation? A series of letters to your mother?[13] Or . . .

## CHAPTER TWO WRITING PROMPTS

- If you have already envisioned your book's structure as an argument or a presentation of information, write an informal paragraph in which you consider one alternative possibility. Which structure would you consider? What makes it appealing, and what challenges would it pose? Write this paragraph informally, as if you were preparing to explain your reasoning to a friend why you might choose it—or why you would not choose an alternative structure.
- When you give a lecture, how do you keep the pace brisk? Do you insert activities, include occasional images or humor, tell stories? Which of those strategies might translate into the lecture of your book?
- To support your throughline, create a running sentence outline for your writing project. Tie each sentence or phrase to a chapter or section of your project. You will be tempted to write just a word or two for each item. The fuller your phrase or sentence, the more clearly you will see your throughline.

**CHAPTER THREE**

# USING EVIDENCE

I have always liked to attend lectures by academic authors visiting the institutions where I have taught. I am more likely to attend events with speakers in the humanities, but sometimes the title of a talk by an environmental scientist or cognitive psychologist will catch my interest. Yet following talks from thinkers in fields far from my own can be challenging. When a speaker starts delving into statistics and experimental design issues, I have to focus really hard to understand what's happening. The longer I have to process slides with tables or graphs or statistics on them, the less and less I will be able to keep track of the main idea. But the best presenters bring their teaching skills to such talks and will often also give an everyday example or tell a story to illustrate their point. Those are the moments when I can pause, catch my cognitive breath, and find my way back into the argument. I like to think that I can learn from different types of research and evidence I encounter in any discipline, but I definitely prefer to process new ideas and research in ways that are familiar and comfortable to me as a literature professor.

Ah, you might be thinking, the pedagogical principle of this chapter must be that we should teach to the *learning styles* of our audiences—I know about those! Indeed, most people have heard of the notion that people have a preferred style of learning new information: some are visual learners, some are auditory learners, some are kinesthetic learners, and so on. Unfortunately, research has repeatedly debunked the idea that we should lock into a learning style and stick with it in or outside school. Multiple experiments have shown that self-identified visual learners don't necessarily learn more effectively when they receive new information through visual forms. They might *prefer* visuals, but they actually might do their best learning when they absorb information through listening. We often convince ourselves that we learn in some specific way, but we are often wrong about that.[1]

I like to share this research with both teachers and writers because we can drive ourselves to distraction if we try to tailor our teaching approaches to every learner we hope to reach in our classrooms and in our writing. That's an impossible dream because human brains have such variety, not only across learning preferences but also in terms of our general neurodiversity.[2] The more realistic way to approach the problem of working with learners across preferences and brains is to expand the variety of methods we use to teach them. A visiting environmental scientist I recall, speaking to a mixed crowd of students and faculty, knew that citing data from studies of local ponds would satisfy much of his audience. But he also knew that the college had advertised his talk across campus, and he expected to see some nature-loving, sandals-wearing English professor in the back row. With that in mind, he cited the work of nature writer Wendell Berry at the outset of his talk and closed with a line of poetry from Mary Oliver; halfway through the talk, he projected a photograph of a local pond and used his laser pointer to explain to nonscientists exactly what we were seeing. By enfolding these other types of evidence into his presentations, he has expanded the audience of people who know about and understand his research.

In short, writers who seek to write for broader publics have to develop their skills in searching for, and deploying, multiple forms of evidence in their writing. Academic writers do excellent work when it comes to marshaling discipline-specific forms of evidence for the articles and books they produce for their colleagues. I analyze literary excerpts; my economist friend flashes his tables; the biologist across campus describes her experiments. Our colleagues get us. But when it comes to writing for wider audiences, we are not always quite as aware of the importance of varying the forms of data and evidence we present to less informed readers who don't share our disciplinary background. But to do so is *essential* for academics looking to break outside their usual publishing outlets—and will thus be the focus of the recommendations in this chapter.

I'll begin with a fuller explanation for the principle that audience-expanding academics must **vary their evidence**. I'll provide one great model for how this can be done and then offer a checklist of potential evidence types. Three other important considerations should guide our use of evidence. I'll let Russian novelist Leo Tolstoy help us tackle the tricky question of **how much evidence** you need—or, more accurately, how much your reader needs. However you might use it, evidence really hits its mark with readers when you **contextualize** it. Don't just plunk it down in front of the reader: introduce it, present it in a variety of ways, and analyze it. Finally, if you are going to use **stories as evidence**—as you should—then you need to tell your stories well. I'll give you a quick checklist you can use to enhance the power of your stories.

As a final note, some readers might disagree with my terminology in this chapter. What I will call *evidence* you might call *data*. But I make this word choice deliberately. As nonfiction writers, we are always making arguments to readers, even if we don't always describe them that way. A memoirist hopes to convince readers that their story is both true and significant; a political scientist lays out their policy recommendations in an op-ed for a popular newspaper; a nutritionist writes an advice book that introduces their program to live a healthy life. In that last case, the writer is giving you advice, yes, but they also must convince you that you should follow it. That's an argument. In almost any nonfiction book or essay, the author brings their collection of data, in whatever form it takes, to the table in service of their argument, which turns it into *evidence*—which is the term I will use in this chapter and beyond.

## VARYING EVIDENCE

We can find a master course in the use of evidence in Eve L. Ewing's 2018 book *Ghosts in the Schoolyard: Racism and School Closings on Chicago's South Side*. Ewing is a sociologist of education at the University of Chicago, who has written extensively about schools in Black communities in Chicago and beyond. Her book opens with the strategy we considered in chapter 1, posing an intriguing question to the reader. In the first two decades of the twenty-first century, many Chicago public schools situated in predominantly Black communities were characterized as underperforming and slated for closure. But in the face of these announced closures, community members rose up in protest. She poses her question at the top of the book's third page: "But if the[se] schools were so terrible, why did people fight for them so adamantly?"[3]

That's a great start for a book aimed at a wide audience, but her skills as a nonfiction writer shine as she gathers many forms of evidence in support of her answers to this question. Ewing started her career as a Chicago schoolteacher, and she describes that background. While she works on the book, she attends community protests and reads transcripts of school board meetings, taking notes and recording her observations. She produces and analyzes public statements from school administrators and local politicians. She provides a historical overview of Bronzeville, the Chicago neighborhood that provides the setting for the book. The book includes statistical tables and graphs explaining shifts in enrollment and student and population demographics. For good measure, she reproduces a few images.

Early in the book, Ewing explains something important about one feature of this collection of evidence in the book. Some readers might come to such a book with expectations that they'll engage with the numbers, the power players, the outcomes. But she doesn't want readers to neglect that an essential plank of evidence comes from citing and analyzing the words and experiences of members of the local community:

> The experiential knowledge of people of color not only is a legitimate source of evidence, but is in fact critical to understanding the function of racism as a fundamental American social structure. So I cannot and do not aspire to tell you an objective story; rather I offer a story that is revelatory based on the experience of my own life and the lives of community members living in the shadow of history.[4]

In Ewing's account, the unrehearsed statement of a community member fighting for the future of her children matters as much to her argument as graphs and statistical tables or the official proclamations from the chief administrator of the Chicago Public Schools.

Aspiring academic authors from disciplines that are more scientific might feel challenged by the suggestion to incorporate this kind of evidence into their writing. But you might think about the ways in which you engage in these practices in the classroom, even if you do it in unplanned moments. You might be demonstrating a scientific principle or using statistics to explain a social phenomenon, and then offer an aside, "This theory reminds me of something I once experienced when I was a child . . ." or "As a side note, we see an interesting example of this issue in the recent uproar about celebrities and their private jets . . ." These statements can seem like throwaway moments in a class devoted to serious stuff, but some students perk up in these moments and might lodge them more firmly in their memories than your beautifully designed statistical table.

Writing for an expanded audience thus means becoming *deliberate* about varying the types of evidence you use. Your deliberate thinking about evidence variety should occur at two levels. First, as you are planning, writing, and revising your work, keep an eye on the mix of evidence forms you are using. It can be helpful to keep a list somewhere of all your evidence types throughout the project, just as an easy reminder of the importance of this work. Such a list might contain:

- Personal anecdotes
- Real-life examples from current events
- Hypothetical scenarios
- Case studies and biographies
- Quotations from works of literature
- Artworks, images, photographs
- Statistical tables, graphs, charts
- Outcomes from research experiments
- Formal and informal survey results
- Casual observations of events and people
- Field notes from you or others
- Research and ideas from authorities in your discipline
- Citations from academic research
- Interviews with experts
- Interviews with relevant subjects

As you are putting your mix of sources together, don't neglect this last one. Many authors interview experts and include their ideas and recommendations in their work. But we should incorporate the lived experiences of people who might not have authoritative credentials but who can inform our discipline with their unique stories and perspectives. If you are writing about teaching, interview some students and teachers and include their voices. If you are analyzing a new economic theory and its potential social effects, talk to members of the communities it will impact and listen to their stories. While you shouldn't base an economic theory on a few conversations, you might hear about an experience that illustrates a key element of your theory and share it in your book's introduction (with the storyteller's permission, ideally in written form for your files).

## GenAI Callout

The use of generative artificial intelligence (GenAI) can serve as a guided research assistant as you seek to diversify your source base. Conventional search engines can serve this purpose, but GenAI can move us more quickly toward the goal of diversifying our evidence when we find ourselves drawing from the same well for all our evidence. You can paste your thesis or a one-paragraph sample of your project into the prompt box and ask the AI tool to produce examples from any of the evidence categories presented in this chapter, especially the ones that are less familiar to you. If you are a social scientist who largely works with survey data, prompt your AI tool to point you toward some interviews with relevant subjects, or to show you works of art that would illustrate your main themes, or to produce a hypothetical scenario. If you work in a humanities field, prompt the AI tool in the other direction, seeing if someone somewhere has developed an experiment or survey that would connect to the argument you are making. You can also ask it to introduce you to experts or stories from people with diverse backgrounds, including women, scholars of color, Indigenous scientists, or LGBTQ+ poets. A quick story on this use for diversity. In 2023 I began a monthly Substack column in which I pair works of literature and philosophy with challenges facing higher education. When I started the column, I had a handful of novels and philosophical works that I already had in mind, mostly ones I had first encountered in my undergraduate or graduate education. But when I was ready to expand my thinking and discover some new (to me) authors, I gave ChatGPT this prompt: "I write a Substack column that highlights connections between classic works of philosophy and the challenges facing higher education. I would like to include more non-western philosophers in my column to diversify my thinking and the thinking of my readers. Can you introduce me to some less well-known Black, Indigenous American, Asian, or East Asian philosophers?" I was thrilled with the results—lots of new books to read! A year later, I am still chasing down and reading the works from the list it gave me. In their classroom presentations and discussions, many faculty have become aware of the importance of including illustrative examples that draw from a variety of races, ethnic traditions, gender identities, and sexualities. The same orientation we have brought into our teaching should be carried into our writing—and GenAI can support that objective.

### STREAMLINING EVIDENCE

The Russian novelist Leo Tolstoy wrote a short story called "How Much Land Does a Man Need?" The answer, in the end, was six feet: the space in which to bury a human body.[5] The story's title and theme critique the very human desire to pile up material goods (like real estate), gathering and displaying far more than anyone should need. That same desire can infect academic authors when it comes to evidence. We are experts when it comes to doing research, and we can go to great lengths to find sources and data and surveys and interviews and more. But we are not writing to ourselves—we are writing for readers. Thus academic authors who wish to write to nondisciplinary audiences have to ask themselves not how much evidence they *have* but how much evidence they *need* to convince their intended audience of their arguments.

The answer: Not as much as you think.

To be sure, academic audiences prefer lots and lots of evidence. They expect to see that you have done your research. But if you are writing to broader audiences, you have to think differently about this issue. Your goal is to convince people of something. An academic article in your subject might contain references to twenty to thirty or more sources, which are needed to convince your audience. But an educated nonacademic reader might be convinced by an article that contains one interesting case study, the statistical findings of two surveys, and a little bit of historical comparison. It will be helpful for you as an expert to have twenty to thirty sources in your internal knowledge base, but your work as a public writer consists of discriminating among them, selecting the most essential ones, and letting the rest go or relegating them to the footnotes or a dedicated "further reading" section.

While I was working on this book, I had a videoconference with an author who had submitted a book proposal for the series I edit. The proposal contained an interesting idea, but it was supported by five or six distinct bodies of research that the author wanted to include in the book. We had a conversation that I'm sure was difficult for him, but in the end I convinced him that much of the research and many of the sources that he was referencing continually throughout the proposal were extraneous to the really interesting idea that he was bringing to the table. At the end of the call, I saw his shoulders sag and he sighed. "I guess," he said, "I shouldn't be putting everything I know about education in this one book." The call, in other words, finished well.

I would love to invent or document some kind mathematical formula that I could pass along to you—the Lang Evidence Ratio—but no such thing exists, because the quantity of evidence you need will depends on the audience and your purpose. I continue to rely heavily on documenting evidence in my teaching books because I am writing to teachers in higher education, and "evidence-based teaching" has become an oft-repeated phrase in that field. If I were writing to students or parents or K-12 teachers, all of whom are interested in education research but who do not normally read articles in academic journals, I would certainly make different choices about the amount of evidence I use. The primary audience of *this* book consists of readers with academic training, who would normally like to see lots of evidence—but I know they are coming to these pages in search of very practical advice. Experts in public scholarship might react with consternation to the light amount of evidence they see from their field, but I write these pages more from my role as a practitioner than from my scholarly chair. The further away you move from an academic audience, the more ruthless you might need to be in narrowing down your evidence base in support of your arguments.

Moreover, the more you rely on the traditional meat and potatoes of academic research—statistics, complex survey data, detailed field notes, archival material—the more you will need to balance that research with stories, examples, quotes, and images. It's very typical in an academic work for the writer to adduce five or ten traditional experimental results in support of even a minor point in support of your idea. You will lose your nonacademic reader by source number three. Instead of trotting out one source after another of that same type, tell your reader in detail about one really definitive experiment, mention one or two others to demonstrate that it's not an outlier, and then tell a great story or two illustrating the phenomenon the experiments were designed to investigate.

Don't underestimate the power of even one great source. I subscribe to several Substack newsletters and blog feeds written by successful nonfiction book authors. All of them share something in common: instead of trying to tackle a large topic and supporting their idea with multiple sources—as we typically do in our academic work—they select one or two especially interesting sources and take a deep dive into the topic. Cognitive psychologist Michelle Miller organizes her newsletter for college teachers by identifying a recent article in her field, providing a summary of it, analyzing the methodology, offering caveats, and spelling out implications for higher education.[6] The Learning Scientists, a group of early-career cognitive psychologists, do the same thing in a weekly blog post.[7] In both cases, they point their readers toward other research that connects to the source they are presenting. Substack newsletters or blogs offer academic authors a regular opportunity to develop and sharpen their writing skills, including an awareness of how to make academic research accessible to nonspecialists. Straining a complex idea through the filter of a single source will appeal to your reader-learners and might prove enabling for you as a writer—even if you then move into a deeper level of research immediately afterward.

As an expert writing to nonexperts, you highlight the evidence that will be most convincing to your reader. That will never be just one source, but it will likely be fewer than you expect. As you are picking the evidence that will feature in the main text of your book, identify a mix that will appeal to as many readers as possible, and focus on the strongest ones. Build your book around those foundational supports.

## CONTEXTUALIZING EVIDENCE

At this point you might be wondering what your writing might look like if you take a hatchet to your mound of collected research and significantly narrow your evidence base. How will you fill up the space you have created by cutting all that research material?

You will fill that space by practicing two essential skills needed by audience-expanding academic authors. First, you have to offer engaging presentations of your traditional academic evidence, which includes providing full context for it (the subject of this section). Second, you should always balance your traditional evidence with great stories (the subject of the next section).

The tradition of the literature review, for all the important work it does for us as academics, is not the friend of a public-facing nonfiction writer. Literature reviews train us to nod quickly at as many previous articles and books as possible. This puts us in the habit of writing paragraphs like this one, which I am not singling out for criticism because this paragraph looks exactly like the hundreds of thousands of literature review paragraphs you can find dispersed in many thousands of academic books and journals:

> Since they were identified, HIPs [High-Impact Practices] have become a foundational strategy to increase student retention and completion rates in institutions of higher education and have been used as a variable to study student success (McGlynn, 2014) and engagement (Sweat, Jones, Han, & Wolfgramm 2013). HIPs have also been used to explore the needs of specific student populations such as first-year students (Tukibayeva and Gonyea, 2014) and students from traditionally underserved or underrepresented backgrounds (Sweat et al, 2013). Frequently discussed across a range of disciplines including university libraries (Murray, 2015), the presence of embedded HIPs during a student's academic career is now considered to be a fundamental metric for an institution's dedication to student success (Kilgo, Sheets, and Pascarella, 2015) and campus cultures that promote and support high-quality and effective educational practices (Laird, BrckaLorenz, Zilvinskis, & Lambert, 2014).[8]

The practice of glancing at such a large number of resources in such a small space makes us forget that every one of these briefly cited studies was conducted by curious people, trying to investigate an interesting question, under a unique set of circumstances. Most pieces of published research (there are exceptions) have uncovered something new or intriguing or just different. Every one of these contextual features can offer nonfiction writers an opportunity to make their evidence more engaging to their readers. Here are some examples of how certain kinds of evidence can be presented to readers:

- **IF YOU ARE CITING AN EXPERIMENT, NOTE UNUSUAL DESIGN FEATURES OR THOUGHT-PROVOKING RESULTS.** The design features of an experiment can seem like second nature to you, but nonacademic readers might be surprised by some of the strange things that researchers get up to in their laboratories. If the researchers did something especially creative or unusual, highlight it: "Most experiments in this field have followed the traditional protocols, but these researchers introduced an interesting twist." And remember that at the heart of every experiment lies the same kind of fundamental question that we considered in chapter 1. Bring the questions to the surface and describe how the researchers tried to answer them.

- **CONSIDER HOW BEST TO PRESENT STATISTICAL OR MATHEMATICAL DATA IN YOUR TEXT.** In theory, offering data in both words and graphics would appeal to the widest swath of readers. Some readers' eyes will glaze over as they are reading text descriptions of the data and focus on the graphics, while others will skim tables and graphs and dive into the numbers on the page. But some publishers will balk at an excessive use of graphics, tables, or images. Whether or not you use visual presentations of data, make sure your textual descriptions are accessible as possible. An essay of recommendations by Martha Coven on writing about numbers starts with an easy-to-apply principle: "Do the math. If you want your reader to easily understand the data you're using and any conclusions you draw, you may literally need to do the math. It's not enough to spill numbers onto the page. Tell your reader what the relationship is between them."[9] As in: If you are presenting a numerical increase from 75.6 to 149.2, provide those numbers but also note that the number of instances "nearly doubled."

- **IF YOU ARE CITING THE WORK OF EXPERTS OR INTERVIEWING PEOPLE, OCCASIONALLY FILL OUT THEIR BIOGRAPHIES.** If making a brief reference to someone's work, this is fine: "According to sociologist Eve Ewing . . ." But if you will be citing Ewing's work for a few paragraphs, or returning it to more than once, introduce her to your readers more fully: "Sociologist Eve Ewing began her career as a public-school teacher in Chicago, where she witnessed firsthand the impact of race on public-school funding decisions. She earned her doctorate at Harvard Graduate School of Education and now is an associate professor at the University of Chicago. She has also built a successful career as a poet and author of young adult fictions, which feature Black protagonists and Black life in America." Put faces and histories on the more important experts you cite, or on the people who feature in your stories and interviews. This practice not only injects a human element into your evidence but also explains why readers should trust this source.

- **OCCASIONALLY QUOTE VERBATIM FROM ESSENTIAL TEXTS IN SUPPORT OF YOUR ARGUMENT.** This is common in humanities research, though not so much in the sciences. But as you are either a practicing or an aspiring writer, you should recognize that words matter. A well-crafted sentence can create new ideas. One caveat: don't use long or dense quotes just to support ideas that you can easily put into your own words. Your quotes should do some important work; for example, provoking a different way of thinking about the topic, celebrating the achievement of a beautiful sentence, or introducing your readers to some famous quotation from a giant in your field.

In the previous section I mentioned the Learning Scientists, whose blog provides a regular dissection of a research study in learning or memory. Because its contributors are academics writing for teachers at all levels of education—some of whom are academics and some who are not—the posts vary considerably in their approach to evidence. Consider the following examples of evidence framing, all from the same post, with the amount of evidence context moving from low to high.[10] Taken together, they might serve as a useful Rorschach test that can force you to consider which level of context you think a reader outside of your field would respond best to.

> **LOW CONTEXT.** Excessive smartphone use is linked to depression, anxiety, and poor sleep quality. [A footnote links to an academic article.]
> 
> **MEDIUM CONTEXT.** One study of smartphone use among American college students found that 25% of students surveyed

reported sleep texting. [A footnote links to an academic article.] Sleep texters were significantly more likely to have interrupted sleep, contributing to overall low sleep quality in college students.

**HIGH CONTEXT.** A recent study by Brailovskaia and colleagues (2022) examined the effects of smartphone use reduction and abstinence on well-being. [A footnote links to the academic article by Brailovskaia et al.] A total of 619 participants were randomly assigned to one of three conditions: Abstinence, Reduction, or Control. The Abstinence group (N = 277) was instructed to not use their phone for 7 days. The Reduction group (N = 242) was instructed to reduce their overall phone use by an hour each day for 7 days. The Control group (N = 232) were not given limitations on their phone use. Several measures of smartphone use and well-being were assessed at baseline (prior to the week-long intervention), post-intervention, one month post-intervention, and four months post-intervention. [A discussion of the results follows.]

I would argue that for writers seeking an expanded audience, the sweet spot seems to fall somewhere between the second and third examples. Both as a reader and as a writer, I want more than what I see in the first example. I appreciate the additional information in the medium- and high-context examples, but the third one includes more detail than a nonacademic reader might want or need—not to mention that such readers might not know that *N* stands for "number," or the exact meaning of a control group. Instead of the numbers and discipline-specific terminology, I would have preferred to know more about the authors, where these studies were conducted, and who the participants were.

But a final point needs to be made here. All three examples come from the same essay. In some cases, you and your reader might be satisfied with a zero-context statement and a footnote because it's peripheral to your argument. But when a writer relies heavily on a piece of evidence to support a core plank in their argument, this reader wants to know more. After all, we teach our students to inspect and question the evidence they find in the essays and books they read, and we all wish that the reading public would do the same; when we fill out the context that surrounds our evidence, we model good critical thinking for our learners.

Your writerly obligations to your evidence include a final task: linking it back to your main ideas. Many academic writers present a piece of evidence to the reader and then walk away. In other words, they forget that the reader has to be reminded what the evidence is *for*. A colleague of mine describes the practice of producing evidence but not explaining its significance as akin to a card player laying their winning hand on the table, scooping up the pot, and strolling away into the night. Everyone playing the game would understand what happened. But envision yourself, having laid out that winning hand, then having to explain *why* your hand won to a bystander who was just learning the game. What would they need to understand to recognize the brilliance of your play? What specific cards or moves would you point to? What was the key moment and why?

The best analyses of evidence draw your reader's attention to the details that matter. If you present a statistical table, put an actual or metaphorical circle around the most important number you want readers to remember. If you give a telling quote from a research subject, present the full quotation and then pull out the key word or phrase and explain its significance. I once cotaught a course on The Art and Science of Learning, and we brought the students to the campus art museum to discuss the learning that can happen outside the classroom. The docent who was leading our tour brought us to a sculpture and explained that it came from a sculpture series devoted to depicting the effects of climate change. Then she had us sit on portable stools and just *observe*. Gradually the details of the sculpture began to pop out for us, ones that we might have missed if we had strolled by it on a leisurely walk through the galleries. We shared these observations with one another, analyzing the implications of posture, hand gesture, and clothing. When we finally resumed our tour, our understanding of the artist's message had been deepened by this work of closely analyzing the details of the sculpture.[11]

Envision yourself as that docent, gathering your readers around your best pieces of evidence, having these readers sit for a moment, and then directing them toward the telling details of an experiment, table, image, idea, or text.

## TELLING GREAT STORIES

Many of us aspiring public authors, this one included, dream of seeing our work in the pages of storied publications such as *Harper's* or the *New Yorker*. These magazines are an excellent fit for experts who do their research and care about the craft of writing—people like you. We love these publications, in part, because they tell great stories. We get statistics, information, new ideas, yes, but we also get that evidence mixed generously with stories. But if you use stories in your writing—and you should—then you should learn two important lessons from great storytellers throughout the ages: provide *descriptions* and give *details*. I'll use two examples from the *Atlantic* to illustrate these principles.

The use of descriptions in storytelling invites readers to imagine themselves within the world of the story and feel it with their senses. If the reader were standing at the scene of the story, what would they see? What would they hear? The following excerpt comes from an essay by Elizabeth Bruenig, a staff writer for the magazine, on the botched execution of a prisoner in Alabama. She describes the process of arriving at the prison with other journalists to witness the execution:

> The van passed through gated checkpoints and razor-wire fences, orange flood lights scattering the shadows. The driver and a uniformed corrections officer who rode with him herded us through a

guard shack outfitted with a metal detector, then took our phones and identification. A second van drove us a negligible distance up the gated road to the execution chamber.

At 10:30 p.m., two uniformed guards guided us, again, out of the van. This time we found ourselves in a cul-de-sac terminating in the high walls and slit windows of Holman's death row. The squat building sat beside us, its heavy door cracking open, occasionally, startlingly, to spill light into the dimness. But no word came from within. And so we paced, and waited.[12]

This scene is set so well that you might not realize how many direct appeals Bruenig makes to the senses. Sight words: *gated, orange floodlights, shadows, cul-de-sac, slit, squat, light, dimness*. Movement words: *passed, herded, guided, cracking, spill, paced*. There are no specific words for hearing, but many details imply what you would be hearing: the van rolling along, the guards asking for cellphones and IDs, the creaking sound of the heavy door opening. Every sense is available to us when we are giving descriptions, but most commonly we encounter words of vision, hearing, and feeling (as when the door opens "startlingly").

We can fill out and complement our descriptions with details that give us other kinds of information about the story. For example, we are told that Bruenig and her companions are released from the van at 10:30 p.m. This detail tells us much. It would be dark outside. It has likely been a long day for the journalists already, and they are tired. The prolonging of the day would intensify the prisoner's fear and the anguished waiting of his family. That ripple effect caused by the execution's timing intensifies the pain for everyone involved. As in this brief excerpt, both the details and the descriptions that writers provide should serve a purpose: they tell the reader something about the characters in the story, give essential information, or connect directly to one of the work's themes.

In this second passage, from an essay on the building and selling of homes in a hurricane zone, nonfiction writer Michael

Grunwald marries descriptions and details in his two opening paragraphs:

> Five years ago, after Hurricane Irma pummeled Florida's Gulf Coast, I rode a boat through the canals of Cape Coral, the "Waterfront Wonderland," America's fastest-growing city at the time. It was a sunny day with a gentle breeze and just a few puffs of clouds, so as I pointed to the blown-out lanais and piles of storm debris, my guide, a snowbird named Brian Tattersall, kept teasing me for missing the point of a magical afternoon. He said I sounded like his northern friends who always told him he was crazy to live in the Florida hurricane zone.
>
> "Come on. Does this feel crazy?" he asked, as we drifted past some palm trees. Cape Coral is a low-lying, pancake-flat spit of exposed former swampland, honeycombed by an astonishing 400 miles of drainage ditches disguised as real-estate amenities, but to Tattersall it was a low-tax subtropical Venice where he could dock his 29-foot Sea Fox in the canal behind his house. When I asked if Irma would slow down the city's population boom, he scoffed: "No way."[13]

The descriptions here contrast the dangers of the hurricane zone—the piles of storm debris—and the hopeful attitudes of the residents, represented by the image of a sunny day with a gentle breeze. Details can often create symbolic resonances like this. But this passage also provides some basic information that gives us context for the scope of the problem: four hundred miles of exposed but precious real estate.

The descriptions and details used in these two passages are all doing *work*; they are not chosen at random.

Learning to tell stories like these two examples takes time and practice. When writers first begin to add descriptions and details to their work, they often overindulge. They layer on adjectives and adverbs, choose unusual verbs, and lengthen sentences. Editors refer to this as "purple prose," filled with ornamentation and complexity. We'll return to this issue in chapter 6, but for now I recommend that academic writers wade slowly into this work of storytelling. Start with the basic plot: what happened, and to whom did it happen? Then add just a few additional details or descriptive words. When I work with writers on developing their storytelling capacities, I first give them a comprehensive set of questions that *could* inspire a rewrite:

- Have you located your story in time?
- Have you located it in space?
- Have you described actions?
- What would someone at the scene hear?
- What would they smell?
- What would they feel?
- What was the weather or atmosphere?

But after they answer as many of these questions as possible about their story, I ask them to step back and determine which of these questions matter most. I suggest that they pick just two or three of them and incorporate some new language in response. That's usually enough. The kinds of stories we tell in our nonfiction writing should not overwhelm the reader with too many descriptions and details. You can hit one or two senses to help readers envision the scene, and then include a few details of helpful context.

Even when the descriptions and details are limited, remember that they should serve a purpose. If you are writing a book about how our daily economic choices shape our lives and you take an economist out to lunch to discuss the topic, it might be worth noting whether they ordered caviar and chardonnay or a grilled cheese sandwich and Pepsi. If you interview an expert on work-life balance via Zoom and there are children screaming and dogs barking continuously in the background while the expert serenely answers your questions, that might be worth mentioning. But if you are interviewing an economist about the secret machinations of the Fed, their barking dog in the background doesn't do any important work for you or the reader.

I should finish by acknowledging that stories are supporting actors in logical arguments: they are not the stars of the argumentative show. They are not definite proofs for anything. Give me a story to support either side of a debatable topic, and I'll find you a story to support the other side. Stories should supplement and illustrate the more traditional forms of evidence you have gathered as an academic and are showing to your reader. But they are great at drawing readers into your arguments, offering new perspectives on your subject, and giving your readers a break from other kinds of cognitive work.

## STRATEGIES: VARYING, STREAMLINING, CONTEXTUALIZING, AND STORYTELLING

- **VARY YOUR EVIDENCE.** As you write to wider and wider audiences, you will find that you are arguing to readers from diverse evidence traditions—and some who come from no particular evidence tradition. Successful nonfiction works thereby ensure that they are appealing to as many readers as possible by varying their evidence through the work. This means keeping an eye on the overall mix of evidence forms, including everything from statistics and lab results to personal anecdotes and interviews with unique voices.
- **STREAMLINE YOUR EVIDENCE.** The amount of evidence you need for your work will depend on your audience. Academic audiences will welcome all the stuff: the journals, the statistics, the experiments. Readers outside your discipline or from outside academia will be overwhelmed by too much of this kind of evidence. If you are concerned about what expert readers might think, move your ancillary research into footnotes (but still fewer than you might like) or archive it onto your website.
- **CONTEXTUALIZE YOUR EVIDENCE.** Once you have pared down your evidence base to its essentials, give at least some of it the

full-day spa treatment. Surround it with writerly love. Put faces on the people whose work you are citing. Explain the forms taken by research in your discipline; don't take for granted that readers know what it's like to design an experiment, dig into an archive, or take field notes. Highlight the important points in the evidence you are showing by drawing the eyes of your reader toward the fine brushstrokes.

- **TELL GREAT STORIES.** Stories live in the descriptions and details. If you have a story that will help your readers understand something important about your topic, put your reader at the scene of the story and help them experience it with their senses. Include details that provide crucial context or that connect to your current themes. Ensure that all descriptions and details serve a purpose; don't just fill out stories to take up space.

## FINAL CONFESSION

If you put your ideas into book form, and you manage to get it published and people actually read it, you will be faced by the prospect of readers commenting on your work. Even if your book isn't featured in the *New York Times*, you can see how people are responding to your ideas and writing on social media or in the comment sections of Amazon and Goodreads. Many authors will say that they don't read their reviews. I don't believe them. I will happily confess that I read my reviews, in part for self-laceration purposes and in part because I would like to continue to learn about how I can reach new readers.

Some of the reader comments on my book *Distracted: Why Students Can't Focus and What We Can Do about It* have singled out my approach to the topic of this chapter, the use of evidence in nonfiction writing. Two of those comments illustrate the reason I have mentioned several times in this chapter why your evidence practices will always depend on the nature of your audience. The first one comes from Amazon:

> Lang certainly did his homework to write this book. If the Amazon preview allows it, I recommend looking at the "Chapter Notes" section of the book. There you will see the extensive bibliography that Lang draws upon to formulate his views. He does a great job at presenting the latest research without getting too bogged in the details of each study. He summarizes and references other studies effectively and always extracts practical pieces of advice and theory from the studies.

The author of this comment is obviously a very smart person and an all-around great human being. Here's the second one, from Goodreads:

> The first half was a bit hard to get through, and, although the author listed his sources, it seemed mostly anecdotal and based off a couple of isolated cases rather than true research. I'm not saying it wasn't correct, just not convincing.

This person was probably distracted on a smartphone instead of paying rapt attention to my unassailable arguments.

But you can see the point made by juxtaposing these two responses. Some of your readers won't blink an eye at your extensive citation of academic journal articles, especially if they come from your discipline or are aficionados in your subject matter. For those folks, pile it on. But as you move further and further away from expert readers, the more you will find people who are convinced (and even impressed!) by a more streamlined presentation of evidence. Those readers will be drawn in by the kinds of recommendations I have made in this chapter: varying evidence types, highlighting the key sources, drawing attention to the key features of your evidence, and telling great stories.

If you're trying to reach a mix of readers along the continuum from expert to novice, as we often are, err on the side of the strategies recommended here. If you are bringing new ideas and research to the table, experts will forgive you for a little overexplaining of how evidence is collected and presented in your discipline. But if you don't explain your evidence protocols to novice learners, they will do the one thing we want readers never to do: close the book unfinished and walk away.

---

**CHAPTER THREE WRITING PROMPTS**

- Drawing from the bulleted list of evidence types in the "Varying Evidence" section of this chapter, brainstorm the list that will support your ideas. Review that list with the arguments of this chapter in mind and add at least one evidence type that will challenge you as a writer. Write a few sentences to yourself about how you would gather that evidence.
- Select three of your more traditional sources that were contextualized in a minimalist way—such as with just a parenthetical citation of a book or journal article—and expand your introduction to it with one of the strategies recommended in this chapter. Remember that you don't have to put a face on every source. Limit this strategy to the most important ones.
- You probably already have some stories in mind to include in your book, or that you have written in other contexts. Select one of them and write or revise it by adding three details or sensory appeals. Don't overwhelm the story—three only.

**CHAPTER FOUR**

# CULTIVATING READER ATTENTION

I don't know of any more demoralizing feeling than standing in front of a room full of students, hoping to inspire them to learn something new—something you love, and have chosen to devote your life to—and you realize that they are completely ignoring you. They're either slumped in their chairs with their eyes glazed over, meandering through the caverns of their minds, or surreptitiously texting a friend about where to meet for lunch. You seem to be the only person in the room interested in the suspenseful climax of your story about a groundbreaking discovery in your discipline.

When I was in college, inattentive students read the campus newspaper, talked quietly, and—my favorite activity in boring classes—wrote witty comments in their notebooks and shared them with their nearby seatmates. Within the first decade of my becoming a teacher, digital devices made it even easier to tune out teachers. First came the laptops, then the wireless networks that enabled them to connect to the internet, followed by the smartphones that didn't even need all that expensive Wi-Fi. When I began conducting the research for the book I wrote on attention and distraction, I would have counted myself among the teachers who thought we should chuck these devices out the window and get back to good old-fashioned book learning. But it didn't take long for me to discover that we have a long historical record of humans generally, and teachers specifically, expressing concern about the fragility of human attention. If you describe the relationship of attention and distraction as a battle, it is one that teachers have been losing for at least two millennia now.[1]

But we don't have to cast it in those terms: instead of *battling* students for their attention, we can instead describe our work as *supporting* their attention. Human attention evolved to be always on the move, a quality that helped us thrive over our long evolution as a species. Our early ancestors needed a constant awareness of their environment, scanning continuously for predators and prey, dangers and opportunities. That was essential for our ancestors' survival, but today's humans face very different environments and demands on our attention. To sit in a chair and listen to a speaking figure for fifty or seventy-five minutes is a pretty strange demand on brains that evolved to survive as hunger-gatherers in grassland environments. We are an extremely adaptable species, so for centuries we have been putting pressure on our ever-evolving brains to sit down, block out distractions, and focus. But when the opportunity arises to check out the flashing lights and movements in our screens—and that opportunity arises all the time now—our brains jump in with both feet. When students lose themselves in these devices instead of paying attention to their learning, we shouldn't be surprised or judgmental.

Instead, we have to help students pay attention. Giving students breaks in the middle of class, varying the teaching strategies we use throughout the class session, interspersing periods of lecture with active learning exercises—all of these have been proposed by researchers in this field, but most teachers eventually intuit them from teaching experiences. It doesn't take long for new teachers to realize that if they give uninterrupted lectures for fifty minutes or more, students will zone out. If they want to keep the attention of their students, teachers have to vary their classroom activities, modify their pacing, and give students cognitive breaks.

If we continue with our premise of viewing the *reading experience* as a *learning experience*, we must recognize that writers have to become just like attention-supporting teachers. However powerful your prose might be, however fascinating your subject matter might be, if you deliver it as the print equivalent of an unbroken lecture, your reader will eventually zone out. Instead of letting that happen—and blaming the problem on your distracted readers—you can be deliberate about using the writer's tools of attention.

The tools used by teachers and writers don't look exactly the same, but four writing strategies can ensure we are giving attention-challenged readers the supports they need. First, the capturing of attention begins in the opening sentences and paragraphs. Stories, striking statistics, curious cases—all of these do the essential work of **capturing attention** in the initial moments of a book, chapter, or essay. From there the support for attention has to be extended throughout the work. Creating **divisions within a text,** in the form of paragraphs and sections and chapters, gives opportunities for our brains and eyes (or ears) to pause and regroup when attention begins to wane. Writers can also rely on a battery of what I call **small attention tools,** which are writing strategies designed to point readers to the most important moments in a work. Finally, **closing strategies** in a text should reward readers for their attention to our writing with a thought-provoking finish.

## OPENINGS

In chapter 1, I argued that questions should drive our writing, and those questions should be shown to the reader in the early pages of an essay or a book. But if you study the openings of some great nonfiction books, or just scan the opening paragraphs of essays in prestigious publications, you'll notice that writers often lead into those questions with a few paragraphs or pages designed to capture the reader's attention with surprise, storytelling, or wonder.

Consider these three examples:

> Every year, 9 million children die before their fifth birthday. A woman in sub-Saharan Africa has a one-in-thirty chance of dying while giving birth—in the developed world, the chance is one in 5,600. There are least twenty-five countries, most of them in sub-Saharan Africa, where the average person is expected to live no more than fifty-five years. In India alone, more than 50 million school-going children cannot read a very simple text.
>
> ABHIJIT V. BANJERLEE AND ESTHER DUFLO, *Poor Economics: A Radical Rethinking of the Way to Fight Global Poverty*[2]

> I sat in my first college class with pen nervously poised, ready to absorb every word my professor had to say. I imagined that he would stand at the front of the class and stiffly, yet drolly... impart the wisdom of his many years in psychology. Instead, the late, great Michael Fleming of Boston University stalked into the room with all of the zeal of the velociraptor. He spent the semester alternatively delighting and terrorizing us, telling shocking tales straight from the therapist's couch; hissing *Mystery Science Theater 3000*–style psychological commentary on scenes from popular movies; and gleefully creeping up on sleeping students to startle them awake. It was my favorite class of a very long educational career, and it was a rollercoaster of emotions.
>
> SARAH CAVANAGH, *The Spark of Learning: Energizing the College Classroom with the Science of Emotion*[3]

> People like to masturbate. They also like to get drunk and eat Twinkies. Not typically all at the same time, but that's a matter of personal preference.
>
> EDWARD SLINGERLAND, *Drunk: How We Sipped, Danced, and Stumbled Our Way to Civilization*[4]

Shocking statistics, personal stories, baffling statements—these openings serve a very practical purpose: the author wants you to keep reading. Such engaging entry points are the stock-in-trade of professional writers, but apparently they challenge many of us academic experts. Casiana Ionita, the publishing director at Penguin Press, has pinpointed uninteresting openings as a sticking point for academic authors trying to find their way into trade publications:

> Start with something really gripping, instead of building and building over many pages, explaining the field, describing what this and that person has done. Get to the point really quickly. We are all so busy, so you want to grab the reader by the neck as quickly as possible. Otherwise, they won't keep going.[5]

As a writer trying to grab the attention of novelty-loving human brains, you are competing with a world of distractions in the reader's immediate environment. Even if you are writing to people who are accustomed to sitting down and reading, they still have many distractions in their immediate purview. Your opening must convince them to join you for an intellectual ride. You are looking to spark their curiosity, make them wonder what will come next. What should we do about those terrible statistics about global poverty? What's the relationship between emotions and learning? What's the relationship between drinking, Twinkies, and masturbation?

In addition to sparking reader curiosity, your opening also announces your personality as a teacher-writer. My reading time is precious, and I might not want to spend it in the company of a writer who lectures me uninterruptedly, cites endless research papers in support of their arguments, and never stops to let me think and wonder. The three examples I provided introduce you to different kinds of educators. You can gather that Banjerlee and Duflo will bring their research expertise to the table, and that will include statistics. Cavanagh is a storyteller and will leaven her research with plenty of examples. Slingerland, a philosopher, wants to provoke the reader. You might not know what comes next from his opening—an evolutionary history of drinking and drug use—but it would be hard to resist at least the next paragraph. In every case, I would be energized to spend the semester in the presence of these teachers.

Because your opening plays such an outsize role in the success of your project, it can create a fatal stumbling block. I know some anxious would-be authors who are so intimidated by those critical opening sentences that they just never start composing. Fortunately, there are plenty of tried-and-true options you can consider as you plan your learner's entry point:

- **STORIES.** In chapter 3 I argued for the power of stories as evidence, and that's because people like stories (see: all literature). Your stories can be personal ones, like Cavanagh's, or they can focus on other people's experiences. They can unfold in a few sentences or spread to two or three pages. Very brief opening stories don't have to have a real dramatic arc; they might just be a scene and a little bit of action. Remember what we considered in chapter 3, and if you are going to tell a story, tell it well, with sensory descriptions and contextual details.
- **SHOCKING STATISTICS.** Don't overwhelm readers with detailed analysis of statistics; save that for later. Instead lay out a percentage or set of numbers that will make a reader pause. Use words in your opening sentences and save the graphics for later when you are digging into the stats in more depth. Opening statistics should have some shock value. Pick out the most surprising or disturbing piece of data from your research, and lead with it.
- **INTRIGUING FACTS.** Tell me something cool about the world, something a little baffling. I don't know much biology, but one of my children does, and every once in a while she tells me something she learned in college that makes me say, "You're kidding me—really?" Academics typically have great hoards of interesting facts, but they sometimes lose sight of how strange those facts might be to outsiders. Intriguing facts are a great way to introduce yourself to readers as an interested and interesting person.
- **QUOTATIONS.** Many people like to start their essays and books with a few lines from famous thinkers (these are called *epigraphs*, and

you see them on the first page of many books, including works of literature), but what I mean here is a quotation from someone we will encounter later in the book. If you interviewed someone who gave you a really great quote, lead with it. Plunk the reader into a scene and let the words emerge from your source's mouth.

- **PROVOCATIVE STATEMENTS.** Make an assertion that runs against conventional wisdom. You can use a little hyperbole here—not *everyone* likes Twinkies. Remember that most nonfiction books are arguments of some sort. As succinctly as possible, how could you state the most extreme version of your position—or the position you will refute? I'm especially drawn in by these openings. After I read someone's provocative claim, I think, "Now wait a minute here . . ." and then I'm primed to start arguing with the author in my head—which means I keep reading.

If you find yourself paralyzed at the thought of writing a great opening sentence, just don't do it—at least for now. Many writers wait until much later in the drafting process to write their openings. I like to draft my opening at the beginning of a writing project, but I always assume that it will be replaced by a new one by the time I have finished. You do need a great opening for your reader, but you don't need one before you start writing the book.

## TEXT DIVISIONS

If you ever come across ancient manuscripts in a museum, or see images of them, you might think to yourself that those ancient peoples had better powers of attention than we do. Some of the older manuscripts I have seen are printed as column after column of text, with no paragraphs or section breaks, and sometimes no visible punctuation. But don't fool yourself into believing that our brains today are somehow fundamentally different from those of our ancient forebears. For ancient writers, paper or papyrus was a precious commodity, so they tried to jam as much text as possible onto every page.

Your publisher will have easier access to paper than a medieval copyist did, and much of our reading happens on screens. Writers today thus should use one of the simplest attention tools in the writer's arsenal: divisions and breaks within the text. These can take the form of chapters, parts, sections, and subsections. The use of such tools recognizes something fundamental about attention: it fatigues. When we have to focus on something that challenges us cognitively—like a lecture or a long section of text—our powers of attention start to erode. Remember the last keynote presentation you attended and think about how much easier it was to pay attention in the first five minutes than it was after forty minutes of unbroken lecturing. You surely have noticed this phenomenon in your classes as well, which might begin with students giving you their full attention, which then gradually dissolves over the course of the hour. Researchers call this "directed attention fatigue," and it can derail a tired reader, learner, or human.[6]

Writers can combat this phenomenon by creating plenty of opportunities for the reader to finish a section of text, pause their attention for a minute, and then return with renewed focus. You are an expert and well-practiced reader, but if I watched you in your reading chair, what I would likely observe would be you pulling your eyes from the page occasionally and taking a few seconds to stare out the window at the falling rain or notice the cat cleaning itself. In these short breaks, you are giving your brain the pauses it needs to refresh and be ready to tackle the next sentence or paragraph. When we build pauses and divisions into our work, we provide the reader with strategic moments to take these quick breaks in the action.

This seems to be something that writers throughout the ages have intuited, since divisions and breaks are ubiquitous in almost every form of literary and even academic writing. Many poems are divided into stanzas or parts, especially longer ones. Plays are segmented into acts and scenes. Works of fiction and nonfiction are first divided into paragraphs, and then usually into chapters and parts. Of course there are exceptions: epic poems that roll along without breaks, as do some of the novels of Samuel Beckett. But even shorter forms of nonfiction writing, such as long-form journalism or thought pieces in intellectual publications, will often include visible breaks in the text.

The use of text divisions also acknowledges the reality that readers will frequently not read a work in one sitting. Readers put books down and then come back to them. Text divisions provide them a convenient spot not only to stop their reading but also to have a place they can return to easily. When they pick up the work again, especially if a day or a few days have passed, they might return to the division point they marked and start by glancing backward to remind themselves what they had already covered. They are essentially doing what we all do these days when we are watching a television series and start a new episode by watching the brief recap of what has come before. Extended television storylines are played out over multiple episodes—another example of the importance of divisions. I might binge an entire television series in a single weekend, but between episodes, I am going to the bathroom or making a snack or responding to a text—and these activities help my attention refresh and renew.

Writers should think strategically how divisions are used throughout the text. Don't push a reader's attention to its absolute limits. There are times when you might need multiple pages to play out a complex idea, and you need the reader to follow you even when it's difficult, but your default thinking should be to look for places where you can create breaks in the text. I don't think I'm alone in this practice, but sometimes when I am reading a work of nonfiction and am in the middle of a difficult part of the text I sometimes will stop and flip a few pages to see when the next break will appear. As the reader in that situation, I am essentially giving myself a little pause in the experience—and doing myself the work that the writer probably should have done. Even when reading a novel, I might page ahead to see when the next chapter or text break will appear so I don't have to stop reading in the middle of a scene.

Practically speaking, the two most common text division strategies are the following:

- **TITLED SECTIONS AND SUBSECTIONS.** In chapter 2, I argued that titles, subtitles, and section headings can keep your reader attentive to your throughline. If you follow that suggestion and use section headings throughout your chapters, the text divisions will take care of themselves. In a book, I would recommend that headings of sections occur *at least* every three to five pages. I wouldn't be too rigid about following that rule in either direction, though. Your use of sections and subsections should be inspired by the needs of the argument and the reader. Package ideas together in a chapter the same way that you package sentences together into a paragraph.
- **TEXT BREAKS.** A section heading is a hard break; a text break is a soft one. At the end of a series of paragraphs, insert a short space before the next paragraph (called a *line space* in the publishing business because it's the same width as a line of text, only blank), and that space indicates that the work will move in a new direction. These breaks are especially common in essays or long-form journalism in periodicals like the *Chronicle of Higher Education* or the *New Yorker*. Soft breaks can be used to mark out the steps of an argument or the way points of an essayistic journey, implicitly saying, "Are you following me so far? Good, now I'll move to the next part."

### GenAI Callout

**SECTION BREAKS AND SECTION HEADINGS.** Once you get into the habit of using section breaks and section headings (which I'll call subtitles), you will notice sensible stopping points as you compose or revise. But if you find it challenging to put this strategy into practice, allow generative artificial intelligence (GenAI) to provide some models for you. Paste a full chapter, or longer sections of a chapter, directly into the chat bar and ask the program to create section breaks for you and subtitle them. I tried this experiment with a previously published *Chronicle of Higher Education* column of mine that contained no section breaks (physician, heal thyself). The version the AI program returned had ten subtitled breaks for a 1,700-word essay, which was obviously too much. I asked the AI tool to pare the number down to three. It returned a version with three subtitles and three sub-subtitles (another lesson in the ongoing importance of analyzing and editing the products of the tool). Having acknowledged that misdirection and eliminated the three sub-subtitles, I will say honestly that the essay was improved not only by the sectioning but also by the quality of the subtitles. They had no creative flair, but a glance at them would have given a casual reader an accurate impression of the argument. I would have no concern about asking the reader of a book to stay focused for 1,700 words or more, but the columns I publish on the *Chronicle* website appear alongside a host of others published on a daily basis, which means giving quick glances at the content provides an important service for busy readers. As always, embracing GenAI tools requires human decision making about context and purpose.

*Of course*, you might feel hesitant about feeding your unpublished work into GenAI. I won't argue with that; feel free to ignore this suggestion. Practically, I already have so many words publicly available on the internet that it seems pointless to me to stop now. But I recognize all the ethical issues that arise when we give GenAI access to our words to feed its algorithms. This writer will respect whichever decision you make, and this editor would never compel any writer to interact with GenAI in any way.

## SMALL ATTENTION TOOLS

The next set of attention tools I will recommend emerge from the fact that reading is usually—although not always—a visual experience. A 2021 survey from the Pew Research Center found that around 75 percent of Americans had read a book in the previous twelve months; 65 percent of these respondents had done their reading in print format, and 23 percent had listened to audiobooks.[7] Most writers will not have control or responsibility for producing audio versions of their work, and the aural versions of the recommendations that follow are the province of actors or trained voice professionals. I will focus here on what writers can control: the use of small attention tools that can be used for words on a page, whether it's on a screen or on paper.

Text treatments such as italics, boldface, and punctuation have the power to draw readers' attention to the important words and moments in an essay or book. Think about the textbooks that your students might be using in your courses; open any page and you are likely to see the key words standing out in *italics* or **boldface** (like this). You'll also notice frequent use of graphics such as charts, images, and photographs. These tools can offer the reader another way to understand the content, just as a teacher might provide information through key phrases scrawled on the board alongside a table or image projected on the screen. Textbooks for students have an overabundance of these kinds of strategies, and many successful nonfiction authors make effective use of them as well.

But the use of such tools comes with an important caveat. The special challenge of the small attention tools described in this section is not to overuse them. Every time you put another word into an italic or bold font, you are slightly diminishing the power of that font. If you have written a full book and boldfaced just two or three words in each chapter, they are going to stand out. If you are setting multiple words per page in boldface, they are playing the role of Aesop's boy who cried wolf, and the reader will pay less and less attention to them. An overuse of tables or images can have a similar effect, disrupting the reader's ability to engage fully with a story or complex idea.

The specific strategies listed in the subsections that follow, with your print or digital reader in mind, can support attention and direct your reader's eyes and brain to where it matters—but should be deployed carefully.

### *ITALICIZED* AND **BOLDFACED** TEXT

Easy to see and use, these two typeface tweaks are the most common tools in the writer's tool kit. They are often used interchangeably for the same purpose: highlighting key words and phrases. Boldface type stands out a little more from the page and to me seems more reminiscent of textbooks and reports; italics are more understated, perhaps better used in academic and serious nonfiction writing. Italics often serve as the typeface equivalent of slightly raising your voice for emphasis when you are reading aloud, or pausing briefly to make distinctions between two or more concepts or ideas.

One of the books that I consulted frequently when I was conducting on my own research on attention was *The Distracted Mind*, a layperson's introduction to the neuroscience of attention and distraction. The authors, Adam Gazzaly and Larry Rosen, use italics judiciously throughout the book for emphasis and clarity. You should be able to perceive the good work that the italics can do in the two examples that follow if you read the sentences out loud and imagine you are relying on them to explain ideas to a student. For the first example, raise your voice a bit and pause for a moment when you hit the italicized words:

> Goal interference occurs when you reach a decision to accomplish a specific goal . . . and something takes place to hinder the successful completion of that goal. The interference can either be

generated *internally*, presenting as thoughts within your mind, or generated *externally*, by sensory stimuli such as restaurant chatter, beeps, vibrations, or flashing visual displays.⁸

The main idea of this paragraph is to help the reader understand these difference between internal and external distractions, and the italics support that purpose. The two italicized words serve as weight and counterweight in the comparison. In the second example, the italics spotlight a phrase or concept that will appear frequently in what follows:

> How can self-perpetuated interference-inducing behaviors be considered optimal from any perspective, when they are clearly detrimental to us in so many ways? The answer is that [at] our core we are *information-seeking creatures*, so behaviors that maximize information accumulation are optimal, at least from that viewpoint.⁹

As you might suspect from the first sentence of this example, the authors don't shy away from challenging sentences that might push the understanding of a nonacademic reader—but, to their credit, they balance such sentences by highlighting key ideas in the ways you see in the second sentence. While I might find troublesome moments as a reader in the paragraph as a whole, I can easily spot the core idea in the italicized phrase.

Boldfacing has a louder voice in print—somewhere between italics and the shoutiness of ALL CAPS . Boldface can be appropriate for subheadings or foundational words or phrases in a chapter. If they are used together, boldface and italics can create layers of emphasis in the text. For example, I could reserve bold type for key words and definitions, and then designate italics for making distinctions or drawing attention to phrases or sentence-level statements (or restatements) of the book's main ideas. There are no clear rules of usage for these typeface strategies, and there are no "type police," so you can be creative and thoughtful about your use of them. Just remember: *don't overuse them*. If I open your book to two random pages and see it littered with italicized and boldfaced words, I'm going to be wary: This writer has trouble distinguishing the trees from the forest. Will I get lost in these woods?

## PUNCTUATION

I have been teaching two writing courses for a long time: English composition and creative nonfiction. For many years I tried to avoid or minimize the time I spent teaching students about grammar or punctuation. But then I realized (and began to teach to students) that we can view punctuation marks as benign or even restricting features of the written word, or we can realize that these are powerful tools that can be used to create rhythm in our writing, emphasize key ideas or words, or even just exercise our creativity. You can write all your sentences with nothing but commas and periods, and that's fine. But you can also use semicolons to yoke together distinctive but related ideas; you can use colons to build a sentence to a dramatic conclusion; and you use can dashes to qualify or offer ironic commentary on the other parts of a sentence. I try to use all those punctuation marks in my writing, but—like Emily Dickinson—I am especially a lover of the dash. Dashes mark the places where my thought process takes an unexpected turn. I did not start this paragraph with the intention of comparing myself with Emily Dickinson, and the three words between the dashes should make you pause for moment and ask yourself: Did he just compare himself to Emily Dickinson? That little dash-induced wink lets you know that I might not be serious.

In the next few novels or nonfiction books you read, study the punctuation marks and see whether the writer does something interesting or deliberate with one or more punctuation marks. Lean into one of those marks and make it your own for a while. Because we are so used to seeing sentences with nothing but commas or periods, the smart use of additional punctuation marks will help sentences stand out, even if the reader might not realize that's what's happening.

**SPECIAL NOTE ON EXCLAMATION POINTS.** *Because of all the informal writing we do now on email, texts, and social media, exclamation points are omnipresent in everyday discourse. They serve as a blunt instrument to convey all kinds of emotions: enthusiasm, outrage, friendliness, laughter. Blunt instruments work just fine for texts and social media posts and emails. When we have the space and time to devote to our writing, such as in the formal setting of an essay or book, we should seek greater precision in infusing emotional tones into our words—more than what a single punctuation mark can convey. Don't avoid using it, but be wary of overusing this one punctuation mark.*

---

## PARAGRAPH LENGTH

Like punctuation, the length of our paragraphs is something that we often take for granted, but it has power to draw attention to key moments in your text. Instead of writing every paragraph to the same basic length (two hundred to three hundred words), occasionally take a single word, phrase, or sentence and make it into its own, single paragraph. Our attention becomes dulled by the view of many pages of paragraphs that look like they were cranked out from the assembly line at the paragraph factory. Experiment with paragraph length, as you can experiment with punctuation. If I turn or scroll to a new page and see a paragraph that consists of a just few words, I am going to be curious about what I will find there.

Biologist Robin Wall Kimmerer wrote a best-selling book, *Braiding Sweetgrass: Indigenous Wisdom, Scientific Knowledge, and the Teaching of Plants*, in which she intertwines her scientific training with the knowledge traditions of her Indigenous ancestors. The book models the use of paragraph length to highlight the key ideas of a chapter. In a section of the book in which she describes her rough introduction into the world of academic plant biology, she laments her experiences with an academic advisor who dismissed her wonder at the plants she observed in the wild, pointing out that loving plants wasn't real science. Cowed by this interaction, Kimmerer chronicles how her successful academic career caused her to lose sight of her passions for plants. At a turning point in the chapter, Kimmerer pauses to share her realization of what had happened in a single-sentence paragraph:

> I was teaching the names [of plants] and ignoring the songs.[10]

That single sentence captures the idea of the chapter, and perhaps even of the whole book. *Braiding Sweetgrass* doesn't diminish the importance of teaching the names of the plants—that is, scientific knowledge. Instead, she seeks to expand our definition of knowledge by incorporating the perspectives of Indigenous peoples on the natural world.

Just remember that if you single out a sentence in a paragraph, it better be an important one—and perhaps even a beautiful one. It might serve as a turning point in an argument or story, a concise formulation of a key idea, or as a question that will lead into the next section of the book. You can easily observe varied examples of this technique in popular nonfiction, since these kinds of very short paragraphs stand out when you flip through some pages of a book or scroll through an article. You'll find writers using the very short paragraph for specific reasons: emphasizing ideas, making a dramatic turn in an argument, or saying something humorous. Again, this strategy only works if you use the short paragraph within the context of more traditional-length paragraphs.

## BULLETS AND LISTS

Bulleted lists (that is, lists of points or items in which each is preceded by a "bullet," or symbol, typically circular, like this: •) have a place in most kinds of nonfiction writing aimed at general audiences. Many academics, this one included, might have a negative impression of lists in writing since they have become the provenance of clickbait listicles: "These Twenty-Five Celebrities Have Moles!" (Darn it, I just wasted one of my exclamation points on a fake headline.) But lists and bulleted points can be used well to help readers categorize and keep track of a small number of ideas. You can present those ideas in standard paragraphs, but if you separate them, I can see more easily that, for example, you are showing me four ideas here, all at the same conceptual level. Think about the headlines in a bulleted list as the main points on a presentation slide, and the text after the main point resembles the explanation you give while the slide is on the screen. It's also much easier for a reader to return to your work and remind themselves of the items from a list than it is to try to hunt down the main ideas in standard paragraphs.

Bulleted lists thus might have priority of place in advice books, where they can house the key pieces of advice in a chapter or a whole book. You will have noticed that while I bullet things here and there in the chapters, the most consistent use of them occurs at the end of each chapter. The longer the book, and the more complex the topic, the more a reader might welcome them as final reminders of the key ideas of the chapter or the book as a whole. An interesting example of this strategy, paired with the use of bold-faced text, can be found in Julian Baggini's book *The Great Guide: What David Hume Can Teach Us about Being Human and Living Well*, published in 2023 by Princeton University Press. Throughout the book, Baggini boldfaces the sentences that present the core insights of Hume, no more than a handful of them in each chapter. Those sentences are then compiled and re-presented at the end of the book as a final list of Hume's ideas in aphorism form. Baggini doesn't technically use bullets in this concluding section; the aphorisms appear as a list of sentences separated by blank space. But a list of key ideas—bulleted or not—makes sense for a book devoted to the thought of an eighteenth-century Scottish philosopher whose works addressed complex philosophical issues in the formal language of his day. The more complex the topic you are addressing, the more likely the reader will be to welcome a list of essential principles, just as students will do when you finish your lecture with a slide of takeaways from the material.

## GRAPHS, TABLES, VISUALIZATIONS, IMAGES

Finally, as someone who is coming from a background in writing about English literature, I'm not accustomed to including tables, graphs, visualizations, or images in my writing. But I appreciate them in the work of others. If you are coming from disciplines that use data, by all means create graphs and charts if they can help illustrate data sets and the results of research. As discussed in chapter 3 on using evidence, don't take for granted a reader's ability to read a table or graph, just as we shouldn't take for granted a reader's ability to understand information in mathematical form. Provide a close reading of any table or graph: direct the reader's attention to the essential items. Individual cells in a table can be shaded; key numbers can be boldfaced; arrows could even direct eyes to the right place.

Infographics have accustomed contemporary readers to the use of visualizations to explain the relationships between ideas or information. The use of visualizations in helping people learn has long been in the toolkits of teachers, as we have been creating quick little concept maps and Venn diagrams on the board for many decades. Teachers' use of slide presentations has also become ubiquitous both in the classroom and in academic presentations we give to one another. As with all the tools we discussed in this section, visualizations have a dual purpose: they give the reader a break from the sometimes monotonous task of processing page after page of similarly formed paragraphs *and* give a learner another pathway to understanding. The farther I am reading outside my familiar subject areas, the more I welcome visualizations that allow me to see relationships, structure, and hierarchies.

Tables, graphs, and data visualizations appear more frequently in works of natural and social science, and less so in the works in the humanities, where readers are more likely to find photographs or images from artworks. Flipping through the shelf of my favorite nonfiction books, I see multiple examples of authors in the humanities who made excellent use of images or illustrations to enhance my understanding of the topic. Jamie Kreiner's *The Wandering Mind: What Medieval Monks Tell Us about Distraction*, a recent entry to the scholarship on attention and distraction, makes a modest use of photographs to enhance the author's analysis of medieval theories about the distractible human brain. Kreiner is a historian, and her research base largely consists of medieval manuscripts and documents from monasteries. Such material might portend dull reading. But when Kreiner's lively prose combines with images from manuscript pages in which we see the doodles and drawings of bored medieval monks, the result is a highly readable and enjoyable presentation of lessons from the past on very contemporary concerns.

I should note that your ability to use graphs, tables, visualizations, photographs, or other images will depend on your editor and your publisher; if you have any of these tools in mind for your project, be clear about this with your editor up front. Many book contracts will ask you to specify whether your manuscript will include any of them, and—if so—how many. Be prepared to make the case for their importance, and be open to the possibility that you might not get as many as you want. If you're writing a book that will be published in print, black-and-white illustrations will cost less than full color and thus be more likely to receive approval.

## CLOSINGS

Finally, a short visualization. Imagine yourself sitting at a conference, in the middle of a long presentation, and you're doing your best to focus but it's been thirty minutes, and you feel your attention drifting. The room is warm, someone has begun setting up fresh coffee and pastries in the back of the room, and you can feel your phone vibrating in your pocket. Just when you are ready to sneak out to the restroom and peek at your phone, the speaker utters some variation of those magical words—"In conclusion . . ."

or "I will finish with . . ." or "My fourth and final point is . . ."—and your attention immediately perks up. With the end of the presentation in view, you gather up your attentional resources and lock in for the final moments.

Because we perk up our attention at the end of a class, lecture, or reading experience, your conclusion is valuable real estate. For this reason, writers are often told to restate the main idea there. It gives you one final opportunity to assert your major claim or idea. Follow that solid advice, but you should be able to do this work briefly. It shouldn't take longer than a few pages or paragraphs or even sentences to reiterate the essential ideas of your essay or book, which means you have room to be a little more creative in your conclusion. The repetition of your thesis can be presented before, after, or enfolded within other attention-rewarding strategies.

Consider your conclusion to have these two fundamental purposes: to reiterate your major idea, and then to give readers one final thing to think about. Here are three strategies that can pair well with the work of restating your thesis.

- **FINAL STORY.** David Gessner's book *Leave It as It Is: A Journey through Theodore Roosevelt's American Wilderness* recounts an automobile road trip he took to understand Teddy Roosevelt's impact on the preservation of wild lands in the early twentieth century. The book concludes with Gessner's story of a chartered flight he took over the lands he had driven through in the main part of the book. Gessner uses this aerial view to give him—and the reader—one final perspective on his subject. From that height, he could see the scale of Roosevelt's work in ways that were invisible to him from the ground. Follow Gessner's lead by concluding with a story: a pilgrimage to a place that played an important role in the life of your subject, a final conversation with a colleague or friend about how your research has changed on you, a description of a final case or news story that relates to your subject. You want your conclusion to stick in the reader's mind, and stories are especially sticky in human brains.

- **CALL FOR ACTION.** One of the most common ending strategies for nonfiction books of every kind is the call to action. As the result of reading your book, what do you want readers to do after they are finished? Tom Vanderbilt's *Beginners: The Joy and Transformative Power of Lifelong Learning* argues for taking up new learning through adulthood, and it finishes by playing with his title word: "My own little experiment, all these little boats I've pushed out, continues. I haven't learned any of these skills, but I'm learning them. Now that we've ended, it's time for you to begin."[11] You can be creative in your call to action; it doesn't have to be explicit. The final pages of Peter Laufer's *Dreaming in Turtle: A Journey through the Passion, Profit, and Peril of Our Most Coveted Creature*, are titled "A Call to Action." But instead of making an explicit plea for turtle conversation, he quotes an email from a turtle biologist: "I am a turtle and tortoise lover because I have always loved the underdog. These noncharismatic species *are* the canaries in our environmental coal mine. As they go, I believe, we go."[12] The obvious implication: if you care about the survival of humans, get out there and protect other species.
- **ASKING OR PROMPTING A QUESTION.** Not all nonfiction books are calls to action, even on a deep level. Maybe they are diagnosing a social trend, laying out the contours of a problem, or expressing admiration or critiquing a person, a work of art, or political trend. But such works should still inspire readers to keep thinking about the book's subject after it ends. You can accomplish this by posing questions to your reader: We've just considered a bunch of proposed solutions to a wicked problem, but we have seen that all of them are partial ones. What would we need to craft an effective solution? You don't always have to give answers; leave space for the reader to keep thinking. Lots of books give life advice drawn from the philosophical heritage of the ancient Greeks, for example, but Edith Hamilton's isn't one of those books. After sixteen chapters about the Greeks, she finishes with a short one called "The Way of the Modern World." She believes that the circumstances that created the balancing of spirit and reason in the Greek world

were unique ones, and probably unavailable to us: "We cannot recapture the Greek point of view; the simplicity and directness of their vision are not for us."[13] For weeks after I closed her book, I kept thinking to myself: I can't alter the philosophical heritage of modern American society, but were there ways in which I could change myself after engaging with the thinkers of ancient Greece? Hamilton prompted that question in my mind but didn't offer answers.

- **CLOSING THE LOOP.** Finally, many nonfiction books close the loop on something presented in the introduction: a story, a statistic, a word. If you began your book with a curious case study, launch your conclusion by reminding the reader of that story. Now that the reader has engaged with your ideas, how will they see that story differently? If you began with a shocking set of statistics, point back to them and explain how the world could be different, at least according to your research. A subtle model of this strategy can be observed in *Teaching to Transgress*, bell hooks's canonical work of progressive pedagogy. The book begins with this paragraph, with one key word bolded by me (the italicized words appear in the original): "In the weeks before the English Department at Oberlin College was about to decide whether or not I would be granted tenure, I was haunted by dreams of running away—of disappearing—yes, even of dying. These dreams were not a response to fear that I would not be granted tenure. They were a response to the reality that I *would* be granted tenure. I was afraid that I *would* be **trapped** in the academy forever." The author begins in a place of confinement; the book ends with the following paragraph, with key words in bold: "The academy is not paradise. But learning is a place where paradise can be created. The classroom, with all its limitations, remains a location of **possibility**. In that **field of possibility** we have the opportunity to labor for freedom, to demand of ourselves and our comrades an **openness** of mind and heart that allows us to face reality even as we collectively imagine ways to move **beyond boundaries**, to transgress. This is education as the practice of **freedom**." From beginning to end, hooks leads the reader from entrapment to freedom. The book's opening and closing paragraphs encapsulate the journey traveled by both author and reader.

I am always exhausted by the time I get to the end of a long writing project, especially a book. I am always tempted to slap on an ending and take a vacation or move onto the next thing. Apparently many academics make this mistake, according to Penguin's Casiana Ionita. Endings are hard, she acknowledges, but we have to put in the effort:

> Land the ending—something even journalists sometimes find difficult. You spend so much time writing the book and getting into the nitty-gritty, and then readers can just feel "And now we have come to the end." Or there's a summary, which is quite dry. The end needs to be as memorable as the beginning.[14]

To help you land that ending, envision yourself presenting your book's ideas in a TED Talk. You have wowed the audience with your research and its implications. You have two minutes left in your presentation, and shortly attendees will stand up and engage in discussions in response to your talk. You want them to keep talking for the rest of the day.

What could you say in your final two minutes to make them linger in those conversations?

---

### STRATEGIES: OPENINGS, TEXT DIVISIONS, SMALL ATTENTION TOOLS, AND CLOSINGS

Don't be the writerly equivalent of the teacher who complains about the kids these days and their newfangled phones and short attention spans. Recognize that reading requires focus and competes with lots of other potential distractions. Give the reader support with the attention tools of writing.

- **START WITH ATTENTION.** The major purpose of your introductory paragraphs and pages is to inspire readers to keep reading.

Entertain them with a story, shock them with a statistic or fact, intrigue them with a mystery, or provoke them with controversy. Make them curious. As you are crafting your opening with this imperative in mind, remember that you are introducing the reader to yourself as a writer. You don't have to do this formally, by reciting your autobiography; instead, give them a sense of what the journey with you will be like. Will they be getting stories and humor? Statistics and academic research? Speculation and perplexity?

- **CREATE TEXT DIVISIONS AND BREAKS.** Attention fatigues and needs renewal. Even short pauses, such as the momentary breaks that readers might encounter in a text, can be effective in calling readers back to attention. The use of titled sections that I argued for in chapter 2 can serve this purpose. But even putting a couple lines of blank space between two sections of the text gives the reader an opportunity to take a sip of coffee, look out the window, or adjust their butt in their seat. Look for opportunities to create such breaks as you are writing, or when you are revising. Sometimes it's easier to see potential break points after you have finished drafting.

- **USE ATTENTION TOOLS.** If your work consists of one paragraph piled on another for many pages, with no breaks or surprises for eyes or brains, eventually the reader's attention will start to drift. Identify a few of the small attention tools listed in this chapter and let them highlight the key words, sentences, and ideas in your writing. But remember that attention tools are dulled by use. If you drive the same route to work every day, you start to tune out the details. But if you see a bear standing in someone's yard, you're going to notice that. Sprinkle some bears around your text.

- **CLOSE WITH ATTENTION.** Your reader should be returning to attentional life in their final moments with you. What do you want to do with those precious moments? You should reiterate your major takeaways, but you should do more than that. A great nonfiction book should leave your reader *thinking*. Tell me a final story, inspire me to get out of my chair and take action, prompt me to ponder what it all means for my life, or close the loop on your introduction.

The conclusion gives the writer one final chance to stick something memorable in the reader's mind.

---

### FINAL ENTHUSIASM

French theorist Yves Citton's book *The Ecology of Attention* offers a final reminder about attention, and how we cultivate it in other humans. From our earliest days on the planet, he explains, we learn to pay attention to the things that other people pay attention to:

> In developmental psychology, people speak of *joint attention* to refer to the fact that, from nine months onward, when a parental figure directs their gaze to look at an object other than the infant, the infant directs its own gaze toward the object in question.[15]

Even if you don't remember your infancy, you should recognize this phenomenon from everyday life. If I stare intently at something, your first instinct will be to look there as well: *What's he looking at?*

The principle of joint attention has a final lesson for writers seeking to keep the reader engaged with the page. Whatever writing personality that you construct for your reader, it should include this essential quality: you are an *interested person*. Not interesting, but *interested*. In other words, you are someone who gets fascinated by stuff. You get excited by your discipline. You believe your research matters. You are willing to show a little enthusiasm for your research and your essay and book. Unless you convey this quality to your reader, you should not expect your reader to turn their gaze toward what you are looking at.

You don't have to do this like a cheerleader with exclamation points. You can do it in subtler ways. Occasionally attach adjectives like *intriguing* or *fascinating* to the research findings you present. Note the times when you encountered a puzzle in the material and you were driven to solve it. When you include an excerpt from an interview transcription, pause and note the place where you were struck by an insight or taken aback by the interviewee's words.

Remind the reader of how your subject matter has impacted your life in positive ways.

These small enthusiasms of an interested writer will help cultivate joint attention and direct the gaze of your readers to the subjects that have played such a meaningful role in your life.

---

**CHAPTER FOUR WRITING PROMPTS**

- Grab a handful of nonfiction books from your shelves. Skim the first few paragraphs of each one. Based on the recommendations from this chapter, and what you read from these books, how will you start your book? Draft or revise your opening paragraph or two.
- When you are finished, follow the same procedure with the concluding paragraphs of those books. What strategies did they use? But don't jump too early to drafting your conclusion. Instead, write a few sentences describing the concluding strategy that appeals to you and stick them on the last page of your book, just so you won't forget your idea later.
- Choose a one- to two-page selection from a previously published work of yours, the more academic the better: dissertation, journal article, previous book. Experiment with making small revisions to it with the simplest tools of attention: boldfaced words, italics, or bullet points. Use your chosen tool sparingly. See what a difference it would make to boldface or italicize a single word or a pair of words.

CHAPTER FIVE

# INVITATIONAL LANGUAGE

The educator who taught me the most about the craft of teaching was Ken Bain, a historian who founded teaching centers at multiple universities, including Northwestern, where I received my PhD. My first academic job was the assistant director of Northwestern's teaching center, where I spent three years working closely with Ken, during which time I observed him conduct many workshops on teaching on campus and beyond. I didn't realize it at the time, but those workshops were the basis for his great work in progress, *What the Best College Teachers Do*, which was published four years after I left Northwestern. In part because of the elegant quality of Ken's writing, that book became a legitimate bestseller, selling hundreds of thousands of copies over its lifetime.

Plenty of my convictions about teaching that you have encountered in this book can probably be traced back to Ken's influence. The impetus for this chapter, though, comes from shifts in language he made in his workshops, and later in his books. Ken paid close attention to the terms we use when we discuss our professional practices. Some words common in the teaching lexicon, he argued, trap us into modes of thinking and teaching that might not serve our students or our aspirations very well. The power of this argument struck me the first time I attended one of his workshops.

On that occasion, he said that he intended to engage the participants in some deep thinking around the "promises" that their courses made to students—and then paused and added, almost as an aside, "which you may know as 'learning objectives.'" This different word choice, I realized in that moment, could reshape completely how those of us in the room thought about our courses. Are we clinicians standing behind the desk, checking off boxes that show us that students have achieved our preformulated objectives—or are we the creators of exciting learning experiences that promise to change students' lives? The language of learning objectives is cold and impersonal; the language of promises is warm and welcoming. The latter language befits a great teacher.

This chapter addresses the craft of selecting words, constructing sentences and paragraphs, and employing other on-the-ground techniques that fill out the writer's tool kit. Writing guides counsel academic writers that their decisions in these areas must reflect an *accessible writing style* that appeals to expanded audiences. But the number of recommendations they make about how to achieve that style can be intimidating, and sometimes conflicting. For that reason, I want to clear the language of writing styles out of the way and replace it with the concept of *invitational language*, which I think better captures the ethos of a great teacher. When I introduce students into my classroom, I want to issue them a warm welcome. I hope they will feel comfortable learning with me and their peers. To be sure, I will challenge them and ensure that they meet the standards of the course. But from the first day to the last, I should remain invitational in my words and practices. One recent book on the power of relationships in higher education argues that teachers need to offer a "relentless welcome" to their students, and that phrase captures well the spirit of this chapter's recommendations.[1]

The problem with describing the patterns of the words we put on the page as "writing styles" is that it puts the focus on the writer. The language of invitation rightly widens the spotlight to include the reader. A writer offers invitations to readers to learn with every word they put onto the page; how warm are those invitations? What does a reader perceive from our word choices, sentence and paragraph structures, and the examples we offer? Too many academic writers—perhaps shaped by our disciplinary norms—issue cold and unwelcoming summons with their prose, filling long pages with complex sentences packed with technical vocabulary. Successful nonfiction authors drop welcome notes at the reader's doorstep and show a genuine interest in helping a reader learn through their word choices or the thought-provoking questions they pose to their readers.

The four sections of this chapter play with this notion of invitations to describe how we can render our writing more welcoming to nonacademic readers. A teacher's first invitation should promise learners that they will be given the tools they need to understand the basic information and concepts. The most fundamental learning tools of the writer are our **words, sentences, and paragraphs**. Especially in the early stages of their learning, readers need extra support in processing new ideas, which means paying special attention to clarity. Because so many academics struggle to write clear prose that invites novices to learn, a short interlude will follow this section in which I will invite you to revise and write some sentences with the guidelines I have presented.

Every teacher wants their learners to move beyond basic understanding, though, which means writers also have to invite readers to think, connect, and reflect. The second section will review some common areas in which writers can encourage readers to see connections between our subject matter and their lives, raise or respond to questions, or even just wonder. I have gathered a few writing strategies under the section heading **invitations to think**, but when you realize how many ways in which writers can spur thought in the reader, you will see that we can only scratch the surface. But I hope seeing a few models, and the category that connects them, should open your eyes to the myriad possibilities you can explore after on your own.

The third and fourth sections, which are focused on the relationship between inviter and invitee, recognize that readers are most likely to accept the invitation of a writer—and continue to accept it over the course of a long book—if the reader believes that the writer will be **good company** for a learning journey; after all, in both education and writing, teacher and learner spend a lot of time together. Finally, the invitations of a writer are also more likely to be accepted if they have been issued to the right people. A writer can throw open the doors of a classroom or their house to the whole world, hoping that everyone will come—a strategy that often results in nobody coming at all. Instead, the best hosts learn something about their guests and tailor the experience to them. For writers hoping to reach new audiences, this means attending to the **readers in the room.** You can best accomplish this by researching the publishers, and their readers, who will respond best to our particular style of invitation.

## WORDS, SENTENCES, PARAGRAPHS

Indulge me for a moment as I move you temporally from the role of the teacher to that of the learner. Imagine yourself at a massive conference which relates only tangentially to your field. Your current research landed you on the program only by an act of interpretive generosity on the part of the conference committee. After you have given your presentation first thing in the morning, you decide to attend a session on a topic about which you know very little. You settle into a chair in the middle of the room and witness the familiar routine of the presenter overcoming a technology hitch or two, being introduced by a moderator, and then clicking the slide remote to advance to their first slide. That slide, to your dismay, contains six full sentences displaying the themes of the presenter's research. Each sentence is two or three lines long. The words pack into every corner of the screen. Several of the disciplinary terms on the screen are only vaguely familiar to you. As a final insult, the slide appears only for twenty seconds, barely enough time to read it, and certainly not enough time to absorb it. As soon as the presenter clicks to the next slide, which looks a lot like the first one, your heart sinks. You understand that you do not belong here. The next forty-five minutes will be long ones.

Now envision a parallel universe, at that moment when the first slide appears on the screen. It contains three verb phrases in bulleted form (e.g., "write like you teach"), none longer than five or six words. Each phrase contains an italicized key word that the speaker points to and explains. They turn to the next slide, which contains nothing but a short sentence, framed against a white background, that describes the question that drove the presenter's research. The first two slides, taken together, have soothed your anxieties about sticking your neck out and attending a talk on a subject in which you have no expertise. You settle comfortably into your uncomfortable chair, happy to be into the presence of a good teacher. You will learn something new today.

In the first scenario, you are facing a double challenge: familiarizing yourself with new knowledge and ideas *and* trying to process long strings of words, phrases, and sentences, all interspersed with unfamiliar vocabulary. You probably could have managed both of these tasks if you had had the time to read and reread the sentences on the first slide, and if you really cared about the subject. But what you really needed were some words and sentences designed to welcome you into the learning process. This was what the presenter in the second scenario gave you—and what writers should offer to readers who are in the early stages of the learning process in your field. Writing invitational prose doesn't mean shying away from difficult concepts or the complexities of your field; the phrase "dumbing down," which academics will sometimes use to express their anxieties about writing for the public, mistakes the intent and practice of writing for novice learners in your field. Invitational prose, which I am arguing for in this section via the three subsections that follow, teaches readers unfamiliar terms, instead of expecting that everyone knows them; it reduces sentence complexity to support learning, instead of writing sentences that pack too many thoughts between periods; it keeps paragraphs focused with strong topic sentences, instead of forcing the reader to follow the back-and-forth swings of the long paragraphs that characterize academic writing.

## MANAGING VOCABULARY

Let's start by setting aside a piece of advice that some writing style guides offer to academics: don't use jargon. Just as I am setting aside the language of "writing styles," I want to set aside the notion of "jargon." Whatever formal meaning the word *jargon* has, most academic writers hear it as an admonition not to use the technical vocabulary of their discipline. That advice is misguided. It would only make sense if words were transparent carriers of meaning. They are not. Words not only communicate but also shape our ideas, and even invent ideas. If your discipline has a word that has influenced the field, one that every scholar knows and uses in their writing, that word or phrase has identified something important, something specific, something that no other word can capture. Your reader deserves to know that word. And whatever else you might have heard, many readers *want* to learn new words from you. Perhaps not every human feels that way, but readers of a nonfiction book written by an academic have come to you to learn. Don't shy away from teaching them new words.

What contributes to uninviting prose, when it comes to vocabulary, is using disciplinary terms without acknowledging or explaining them—or even explaining that readers will encounter some new vocabulary. Nobel Prize winner Daniel Kahneman's book *Thinking, Fast and Slow* uses a helpful comparison to put his readers at ease at the outset of a long and challenging book, especially when it comes to the vocabulary. He explains that he will be using some technical language from his home discipline of psychology, and he wants readers to understand that writing choice:

> To be a good diagnostician, a physician needs to acquire a large set of labels for diseases. . . . Learning medicine consists in part

of learning the language of medicine. A deeper understanding of judgments and choices [the subject of his book] also requires a richer vocabulary than is available in everyday language.[2]

In other words, complaining about an author's reliance on disciplinary language would be like wishing doctors would just say "you're sick" instead of naming your actual disease. We don't blink an eye at learning new words at the doctor's office; that's how our understanding of our bodies and their malfunctions grows. Your book promises to grow the understanding of your reader, which will include expanding their vocabulary.

Every nonfiction book doesn't have to make the explicit argument that Kahneman does. But invitational prose will *always* draw attention to, and explain, the words that might baffle a first-year student in one of your courses. In chapter 4 I noted that attention strategies like boldfacing and italicizing words can draw attention to them, and that might be one approach to calling out such words. Having done so, do what you do best: teach them. This doesn't have to entail some complex writing strategy. Phrases that lead into or follow the first use of the word will do the trick:

- Researchers in this field have coined a useful term for this phenomenon...
- You won't understand the results of this experiment unless you are familiar with the term...
- [*Word.*] That's the word that scientists use to describe this strange finding.

Having called attention to the word and framed it with such a phrase or sentence, you then define it in plainer language. This might be the one place where you should heed the admonition to restrain your vocabulary skills. Don't ask the reader to wrestle with technical terms while they are trying to understand a technical term. Envision yourself in the classroom, and a first-year student has raised a hand and pointed to a word in your presentation that they don't understand: how would you define it for them?

## SIMPLIFYING SENTENCES

In the conference presentation scenario with which I started this section, I argued that unwelcoming prose can present readers with too much of a cognitive challenge: trying to process new ideas while they also have to make basic sense of words and sentences. Sentence complexity is a major culprit here, which implies (correctly) that simplifying our sentences is the solution. Academic writing likes long sentences, and such sentences can have a place in writing even for nonspecialists. But the longer a sentence, the more intellectual work you are asking your reader to undertake. If the reader encounters nothing but one long sentence after another in your prose, they will feel fatigued by your writing and make an early exit. Fortunately, most long sentences can be simplified with two remedies: reducing the number of clauses and phrases, and using active verbs. A quick review of some of the basics of sentence construction should enable you to understand how to apply these techniques.

Harking back to your elementary school days in Sentence 101, every (grammatical) sentence must include one independent clause: "Successful writers vary sentence length." We can add a dependent clause to that to fill out the idea: "Successful writers *who hope to expand their audiences* vary sentence length." Still short, still simple. Now tack on a prepositional phrase: "Successful writers *who hope to expand their audiences* vary sentence length *in the service of clarity and challenge*." We're probably still good at this point. But sentences can conjoin two independent clauses, as in: "Successful writers *who hope to expand their audiences* vary sentence length *in the service of clarity, but they should remember that sentence complexity matters more than length*." We could continue adding dependent clauses here—sticking a final prepositional phrase at the end ("especially with difficult subject matter")—but you should get the point now. Each clause in a sentence contains a unit of sense or meaning; as a reader processes a complex sentence, they are collecting and trying to hold in their minds multiple such units. Their cognitive burden gets heavier and heavier.

The last version of the model sentence in the previous paragraph has nothing technically wrong with it. It makes sense and follows the rules of grammar. But you can see that it contains a basic idea that I then qualify or expand in multiple directions. Academic writing, and academic brains, *like* to qualify and expand. We sometimes mistrust simple ideas, which might lead to suspicion of simple sentences (i.e., the unadorned independent clause). Invitational prose doesn't demand simple ideas; it suggests instead that you reduce the number of meaning units that a reader has to keep in mind *during the space of a single sentence*. The good news is that garden-variety punctuation marks like periods and semicolons can ameliorate most sentence complexity problems, as in: "Successful writers who hope to expand their audiences vary sentence length in the service of clarity. Sentence complexity matters more than length, though, especially with difficult subject matter." Same ideas, fewer meaning units packed into the individual sentence.

Another common piece of writing advice can help reduce sentence complexity: using active verbs. You probably have been told or read that writers should prefer active verbs over passive ones. Style guides argue that sentences with active verbs are livelier and more concise, and both of these things are true. But a sentence constructed with an active verb can also reduce the workload for a reader's brain. The most basic form of an English sentence contains three parts, in the following order: *subject-verb-object*. As in: *I (S) wrote (V) the book (O)*. Not all languages work this way, but English does. The first sentences that we mastered in kindergarten took this form. We cut our reading teeth on SVO, and it dominates conversational language. The traditional word order of a sentence can be reversed with the passive voice: *object-verb-subject*. As in:

*The book was written by me.* Making a reader of English wait until the end of the sentence for the subject doesn't matter in a six-word sentence. But a long, multiclause sentence constructed with a passive-voice verb creates a heavier cognitive load for the reader.

Worse still, writers who rely on the passive voice often omit the subject of their sentences, as in: *The book was written.* In a passive-voiced sentence in which you have not identified the agent of the verb, you have now added a little further cognitive work for the reader, who has to sort this out: who wrote the book? The kindergarten teacher who lives in my house tells me that the sentences that baffle new readers are the ones with implied subjects and objects. The verb is there, but the writer doesn't explicitly identify the agent of the action or the object of the action. Our expectations about how sentences operate are formed early, and likely continue to shape our reading brain however old or educated we may become. Hence when we are put in the position of learning something new and complicated, we benefit from sentences with clearly stated subjects and objects, in that order, surrounding their verb.

Passive-voiced sentences do have a place in the language; you don't need to banish them from your stylistic tool kit. In our brief example sentence, the use of passive voice would make good sense if I wanted to emphasize that the book was written *by me*. But active-verb sentences, even if they are longer ones, will lighten the burden carried by your reader.

---

### PARAGRAPHS

Finally, complexity in academic writing occurs both at the sentence level and at the paragraph level. Sentences are meaning units of their own, and they come together to present the major idea of a paragraph. Just as sentences can contain too many meaning units, so can paragraphs. The writing in more-public media outlets will typically contain paragraphs with just a few meaning units (i.e., three or four sentences). Academic paragraphs can contain up to a dozen or more sentence-level meaning units, each of which must be held in the reader's mind as they move from the first word to the final period of a paragraph. As with sentences, volume reduction can help. The further away you move from writing for your academic colleagues, the more editors and readers will expect you to trim your paragraph length. As with sentences, this doesn't mean simplifying your ideas; it means becoming more deliberate about searching for break points as those ideas are gradually unfolded for the reader.

With paragraphs, though, the volume might not be the only problem. The challenge of a difficult paragraph might stem from a different source: the paragraph starts in one place and finishes in another. The paragraph has lost its single focus. I flag this problem as much as anything else I see in my work as an editor. Fortunately, one wonderful remedy exists for paragraph focus: a strong topic sentence. The controlling idea of a paragraph—one might even label it the paragraph's thesis—should be encapsulated in a single sentence. Typically topic sentences occur near the beginning of a paragraph; in many cases, unlike this paragraph, they are the first sentence. But they can appear anywhere (the one in this paragraph began with "The controlling idea of a paragraph . . ."). A writer can start a paragraph with a question or problem and then work toward its solution, in which case the topic sentence comes at the end. A paragraph can consist of a transition sentence, a little setup, the topic sentence, and then some further explanation of the idea. You don't need to build every paragraph from the same template, and not every paragraph will have a topic sentence. Descriptive or narrative paragraphs might not need them. But every paragraph of explication should have a clearly identifiable one.

While I was working on this chapter, I had a meeting with a writer who was in the stage of revising her book. She shared with me a genius method for ensuring that she writes with strong topic sentences. After she has drafted something, she reads through it and highlights in green marker every topic sentence. She then sees if she can follow her argument through the ideas expressed in her topic sentences. Not only does this strategy reveal any logical flaws in her writing, it does the basic work of confirming that each paragraph has a topic sentence.

A final image might drive home the essential task of writing good paragraphs. In "Superman and Me," novelist and essayist Sherman Alexie describes learning to read as a very young man and gradually understanding the operations of the written word. His first dawning occurs when he perceives the purpose of paragraphs:

> I still remember the exact moment when I first understood, with a sudden clarity, the purpose of a paragraph. I didn't have the vocabulary to say "paragraph," but I realized that a paragraph was a fence that held words. The words inside a paragraph worked together for a common purpose. They had some specific reason for being inside the same fence. This knowledge delighted me.[3]

Keep that image of a word fence in mind as you draft and revise paragraphs. Don't let stray wolves bring chaos into your little field of closely related sheep. Gather them around that topic sentence and keep them safe.

---

### PRACTICE INTERLUDE

To help you both identify and create warm prose, I invite you to complete a quick review and practice activity. In chapter 4 I mentioned one of my favorite nonfiction books, Jamie Kreiner's *The Wandering Mind: What Medieval Monks Tell Us about Distraction*, a witty and accessible history of the obsession that medieval monks had with controlling their attention. Here's an excerpt from that book:

> Today when we feel helpless against our distractions, we unplug. We announce on our social media accounts that we're

> staying off our social media accounts, take digital detoxes, retreat to the cabin in the woods. It's a relief while it lasts, a reminder that our minds are still capable of calm—but because such fixes are only temporary, and somewhat privileged, they're not, in the end, all that satisfying.[4]

Because this is an excerpt, you won't be able to see the first invitational feature of this paragraph: it opens the first chapter. That's worth noting. We can attend to the invitational features of our prose on every page, but introductions to books, chapters, or new topics deserve extra care. Kreiner can write complex sentences and long paragraphs with the best of them, but she doesn't do that in these entry sentences. Invitational prose does its best work in the early stages of learning. Beyond that, what else do you see here that makes this prose invitational? How does it perform in terms of the strategies presented in this chapter?

Now review the next two three-sentence paragraphs on the same subject. The first paragraph was produced by ChatGPT:

> Tech fasts, while initially effective in reducing immediate distractions, do not lead to sustained improvements in attention. This is because attention is a complex cognitive process influenced by various factors beyond technology use, such as cognitive capacity and environment. Additionally, once individuals return to their normal tech usage, they often revert to previous levels of distraction, highlighting the limited long-term efficacy of tech fasts in enhancing attention.[5]

The second one is the first paragraph of an article in an academic journal:

Organizational pervasive IS are technologies that may be used almost anytime and anywhere, thus they do not constrain employees to the physical location of their organization. For example, mobile email users can access work-related email while commuting, dining with their families, or on vacation. Although these technologies can augment productivity by allowing employees to be more connected and responsive to work issues, they may promote negative outcomes, such as addiction, work overload, and conflict, which stem from the potential excessive technology dependency and use.[6]

Now analyze these two paragraphs in the same way. How would you describe them in terms of vocabulary, sentence, and paragraph? At the sentence level, how would you improve these paragraphs for a nonacademic reader? If you are reading on your own, mark them up. If you're in a reading group, discuss and debate what you see. Do you see any positive applications of the recommendations I have made? How would you make those paragraphs more inviting to a reader?

I hope these three examples provided enough modeling for the following practice exercise, which you can complete in the blank space at the end of this section or in your notebook or device.

**PROMPT:** Write a paragraph to open an essay, chapter, or book you have drafted or hope to write. Ensure that it has a strong topic sentence. All verbs should be active. Limit abstractions and complexity. Bonus: include one short, sharp sentence.

**INVITATIONS TO THINK**

Teaching new vocabulary (instead of assuming that readers already know it), reducing complexity in sentences, and bringing focus to our paragraphs—these strategies invite readers into their first engagement with our ideas and research. But no great teacher would be satisfied with producing basic comprehension in their learners. We want to invite *thought* in readers: we want them to connect our book to their lives, raise questions about it, argue with it, and even allow it to guide their way of being in the world. (The distinction I am making here between "comprehension" and "thought" is a completely unscientific one—but I expect you know what I mean.) In his book *The Elements of Academic Style*, Columbia University's Eric Hayot argues that our readers deserve more than explainer videos or infographics on our topic. Such writing, he argues, "doesn't change minds, or lives." Further, he suggests, "many audiences *want* to be startled, engaged, disturbed, and otherwise shocked out of their familiar habits."[7] In the classroom and in our writing, good teachers should encourage readers to turn ideas around in their brains, probe into the weak or unclear spots, and even feel challenged or discomfited by our ideas and arguments. Teachers in higher education have the exact skills needed to engage readers in these ways—and to do it warmly, as many of us do in the classroom.

The words after that dash matter, because certainly educators can provoke thought in more and less invitational ways. For a less invitational example, consider the stereotypical teacher stalking the aisles of an auditorium, pointing to students and demanding answers to difficult questions. A warmer approach might invite students who have been introduced to a new topic to brainstorm real-life examples of the phenomenon in action, share them with each other, and then evaluate them together in a whole class discussion. We can't use think-pair-share or team-based learning to engage readers in a print-based learning experience, of course, so we have to deploy other tools to invite thought from our readers.

For this section, I have collected a handful of common strategies in nonfiction writing designed to make your reader pause for a moment in their reading to scrawl a note in the margin, or bring up your book in conversation later that day. No book, and no writer, will need or should feel compelled to use any or all of them, but I hope that one or more will appeal to you and even encourage you to observe thought invitations in the works of others, and then replicate those or invent your own.

## EVERYDAY EXAMPLES

The gentlest invitations to think take the form of providing examples of how our topics connect to daily life. We could say a learner has a basic comprehension of a topic when they can observe or even explain it in the context in which it was introduced—but only there. In other words, I explain a learning principle to you in connection to classroom education, and you are able to explain that principle back to me in that same specific context. But a deeper level of thinking must occur for you to explain how that learning principle manifests in *another* context: how it would apply to a child learning at home, or an older adult taking a tennis lesson, or a new instructor teaching their first yoga class. You can only create such connections if you understand the theoretical contours of the principle and notice them mirrored beneath the surface of a different context. Teachers in the classroom regularly offer everyday examples of their subject matter and invite students to come up with examples of their own. While we don't sit in the classroom with our readers, we can still model the power of everyday examples with the hopes that readers will push beyond *our* examples to see connections to their own experiences.

Not all subjects will lend themselves to everyday examples; I once worked with a writer who wanted to write about her research on dark matter, and I was hard-pressed to offer her much help in finding such examples. But most of us are able to see the places where everyday phenomena intersect with our subject matter, and we should make a habit of including them in our writing when we are explaining theories or concepts that otherwise feel very abstract. Philosophers trade heavily in abstract theories and concepts, and as a result, they have learned the power of everyday examples, as I was reminded while reading *The Path: What Chinese Philosophers Can Teach Us about the Good Life*. The authors, a philosophy professor and a former graduate student turned journalist, begin a section on the ritualistic thinking of Confucius with this:

> Most of us have certain "rituals." Whether it's a morning cup of coffee, family dinners, a couple's regular Friday date night, or a piggyback ride for the kids at bedtime, we consider these moments important because they give our lives continuity and meaning and bond us to our loved ones.[8]

These rather generic examples are followed by the authors digging into the specific example of daily greetings. The everyday examples that connect our subject to everyday life can be just like these—quick and suggestive. The foregoing excerpt actually points to fruitful places where we can search for examples: daily routines. Preparing and eating meals, commuting back and forth to work, interacting with colleagues, pursuing hobbies, playing or watching sports, unwinding after work, socializing, sleeping or not sleeping—all of these can become fodder for thinking invitations to your reader.

## METAPHORS

Our literary traditions suggest another pathway to context-broadening thought: metaphors and similes. (Quick English professor note: Metaphor compares two unlike things; simile is just a form of metaphor that uses "like" or "as" to make that comparison; I'll use the broader term of *metaphor* here to cover both.) Metaphors in teaching contexts, just like everyday examples, typically compare an unfamiliar concept in our disciplines to one that will be more familiar to readers. Each of the following metaphors appeared in each of several books that helped me understand brain mechanics, an area in which I have a strong interest but no formal education: *attention is like a spotlight; the axons of connecting neurons shake hands; working memory is like a conductor working with a tiny choir made up of our hippocampus and the neocortex.*[9] With metaphors, we can move beyond the playground of everyday life into imaginary realms, as evidenced by the fact I have never observed a conductor working with a tiny choir of two and likely never will—but I still was able to conceive of the image from my knowledge of conductors and choirs.

Whether they are real or imaginary, metaphors push us to grasp the principles beneath specific contexts, a core marker of deeper learning. At the same time, a good metaphor can also spur the reader's creative or critical thinking about the concept you are trying to teach. For example, initially I found the "attention is a spotlight" metaphor illuminating (!), but over time I began to question its dominance in explaining the complex concept of attention. What does that metaphor elide? What alternatives might exist to it? The metaphor first explained and then provoked. Novice readers might not make this final questioning move, simply accepting your metaphors as helpful and moving on. Dissecting a metaphor for them, though, can model critical thinking. Michelle Miller begins a chapter on memory by referencing the spotlight metaphor, then adds that plenty of other attention metaphors exist—a camera lens, a highlighter, a computer processing system—and then concludes that each of them falls short in describing the complexity of our attention systems, which are tied to so many areas of our brain. Attention is too diffuse to have it captured in a single metaphor.[10]

The creation of metaphors seems to come more easily to some writers than to others. If you don't use them regularly in your writing, experiment. Don't worry so much about inserting metaphors into your prose when you are getting your thoughts down. But when you are reviewing what you have written, and you are concerned about your presentation of a challenging idea, see if a metaphor can invite readers to see it in a new context or spur them to think about it in a new way.

## ALLUSIONS

A third and final method for helping readers put theories, principles, and concepts in relation to other contexts comes from our artistic traditions: allusions. Especially common in works of literature, allusions are references to other works of literature, art, music, or cultural products of any kind. Construed broadly, allusions can even reference historical events. Many academics write about cultural products and historical events as their main focus, but allusions typically are more glancing references. An allusion in a poem or a movie might consist of a single word, or even just a quiet echo of some other work; I am broadening the notion of allusion here to include sentence- or even paragraph-level references to cultural works that connect to our subject. Unlike everyday examples, which are designed to show the manifestations of the subject in the familiar places around me, allusions show the reader that the subject under discussion has long arms, reaching out across cultures and time periods.

Long story, but not long ago I had reason to be paging through a book connected to the history of gardening: Judith Larner Lowry's book *The Landscaping Ideas of Jays: A Natural History of the Backyard Restoration Garden*, published by the University of California Press. Partway through, I was a bit startled to find a science writer alluding to a favorite poem of mine, John Keats's "On First Looking into Chapman's Homer":

> When I first read about coarse woody debris and discovered the classic "decay literature" of the 1960s and 1970s, I felt like Keats first looking into Chapman's Homer. . . . A whole word opened up, and I was forever changed.[11]

That allusion appeals to me because I have taught that poem many times in British Literature Survey (not to mention the fact that the subject of the poem is Homer's *Odyssey*, another favorite). For other readers, that allusion might fall flat. The use of allusions thus comes with a major caveat: they only work if the reader knows the work you are referencing. An unfamiliar allusion or two won't necessarily get in the way of an unaware reader, but if too many of them miss the mark, your reader might feel like an uninvited guest at your highbrow literary soiree. Allusions are not limited to classical works of literature; they can refer to any cultural product that you believe might resonate with your readers: Taylor Swift songs, Netflix series, a Broadway musical, a Banksy artwork. When allusions work, they offer one more way to expand your reader's ability to see your subject matter across contexts.

## THOUGHT EXPERIMENTS AND HYPOTHETICALS

Speaking of allusions to classic works of Greek literature, one of the most famous works of philosophy of the Western tradition is Plato's *Republic*, which takes the form of an extended thought experiment. Socrates and his companions are returning from a festival and get waylaid at the house of a friend. The group begins to debate the nature of justice, which then evolves into an exercise to imagine the creation of a city-state, and its political and legal system, from scratch. The deepest questions we can ask about the human condition are enfolded into this thought experiment, which has remained required reading in courses of politics and philosophy two millennia later. (The thought experiment of the *Republic* as a whole contains smaller ones inside, such as the story of the Ring of Gyges, which renders its wearer invisible.)

Thought experiments invite readers to think more creatively about our subject matter. They constitute the flip side of the familiarizing work of everyday examples, pushing readers to imagine worlds that don't or could never exist. They nudge us to question the premise of the experiment, envision alternative ways of thinking about a subject, and see how principles or theories *could* be applied beyond what already exists. While they might seem more appropriate for philosophy or political theory, thought experiments can work in any discipline. A physicist could invite readers to imagine a world without the moon in the earth's orbit; a theologian could encourage us to imagine how it would change Christianity if the Bible had only two of the four gospels; a management instructor could create a scenario in which the government has issued a new regulation and ask readers to imagine how they would respond to it. While such learning invitations move readers far beyond everyday examples from the world around us, ultimately they do the same work: to imagine how a person or society would respond to one of these scenarios, I have to challenge my brain to find and apply relevant theories and principles.

Your discipline, and your topic, might not lend itself to book-length thought experiments—we can't all be Plato—but any writer can make use of small-scale thought experiments, which might be more familiar to you as hypothetical scenarios. Just a few pages ago I asked you to *imagine yourself at an academic conference* in the service of my arguments about the importance of clarity techniques. In *Remembering and Forgetting*, Michelle Miller prompts readers to "picture [your]self in the midst of a conversation about the *Guardians of the Galaxy* movies, when you realize you can't remember the name of the guy who played Dr. Strange."[12] She prompts this visualization to illustrate the common phenomenon of having a memory or word right on the tip of our tongue and not being able to express it. Of course a reader can always refuse such prompts that ask them to imagine a scenario or conduct a thought experiment, but issuing them can be a regular feature of a writing practice that invites readers to think.

### PROMPTS AND QUESTIONS

A final level of thought invitation comes when we actually ask the reader to engage in a specific activity designed to prompt some mental or physical action. This comes more easily in the classroom, where I can stop class and give a quiz, share a writing prompt, or tell students to pair up and solve a problem. I have no control over whether my reader will follow any instructions I give in a book—I have at least a modicum of control in the classroom—but that doesn't mean I can't offer the invitations. I read lots of books about teaching and learning in higher education, and many of them contain workbook-like sections in which readers are encouraged to reflect about their experiences, answer some questions, or solve a problem. Such opportunities for active-learning-in-a-book fit well into books about teaching and learning, as they do in a writing guide like this one. You see them in the writing prompts at the end of each chapter, in the practice exercise in this chapter, and in the book's concluding "syllabus" for publishing a book.

But I won't argue that they belong in every book. To be honest, I have mixed feelings about including them in mine. As a reader myself, I tend to skip such prompts and keep reading. But for me to not include them in a writing guide, or not recommend them to others, would mean that I have fallen into a trap that every teacher must take great pains to avoid: assuming that everyone learns the way I do. You might be like me, and feel some hesitation about inserting questions or prompts into a text, but other readers might expect or welcome that. Indeed, from a learning perspective, they are an excellent idea. We use active learning techniques in class for good reason: they work. If you think your book might benefit from including any kind of formal questions or prompts—which might even take the form of reading questions for book groups—discuss the possibility with your editor. My experience has been that editors are very open to these components in books, and they might have good suggestions for the best form they could take.

### BEING GOOD COMPANY

Several strategies from the previous section invited readers to make connections between the subject matter of your book and other realms of life. But readers tend to welcome one final category of examples—ones that come from the author's own experiences. Our academic writing traditions discourage us from revealing too much about ourselves. The authors of essays in academic journals are not encouraged—or are even forbidden—to inject personal stories into their writing. When we write for more-public outlets, though, we can add to our repertoire of examples ones that illustrate how our subject matter reveals itself in our own experiences. Academic writers tend to prefer discussing theories and principles over providing examples, and they tend to need nudging to offer more examples, so we should not neglect this additional well from which we can draw more of them.

More important, the practice of using personal examples in our writing, and revealing something of ourselves to our readers, contributes to the invitational nature of our prose. People can learn from strangers—college students do it at the start of every semester. But over the course of fifteen weeks, those strangers become more familiar. Very few college teachers walk into the classroom, jump directly into the content, and then walk out without ever referencing their lives outside the classroom. We complain about a traffic incident on the morning commute; we explain that we had to cancel class last week because we had a sick child; we might even mention that we have tickets for an upcoming event and engage in a preclass discussion with some students who share our passion for that artist. I still remember an American literature professor from my undergraduate days who made frequent references not only to films we were discussing but also to the contexts in which he had viewed them: in the local theater, on the couch with his wife, when he was a student himself. At least for me, these stories revealed a person who was living a life dedicated to art and literature—just as I was hoping to do myself.

Students appreciate and often remember such glimpses of their teachers; your readers will feel the same way. I'm not sure I can point to any specific body of research to defend this statement, except a lifetime of teaching and learning and studying teaching and learning: humans like to learn from humans. Perhaps not for everything: I don't need someone to fly over from Sweden to show me how to put my IKEA bookshelf together. But for the things that matter, I want to learn from a human. Invitational prose recognizes this preference and allows readers to at least catch glimpses of the person from whom they are learning.

When I give this perspective to academic authors seeking to expand their audiences, they want to know *exactly* how much they should—or have to—reveal. Writing style guides also can get too caught up in the specific question of whether we should reveal more or less of ourselves in our nonfiction. To cut through such questions and debates, I offer one simple piece of advice about the extent to which we should reveal ourselves in our nonfiction: *Be good company*. If you have written a three-hundred-page work, and it contains the fruits of your academic research, it could mean that an average reader might spend a dozen hours in your company. That's a lot of time for two people to spend together. I have friends I see less often than that over the course of a single year. Your readers are companions who will accompany you on an intellectual journey. What kind of company do you offer to your reader?

Being good company doesn't dictate any particular number of examples you should use or self-revelations you should make about your life as a teacher, researcher, or human. Approaches and results vary. On one end of the spectrum, we find Lulu Miller, who provides a successful example of a writer who throws the doors of her house wide open in her book *Why Fish Don't Exist: A Story of Loss, Love, and the Hidden Order of Life* (note the implied question in the title; refer back to chapter 1). Miller is a science writer whose book profiles David Starr Jordan, a twentieth-century biologist who dedicated much of his life to taxonomizing the nonmammals that swim in the sea (as the book's title implies, calling them fish is complicated). The book contains an engaging mix of biography, biology, and philosophy.

But it also contains a lot of the life of Lulu Miller. As she conducted her research on David Starr Jordan for the book, she struggled with depression and existential dread. She traveled to important sites in Jordan's life. She remembered stories from her childhood and of her father. All these experiences are interwoven into her research narrative. They are designed to give readers a sense of the emotional consequences of learning about the chaos underlying our orderly visions of the world. She demonstrates what can happen when we recognize that the systems we have invented to beat back the randomness of the world—such as species taxonomies—are completely artificial ones. The feeling of desperation that she chronicles, the book implies, *should* be the rational outcome of such a systematic collapse.

Miller's no-holds-barred writing voice is not necessarily the best or even the right approach for many nonfiction writers. You might not be as willing to share your experiences and emotions to the extent that Miller does, and there might be good reasons for that. Perhaps you view your research field as being fascinating enough that you don't need to mix in your personal experiences. Maybe you have difficult emotional memories connected to your subject matter. Or maybe you are just a private person and you don't feel comfortable inviting readers through your front door. Intertwining research and personal narrative requires a writerly dexterity that can test even the best professional writers.

But without braiding your life story into your nonfiction writing, you can still inject some sparks into your narrative persona with the occasional personal anecdote. This has always been my approach, in part because I have seen the positive effect it has on readers. When I meet readers after keynotes or workshops, people will often remember personal stories that I have told in my books and share a similar story from their experience. In *Small Teaching* I tell a story about ordering green tea at a coffee shop near my house, and many of my hosts have made a special point of offering me green tea before my events. We have a laugh. Cognitive psychologist Michael Corballis takes a similar approach in *The Wandering Mind: What the Brain Does When You're Not Looking*, a book that packages a lifetime of research on the human brain into a short volume published by the University of Chicago Press. In a paragraph on the stickiness of learned skills, he uses a quick personal anecdote to qualify the general principle:

Once learned, skills tend to stay with us. It's said that you never forget how to ride a bike, although old age and arthritis eventually take their toll. Yet some skills, especially those learned late, can be lost. I once accompanied my four-year-old son to recorder lessons and learned to play rather badly, but I now find I can't remember a single configuration.[13]

Nothing too major in terms of a personal reveal, and yet I still get some glimpses of the person authoring this book: in addition to learning the fact that he seems like an engaged father, I also observe that he welcomes new learning experiences. He could have stayed in the car during those recorder lessons; instead he embraced the opportunity to develop a new skill. Since I love learners, he seems like good company to me.

But even if that small level of personal sharing turns you off, writers can still find ways to interject their personalities into their writing in more subtle ways. In the practice exercises earlier in this chapter, I showed you an excerpt from Jamie Kreiner's book on attention and distraction in medieval monks. This book was my favorite nonfiction reading experience of 2023, and yet—after I closed it—I realized that I knew not one single fact about Jamie Kreiner, in spite of my felt sense that I had learned from a human. Paging through it afterward, I started to notice the moments when she gave the reader a wink or a nod, as in this sentence, which follows a description of a monk falling over asleep over a book: "The struggle feels awfully familiar."[14] Thinking further about where I caught glimpses of her personality, I realized as well that a lively sense of humor was peeking through the specific examples she chose to present from the manuscripts, including one caption in which she explains that the Latin marginal comments we are seeing on a manuscript page noted that the monk had a "massive hangover."[15] While Jamie Kreiner did not share personal anecdotes or discuss her emotional states, her personality was layered into the prose through these small decisions about the examples she chose to share, or her descriptions of them.

To put this section into one final context, which might give you one more way to approach the challenge of writing as a human to other humans, academics are often put in the position of having to dine and drink with strangers in interviews or conferences. If you have success with your writing, you might find yourself invited to speak to an organization and then have a meal with the organizers. In those situations, most of us try to be good company. We do our best to contribute to the conversation. We might mention prior careers we might have had, hobbies we pursue outside our academic work, travel experiences, books we are reading, or films we like to watch. But just as in a job interview, we don't necessarily have to mention whether we are married, have children, struggle with depression, or have a chronic illness. The specifics of what we might reveal about ourselves in these situations remains entirely in the hands of the interviewee, just as it does in the teacher and the writer.

I can find good company in someone who opens themself up to me—but I can also find it in the presence of a lively teacher who reveals little about themself yet who issues me a warm and enthusiastic invitation to learn something new.

**THE READERS IN THE ROOM**

To complete the notion of writing invitational prose, we have to acknowledge the other party in an invitation exchange: the reader. When we throw a party, we typically curate our guest list, identifying the people whom we think will enjoy the experience. Writers have to take this same orientation by learning about their potential readers. When I first start working with a writer who has a book idea, the first question I ask them is about their audience: Who do you think should read this book? Most of them will respond by saying, "Well, I want everyone to read it!" At which point I share (gently) an oft-repeated maxim in publishing: if you write a book intended for everybody, nobody will read it. Your best chance of having lots of guests at your writing party will come from you doing your research on your potential readers—their backgrounds, their interests, and their needs.

Obviously you can't dig into this level of detail on every potential reader of your writing without alerting the authorities, which means you have to do your research on a proxy: the publications or publishers you are targeting for your work. The process of researching publications (and their audiences) is an automatic habit of professional writers, and I have learned from them how to do it with my own nonacademic writing. As I move from one publication to another, I have a background awareness of the implications of these moves for the ground-level choices I make. Especially when it comes to shorter outlets—newspapers, magazines, websites, newsletters—I know that publisher/audience research will improve my chances of seeing my essay in print or online. The following questions are ones that I will ask myself when I am considering a new publication that might become an outlet for a shorter piece of writing—and some of the alterations I might apply to my writing style:

- What **audience** does this publication target—academics, the general public, or some other audience? If I know I am writing to academics, I will lean on personal stories that speak to common work areas for us: teaching, researching, administering. I will favor a more serious tone of voice. I won't be afraid to push the reader with some syntactic complexity or challenging vocabulary. If there will be humor, it will come from occasional self-deprecating asides, not from a long story with a punch line (although if I ever see you at a conference, ask me to tell you my favorite joke, which comes with a long story and a punch line).
- Does the publication have a **specific focus**? General-interest publications aimed at the entire world are pretty rare. Most of them are aimed at someone: readers of literature, religious believers, climate change activists, sports fans, hobbyists of every kind. The examples I give should appeal to my specific audiences. A private equity investor who needs to teach their staff about distractions

in the workplace doesn't want to hear about a funny thing that happened to me while I was working on my dissertation. They want stories that come from comparable environments. My tone will also shift in response to my audience. If I am giving advice to specialized readers looking for help in developing a specific skill, I will favor encouraging words over dispassionate ones.

- Does it have a **regional focus**? People like to believe they are different from one another depending on where they live. Having grown up in Ohio, and then having spent the last two decades in Massachusetts, I can confirm at least one example of this: New Englanders are a little frostier than midwesterners when you first meet them. But even if people were the same everywhere, the places they live shape what appeals to them. Metaphors or everyday examples about life beside the ocean won't play very well in an editorial in the *Omaha News*. I don't have to adopt the local dialect to write for a local publication, but I should be aware of the life circumstances of my readers.

- Does it have **political leanings**? Most of us would know the political leanings of national publications like the *New York Times* (left) or the *Wall Street Journal* (right). But many other publications tilt in political directions. If I want to submit something to the magazine of the *Mass Audubon Society*, I should be aware that they are advocates for environmental protection. In an essay written for them, I'll flash my credentials as a lover of walking in the woods or mention my lifelong passion for reptiles (which is true; at the age of ten, I was a junior member of the Northern Ohio Association of Herpetologists). Political leanings don't necessarily mean that you are restricted to submitting to publications that match your political affiliations. The *Wall Street Journal*, for example, gives an occasional pat on the head to a liberal writer, if only to remind its regular readers what it typically disagrees with.

These are not the only questions you can ask about potential audiences for your work, or the only kinds of adjustments you might make to the invitational nature of your prose. But if you are just getting started as a writer for nonacademic audiences, these four categories will provide a healthy foundation for your research.

They will also apply to the book publishers to which you might submit a proposal or manuscript. Generally, book publishers are casting a wider net than a specialized magazine when it comes to reader audiences. The editors of *Cigar Aficionado* don't really expect anyone who doesn't smoke cigars to buy their magazine at the airport. A book publisher hopes that your book will draw in new readers, including those who might not have a prior interest in your specific subject. While they probably have marketing research that tells them who buys books like yours, they are always searching for new book buyers. Because their audiences might be slightly less defined than those for a specialized publication, pinpointing audiences and adjusting your style for them will not lend itself to an easy formula. Still, even when it comes to book publishers, you can always practice two simple strategies. First, every publisher's website will have an "About" section that will give you some basic information about its audiences; glean what you can and review the full catalog of books in your subject area. Second, and better still, make sure you read some of the books this publisher has released. Nothing will beat analyzing the invitational qualities of the prose that you find there.

Good teachers think about the audiences in their classrooms; good writers think about the readers they are inviting to their prose rooms. Both kinds of educators shape their invitations with their learners in mind.

---

**STRATEGIES: WORDS, SENTENCES, PARAGRAPHS; INVITATIONS TO THINK; BEING GOOD COMPANY; AND THE READERS IN THE ROOM**

- **WORDS, SENTENCES, PARAGRAPHS.** Warm invitations from a writer begin with words, sentences, and paragraphs written to launch the reader's learning journey. As readers are finding their footing in your subject, we shouldn't double the burden we have put on their brains with unexplained vocabulary, complex sentences, or meandering paragraphs. Especially in the openings of books, chapters, or sections, clarity should be a priority. Your prose should offer a warm welcome to readers who don't have the expertise that you do.

- **INVITATIONS TO THINK.** When we don't have learners in our presence in classrooms, we have to find other ways to prompt the deeper thinking that changes perspectives and even lives. Some common writing techniques that provide invitations to think include everyday examples, metaphors, and allusions. These techniques encourage readers to make connections across contexts, an essential marker of deeper learning. We can prompt thinking further with thought experiments, hypotheticals, and active learning moments built into a book's structure.
- **BEING GOOD COMPANY.** Humans like to learn from humans. When appropriate, at whatever level is comfortable for you, give the reader glimpses into the person behind the prose. Don't feel compelled to share things that you would prefer to keep private. Tell the stories and use the examples that will foster connections with your readers. Share your passion for your subject or some examples of how it relates to your life. Let your personality peer through your prose with the examples you choose.
- **THE READERS IN THE ROOM.** The invitations we craft need to reach the correct addresses. This means that we should do the basic legwork about publishers, and their readers, that will shape some of the decisions we might make about our word choices, thought-inviting strategies, and even the level of personal disclosure our writing contains. To expand the number of people who accept your invitations, keep your intended reader always in mind.

---

### FINAL IMPERATIVE

Invitational prose, crafted by a human for other humans, has become even more important in a time when generative artificial intelligence (GenAI) can compose humanlike prose. When artificial intelligence can do some—or even much—of the work that academic writers have traditionally done, we have to consider what we are offering to readers. To be sure, we want to provide them with information and research that fuel our ideas, arguments, and advice. Accomplishing those objectives might become easier to achieve with the assistance of GenAI and its now less-exciting predecessor, the internet. AI tools can power our research and information gathering, help us discover new audiences for our work, and even sharpen our paragraphs and sentences. As the "GenAI Callout" sidebars in this book testify, I recognize its potential to support nonfiction writers.

But the dream/nightmare of teaching machines replacing human teachers in the classroom offers an instructive lesson for writers. When learning management systems and artificial intelligence tutoring programs seemed to threaten the future of the teaching profession, educators had to step back and reflect: what value do I bring to the learning process for the student? The result of that reflection was a profession-wide awareness of the importance of the relational nature of the teaching-learning transaction, as documented in books like Peter Felten and Leo Lambert's *Relationship-Rich Education*. Pedagogy machines can deliver content; human teachers care about their students, tailor content to their distinctive needs, and inspire them with their stories and examples.

Writing machines can likewise deliver content. Let them write the technical manuals or executive summaries we need or assist us as we build the foundations that will support our essays and books. But the essays and books that will educate learners most effectively should emerge from human minds because only a fully human mind can understand what it means to exist in a physical body, with a unique history of experience and education, subject to the strictures of time and space, and in community with others. The more that we can enfold an awareness of those conditions into our writing style and our projects, the more effective we become as educators for our readers. Perhaps more than anything else in this book, the advice in this chapter will likely become more and more important as GenAI tools gain in power.

To write like you teach means to write like a human educating other humans.

---

**CHAPTER FIVE WRITING PROMPTS**

- Review a few paragraphs of your own writing from an academic context: a thesis or dissertation, a journal article, a previous book. How do they stand up in terms of the invitational quality of your prose?
- Will you incorporate active learning into your manuscript? Where are the opportunities for you to make your readers stop and think? Review the possibilities in this chapter and play with one that you have not used in the past.
- Remind yourself of a personal experience that sparked or developed your interest in the subject of your book. Write a one-paragraph version of it and then consider where it might belong in your manuscript.
- Describe the reader whom you think will most enjoy and benefit from reading your book. Be as specific as possible: their occupation or field, their hobbies, their identities, their normal reading habits. What kind of writing would most appeal to that person?

# CHAPTER SIX

# REVISING AND EDITING

Producing a first draft of an essay or book feels a lot like teaching a course for the first time. I design a new course expecting that it will follow a determined plan, but such plans are useful fictions. No new course unfolds exactly as anticipated. No matter that I have been teaching for a few decades now, I will probably still make some classic new course blunders. I will assign too much reading. We will get to the first due date for an essay assignment before I have finished covering the material that students will need to complete the essay. I will realize that a basic interpretive skill that I assumed all the students will have mastered in a previous course needs review and practice. In almost every case, these mistakes won't doom the course for me or my students. I'll adjust on the fly, ask for goodwill from the students, and we'll cross the finish line eventually.

The real sweet spot for a new course occurs when I get a second crack at it. In the rearview mirror I can see the basic mistakes I made and correct them in the course schedule. I'll cut one novel from the reading list. I'll remove one of the major essays and add those points to in-class writing exercises. I'll redesign the final project to give students more room for creativity. But I won't just be fixing problems. I'll also do some basic rethinking. I thought the focus of the course was about the mechanics of storytelling, but the discussions and student essays made me realize that what captured the imagination of the students was the role that literature plays in constructing our own life stories. I'll tweak the course learning objectives, rewrite the course description, and change one of the essay topics to take this shift in focus into account.

These actions to revise a course for its second iteration resemble what a writer does in the movement from a first draft to the second. The composition of a manuscript begins with a spark of creativity, a burst of energy and ideas, just like the one that animates the first days or weeks of a new course. After that short honeymoon, we have to put in the daily work—piling up words on the page or showing up in the classroom three times a week. In writing as in teaching, we encounter unexpected obstacles; we find solutions and keep moving forward. At last we reach the end, grateful and exhausted. We might feel satisfaction with the experience—but we also know that we could have done a better job. It's time to revise.

The revising process demands that we reorganize, fix problems, and do detail work. The detail work tempts us first. Basic mistakes can be easily corrected, word choices can be improved, and citations can be completed. I find it satisfying to check off these kinds of tasks from my revision list. But always calling from the back of mind are the major tasks, which require effort and resolve—perhaps even courage. I have drafted a chapter that *could* work, but deep down I know it's tangential to my argument and should be cut. After I have chopped it, I look at my argument with fresh eyes and see for the first time that I need a new chapter that addresses an essential issue. Perhaps I also then notice that the long case study in chapter 8 really belongs in chapter 10, which means rewriting lots of contextual and transitional material. These are the more important tasks of revision, and they can be *exhausting*.

This chapter will walk you through four major acts of revision. The first three are the most substantive ones: **moving**, **adding**, and **cutting**. The nature of these acts themselves is self-explanatory, so I will focus on techniques and tools to help you get the work done.

Once we have tackled the strategies that support major revision, we'll finish with the detail work: improving your word choices and catching your mistakes. I'll make the case for a simple practice that will not only accomplish these two tasks but also improve the quality of your writing voice: **listening** to your prose.

An early reader of this book responded to this chapter by noting that it drifted somewhat from the book's premise: that nonfiction writing strategies align closely with good teaching practices. I acknowledge the truth of this criticism: not every strategy in this chapter has a direct pedagogical equivalent. Some of the advice here mirrors advice you might find in more general writing guides; you will see I especially echo recommendations from William Germano's book *On Revision*. Even though this chapter extends into areas beyond the book's premise, I still decided to include these ideas because I am aware that some academic writers, even those who have successfully published articles and books, may have never had any formal instruction in word crafting, revising, or editing. I *do* see connections between the revision tasks of writers and teachers, but ultimately I hope both experienced and novice writers will find in this chapter useful suggestions—or reminders—for the finishing work of putting a piece of writing through its final paces.

## MOVING

The best scenario for major revision occurs when you realize that you have written good stuff but it's not in the right order. Whereas adding requires that you write new material and cutting demands emotional fortitude, moving feels like solving an intriguing puzzle. Practically speaking, the act of moving words around and reorganizing your existing material will often lead to adding and cutting. But not always. In this section I introduce three tools that facilitate reorganizing your prose and then narrow down our focus to a single writing feature that every prose mover (and prose creator) relies heavily on: transitions. Mastering some basic transitional strategies in our writing makes revision a much less onerous activity, and a more effective process.

### REORGANIZATIONAL TOOLS

To move words and ideas around in your project, you have to step back and see the whole work as a composition of its many parts. You can conceive of those parts at several levels: chapters, sections, paragraphs. You are making one major argument, but that argument can be broken down to its components: your major claim, your supporting claims, your premises, your evidence. A college course can usually be broken down in the same way, into its units or weeks. In some cases, those units might have an internal logic to them—the students have to learn *this* before *that*—but in others I might have options available to me. When I teach Introduction to Literature, in which students are introduced to the major genres in literature, I have three major units to work with—poetry, fiction, and drama—but they can be taught in any order. In his book *On Revision: The Only Writing That Counts*, William Germano regards the movable parts of our written works as "small island[s] of prose."[1] Yes, and I would add that it is helpful to think of them as unmoored, floating islands, and we have to arrange them into the most pleasing archipelago. You're a sea god, and you can swirl your little land masses around with your trident.

When writers sit down for major revision work, they are challenged by their sense of their current organization as a fixed structure. Their islands are anchored to massive mountains beneath the ocean's surface. The three recommendations in the list that follows are all designed to shatter this mindset and instill the habit of seeing the parts of your project as the English poet Percy Bysshe Shelley saw this contingent world: as a place where nothing is fixed or eternal, and "nought may endure but Mutability."[2]

- **CREATE A MOVABLE TABLE OF CONTENTS.** We tend to think about revision as something that happens when we are finished with a complete draft, but it can happen throughout the drafting process as well as afterward. My first recommendation repeats a suggestion I made briefly in chapter 3: at the start of your project, create a *movable table of contents* and then revisit it regularly throughout the whole drafting and revising process. The entries in that table should be more detailed than one-word descriptions of each section, but you can get away with just a phrase or sentence for each major section. I keep such a table as a digital document, print it out and have it front of me when I am writing, and sometimes will excerpt parts of it onto a whiteboard in my office. Shuffling around the items on that table—digitally, on paper, or on the whiteboard—guides my revision process. Don't feel like your table of contents has to be complete at the outset of your project. Lay out whatever you have as you start, and then add and delete and move as you go. But every time you finish a section or chapter, update the full table. Every time you revisit the table, you might spot an island that needs to be floated into another part of the sea.

- **GET OUT THE SCISSORS.** Christine Tulley, the author of several books on scholarly productivity, hosts a podcast that introduces faculty writers to tools, ideas, and resources. Many of these are digital ones, but in one of her podcasts she recommends a very old-school way of reminding yourself that the organization of parts remains under construction, especially for shorter works. Print out your piece, get out your scissors, and cut it up into its constituent parts. Play with those parts for a while, arranging them in different orders. What would it be like for you to move that introductory story to the end? I have used this technique with my own writing and in my writing classes. In this digital era, it might seem silly to be printing and scissoring your prose. But that might be the best reason to give it a try—it will shake up your usual revising habits and inspire a new vision. The ability to completely change the nature of an essay with some physical snipping remains one of the best ways I know to remind yourself of the essential point about a first draft: "It doesn't have to look like this." Revising a book manuscript with this technique doesn't make much sense unless you have a warehouse-sized office, but you can always use index cards. On each card, write a phrase describing each chapter or section and put them in their current order, and then shuffle them and see what you observe.

- **TRY OUT DIGITAL WRITING PROGRAMS.** The two previous strategies are ones that work for a linear writer like me. I tend to write articles and books from beginning to end. But many other writers I know prefer to approach their projects like mosaic artists. They have a grand vision, and all of the work's sections will eventually all contribute to the final product, but they might not compose the sections in the order in which they will appear in the essay or book. If you would like to test out a digital tool that facilitates this approach to drafting *and* promotes revision, try out digital writing platforms like Scrivener (paid) or Quoll Writer (open source). These help you create a movable outline that can be filled with sections of text, which you can compose whenever inspiration strikes—and then drag them around and drop them wherever you would like in the outline. I tried Scrivener for a while and was impressed by its many features. I believe it could inspire any writer to adapt the right mindset toward their finished prose: it's never as finished as you think as it is. I continue to enjoy my old-fashioned analog revision tools, but I know plenty of writers who have gone digital and aren't looking back.

Only you (and perhaps your editor) can decide what actually needs to be moved around in your prose. But if you use any of these tools, you will get a better view of the possibilities; exercise a little patience as you move parts around, and new pathways will eventually come into your view.

## TRANSITIONS

Whenever you move prose around, you'll have to rework your transitions. The words that guide your reader from one place to the next are not strictly a revision tool—transitions are a basic component of any piece of writing. They provide bridges between words, sentences, paragraphs, and parts.

But I'm addressing this topic in this chapter because the quality of your transitions—and especially their absence—will point you toward the places where you need help with your revision work. In my work as an editor, I almost always spot problems with a work's organization because the author has neglected to put robust transitions between paragraphs or sections. Sometimes this happens just because the author doesn't have a great mastery of transitional strategies, but more often than not the lack of transition reveals a deeper organizational problem. Adjacent sections don't really belong together. A new section doesn't really follow from the last one. The missing transitions are the symptoms; the disease is the manuscript's ineffective organization.

Writing strong transitions thus supports the revision process, but having great transitions will also improve your prose in a more general way. Transitions reveal the logic of your organization to your reader. Academic writers often neglect transitions because of what one team of researchers termed *expert blind spots*.[3] When I have mastered a skill or body of knowledge, I can lose track of basic steps or background information that a novice needs. As I try to explain what I know to a new learner, I jump quickly from idea to idea, and my expert brain doesn't realize that I am unconsciously filling in knowledge gaps. The novice learner gets stopped at every one of these gaps and needs bridges to cross them. Transitions provide those bridges. Use any of the three transition strategies that follow when you are drafting, but then pay special attention to them when you are revising and moving prose islands around.

The use of *subtitles and headings*, already recommended in chapters 2 and 4, offers a first-line opportunity to link parts of your writing together. When you put a break in your prose, and add a section heading to whatever comes next, you are making a transitional announcement: "We've finished that idea, and now we move on to the next." When they see a section break, readers will assume that you will eventually show them the connection between the two sections just because they are adjacent. For this reason, you can sometimes delay the transitional words or phrases at the top of a new section. In the transitions in longer essays or books, you can start a new section with a story or an example in the first paragraph, and then point back to the previous section in the second paragraph.

The second strategy relies on words and phrases that are recognized *words of order and relationship*. Ordering incorporates words of enumeration: *first,* I'll do this; *second,* I'll do that; and *third,* I'll finish up with my final idea. Ordering words can also be hierarchical: my *primary* point, a *secondary* reason. Relationship words fall into various categories, but all of them demonstrate how two ideas or parts connect to each other. Relationship words can be grouped into the following categories: addition (*additionally, furthermore, moreover*), elaboration (*for example, consider the following*), contrast (*by contrast, despite, on the other hand*), conclusion (*finally, my last point*). These kinds of transitions will be welcomed by readers when you are making a complex argument or explaining a difficult idea, and keeping track of relationships between components will challenge readers. But they shouldn't be overused. As with "to be" verbs, if you always present your ideas with numerical transitions, it can render your prose flat and repetitive. An editor friend once told me that she heard an academic speaker at a conference use ordering words in his presentation, starting with "firstly" and continuing through "eleventhly." If you've gone beyond three, you've probably gone too far.

A third transition strategy uses *repetition and echo* to illuminate the path from one paragraph or section to another. You can see this strategy displayed in the work of Roxane Gay, who contributes an opinion column to the *New York Times* and has authored multiple best-selling books including *Hunger* and *Bad Feminist*. When nineteen schoolchildren were gunned down in a classroom in Uvalde, Texas, in the spring of 2022, Gay published an essay for the *Times* that included these three paragraphs:

> The scale of death in Uvalde, Texas, is unfathomable. At least 19 **children** and two teachers are dead. **These staggering numbers** will not change one single thing.

Time and again we are told, both implicitly and explicitly, that all we can do is endure **this constancy of violence**. All we can do is hope these bullets don't hit our **children** or us. Or our families. Or our friends and neighbors. And if we dare to protest, if we dare to express our rage, if we dare to say *enough*, we are lectured about the importance of **civility**. We are told to stay calm and vote as an outlet for our anger.

**Incivility** runs through the history of this country, founded on stolen land, built with the labor of stolen lives.

If you look at the boldfaced words in these paragraphs, you will find an almost invisible thread that links each paragraph to the next. The world **children** in the first paragraph appears in the second sentence of the second paragraph. In the second paragraph, she uses the phrase **this constancy of violence** to point back to the **staggering numbers** in the first paragraph. The second paragraph begins her primary argument by referencing the word **civility**. The third paragraph picks up an echo of that word in **incivility** as the first word of the third paragraph.

Like any good nonfiction writer, Gay knows that readers need transitions to follow her thinking. But like a *great* nonfiction writer, she wants to guide you gently. Her writing doesn't lay out her ideas as numbered points on the prose whiteboard. Her transitions beckon you along like a friendly guide. The basic strategy isn't complicated: begin a new paragraph with an explicit repetition of a single word or phrase from the previous paragraph. As you approach the far shoreline of each island of prose, grab a rock; place it on the beach of the new island when you arrive there.

---

### ADDING

You'll be a fortunate writer if all your revision work consists of moving your perfect prose around and tuning the transitions, but most of us are not blessed in that way. As you reorganize, you'll realize that you still have to do some new writing. An editor or an early reader will raise a question about something you have written, and you will have to find a way to answer it. Some of those questions will baffle you because they will be about things that you thought were common knowledge. Especially when you are writing to readers outside your discipline, you will often need to fill in knowledge gaps with background context. In chapter 5, I suggested that obscure vocabulary might demand that kind of work, but it might be demanded in other parts of your manuscript.

## MISSING PARTS

I once edited a manuscript about teaching that promised to guide readers through the process of designing course assignments—such as papers, projects, or presentations—from beginning to end. The author did indeed walk readers through the work of designing and introducing assignments to students, but then she left out the final piece of the puzzle: giving feedback on the complete assignment. In the revision phase she had to add a final section to address what happens after students turn in their work. You can sometimes identify missing parts in your project by returning to your introduction and reminding yourself what you promised to the reader. Did you fully answer your question? Did you outline a structure that was used for the first two hundred pages and then dropped in the last few chapters? I have often returned to my introduction after a complete review of a draft and realized that I had promised more than I had delivered in the full manuscript—at which point I either had to revise those promises or do some new writing.

## BACKGROUND KNOWLEDGE

As mentioned earlier, scholars or practitioners in a field can have blind spots that make them lose track of the barriers to understanding that are faced by new learners. For an academic expert, the revision process should include your thinking about this question: What do I take for granted in my discipline that readers outside my field, or outside the academic world, would not be familiar with? I have written multiple essays about faculty life for nonacademic publications, and sometimes I forget that not every American knows what it means to be adjunct, or the difference between an assistant professor and a full professor. These distinctions are such an integral part of my world that I neglect to explain them. This problem was once pointed out to me by an editor at the *Boston Globe*, who was reviewing an opinion column I had written and asked me to explain what tenure *was* before I made a case for keeping it. Remember to write like you teach and take little for granted when it comes to the reader's background knowledge. A writers group that includes members coming from outside your discipline will be especially helpful here.

## BECOMING EVEN BETTER COMPANY

In chapter 5, I argued that giving your reader glimpses of the human behind the book creates more invitational prose. Especially if you are writing to nonacademic audiences for the first time, you might not have done much of that work in your first draft. You wanted to get the ideas down on paper. Or maybe you started with a good story but then shifted quickly to your scholarly style. Revision gives you the opportunity to search for places where you can enhance the company you offer to readers. Page through your paragraphs and note anywhere you see long passages focused on content presentation. Be deliberate about inserting stories or examples in those areas that will bring your topic to life for readers. Put some flesh on your argumentative skeletons.

## MORE INVITATIONS TO THOUGHT

With a draft in front of you, now might be the time to experiment with adding thought invitations such as everyday examples, metaphors, or allusions. As you move through the process of revising, during which time you will be living and reading as usual, keep an eye open for new ways to explain your main ideas. After I had written my book on attention and distraction, I encountered a metaphor by the Roman philosopher Seneca that describes how individual interests guide the attention of learners: "Nor should you wonder that it is possible for each of us to collect information benefiting their own studies from the same source, for in the same field the cow searches for grass, the dog searches for the rabbit, and the stork searches for the lizard."[4] This engaging metaphor was too late for that book, but now I include it in my faculty presentations on the subject.

The major additions to your work will likely come from the need to fulfill broken promises or fill knowledge gaps; the minor additions will come from an awareness that you need one more way to explain an idea to the reader, or some way to break up with a long stretch of expository prose.

## CUTTING

I was finishing the first draft of this chapter, which was clocking in at around six thousand words. I had literally one paragraph left to write. I stepped away from the computer because something just wasn't feeling right about the chapter. I was driving to dinner with my wife and the realization hit me: I had written a narrative introduction that had locked me into a structure that wasn't working. Over the course of that evening and the next morning, I thought really hard about what parts of the chapter draft I could salvage. Finally, I accepted the inevitable. It all had to go. I copied and pasted all six thousand words into another document I have that contains all the chopped material for the manuscript. I took a walk, had a consolatory cup of tea, and started over from scratch.

We finish with the act of cutting because it requires the most resolve. You have drafted something, put your tears and sweat into it, and now you have to bid it farewell. Your first impulse will be to trim it here and there, see if you can reuse as much of it as possible. Sometimes those small tweaks work. But more often than not, your best move is to excise everything that you are concerned about and either fix the transitions or start adding. I've done this a thousand times and it never gets any easier. Most writers will have heard the phrase "kill your darlings," which has been attributed to multiple authors, including Eudora Welty, William Faulkner, and Oscar Wilde.[5] As Stephen King points out in his book *On Writing*, this homicidal conceit seems to have originated with the early twentieth-century British writer Arthur Quiller-Couch, who said, "Murder your darlings."[6] But you might also consider this act of excising things that have outlived their usefulness from a teaching perspective. I have developed creative essay assignments in my literature courses that I used for too many years because while I enjoyed assigning and reading them, the students or the course changed, and they no longer fit. Likewise with the course readings—usually a lag existed between the time when I *should* have moved on from a novel or poem and the time when I finally did move on.

Letting go is hard, both for teachers and writers. Typically when I schedule a conference call with an author who has a manuscript that needs cutting, I find myself approaching this delicate task by asking two distinct sets of questions.

- **DOES THIS STORY/EXAMPLE/CASE *REALLY* DESERVE A PLACE IN THE PRECIOUS REAL ESTATE OF YOUR MANUSCRIPT?** I have written many essays that originated with my desire to tell a story about a specific experience. For many of us who write, narrating our experiences can be therapeutic. We make sense of the world with our stories. But as I have discovered multiple times, our nonfiction writing often moves past the initial stories that inspired us to write. We should celebrate this because it means we are learning through the writing process. Our thinking about the subject matter evolves and improves. But then we are stuck with the stories we started with, and we have an emotional attachment to them—they inspired us, and we want to preserve a place for them. The power of the phrase "kill your darlings" comes from the fact that they are our "darlings": who wants to kill the things we love? But if our thinking has progressed beyond a story—or a clever sentence or a fun fact or any other part of our writing—we have to let it go. We can still acknowledge the work it did for us, and console ourselves with the fact that it played a role in the drama. We can also save them for the presentations after our books have been published, or dole them out in social media posts. But every story or example has to make its own case for its place in the precious real estate of your manuscript. Put them all in the docket.

- **IS IT A DETOUR FROM YOUR THROUGHLINE?** In chapter 2, I emphasized the importance of the throughline, the path that the reader can follow from beginning to end in your manuscript. The false paths that lead away from the main route belong on the chopping block. When the COVID-19 pandemic disrupted higher education, the teaching and learning community turned their attention to the health and well-being of students. Every potential author wanted to make the case that we should treat students with compassion and attend to their flourishing as humans—even if that wasn't the focus of their potential book. We should, indeed, treat students with compassion, but everyone doesn't have to make that argument in their book. Academics have passions and hobbyhorses like everyone else. When you have an outlet to express them—especially when you are writing a book, which can seem like a big container—it can be difficult to resist throwing them into your project. And something striking might happen in the world while we are writing, and we have something to say about it. Instead, keep your throughline focused, write a great book, and then publish an op-ed that lets you apply your book's ideas to a recent event.

Most writers I know have a file where they keep material they have excised from their current projects. Having such a space can ameliorate some of the pain you might feel from cutting carefully crafted words from your writing. Every book I have written has a digital file called "[Book Title]—Runoff." Into the runoff file goes anything longer than a sentence or two. For a 75,000-word book, the size of that file will top out at 20,000-plus words. I've often found that the more words I push into that space, the more successful the final book will be.

Some of those words will reappear in other places. The "recycling file" would be a more accurate name for my runoff material because I dip back into it and resurrect old sentences, paragraphs, and sections all the time. There have been times when I have been sweating away at a late section of a book and suddenly feel a sense of déjà vu. I glance back through the runoff file, discover that I had already written something similar, and drop it into the current chapter (with new transitions). I could always paste such discarded prose at the bottom of a chapter file, instead of moving it into a separate runoff file, but I want the cut material to be out of sight and mind; otherwise it becomes too tempting to cram it somewhere even if it doesn't quite fit.

This section has focused on the most difficult acts of cutting, the ones which demand that you excise substantial material over which you have labored. While such cutting should take priority in your revising process, I've never encountered a piece of writing from an academic that couldn't have been improved with some word-level cutting as well. Many of us write like we lecture: using more than words we probably need to. You can find lots of ideas for how to sharpen your prose in the books of Helen Sword, two of which appear in the bibliography. But as a final piece of advice from me, I recommend an incredibly blunt but effective method for honing your prose: after you have completed your first draft, get an exact word count, and cut 5 to 10 percent of it. Don't cheat. Set your mark and don't finish until you're done. Do this enough times and you'll start to notice the specific phrases that bulk out your prose, and develop your own solutions for trimming them.

## LISTENING

The last acts of revision focus on the word level. Editing your prose makes your sentences clearer, improves your word choices to make your writing more engaging, and identifies and corrects any mistakes in your prose. One of the recommendations from chapter 5 will help here: attending to the construction of your sentences—length, complexity, variety. That's work you can do twice: first as you write, and then as you edit.

But my best recommendation for these final stages of revision comes both from the collected wisdom of writing tradition and from learning research. People who work with words regularly know what William Germano argues in *Revision*: "The best rule for revising your writing is the simplest: listen to it."[7] In other words, read your prose aloud. When I was a younger writer, I would save this task for the end of the writing process and read an entire manuscript aloud. Now that I'm a little older, and I parse out this task over more time. I agree with Germano that this one action will do most of the work you really need when it comes to the last stages of revision. If we just took the time to read our prose out loud, we wouldn't rely on spell and grammar checkers so much, and our prose would sing more beautifully.

However, I'm not quite as convinced as Germano that *listening* is what makes the difference. I always felt what was helping me—because I have been reading my prose aloud for a long time—was the *speaking* of it, either to another person or just into the empty air. When you just skim over your sentences in your brain, you aren't really reading them carefully. When you pronounce them aloud, articulating every word, it slows the process. You're hiking over the landscape instead of barreling through it in an SUV with tinted windows. You notice when you have skipped a word, spelled a word correctly but it's the wrong word, used the same verb four sentences in a row, or skipped a transition. Reading your prose aloud makes it   look   like   this   to   your   brain.

That slower pace does more than help us catch mistakes. It helps us notice writing habits that we might want to reshape or abandon. I am a member of the Cape Cod Writers Community, which offers monthly webinars on the craft for writers in every genre. While I was working on this chapter, I attended one hosted by Nancy Gaines Bober, a voice actor who has produced many audiobooks for various publishers.[8] Coming from her daily experiences of reading prose aloud, she pointed out three writing habits that most writers should probably break if we can:

- **RELYING ON FAVORITE WORDS.** Everyone prefers some words over others and has favorites that they trot out for any occasion. Nothing wrong with that; we are writers, after all, and we should have love affairs with our special words. But if you read your prose aloud, you might hear that you are using a few words A LOT more than others. If you are starting to get a hunch that this is happening, use the Find button in your word program and see whether your hunch is correct. You shouldn't excise your favorite words entirely, but look for occasional substitutes.

- **RELYING TOO HEAVILY ON COMMON OR TIRED WORDS.** Even if you don't care much about a word, you might find yourself repeating it just because it covers much ground in the language. The word *logos* in Greek has many meanings, depending upon context. It can refer to words, speeches, written accounts, arguments, and more. Every language has these words; they are useful in part because they are imprecise. For example, verbs like *make* or *do*—which are often translated with the same word in other languages—are useful but utilitarian verbs. Let their appearance inspire you to attend more closely to your language choices. Search for more precise substitutes.

- **OVEREXTENDING PHRASES AND SENTENCES.** The need to breathe as we speak can spur a greater awareness of when we are pushing readers too far in a single sentence. Envision an audio narrator reading one of your longer sentences aloud; will they be gasping for their breath when they finish? Even better, read it aloud yourself and see how your lungs feel at the end.

I would finish by noting that reading aloud does help us identify our mistakes: typos, grammatical snafus, missing or extra words. Spelling and grammar checks do much of this work, but they are not foolproof. Finishing your prose always requires human effort, either by you and your reading voice or by a trusted friend (or both).Learning researchers have given us new support for the value of reading written work aloud to catch those final mistakes we might have left in a manuscript. A 2022 article in the *Journal of Applied Research in Memory and Cognition* describes the result of an experiment in which subjects were asked to revise a passage of prose under three conditions: reading it silently, reading it aloud, and reading it in a disfluent font (i.e., a font that forces us to concentrate, *such as this one*.) Those who read it aloud, to no surprise of this writer, caught the greatest number of mistakes.⁹

> ### Artificial Intelligence Callout
>
> All my previous Callouts have referred to generative artificial intelligence programs that mimic human writing. The general category of artificial intelligence encompasses much more than such programs, including ones that can support the final recommendation of this chapter. While I would argue that reading your own prose should become a habit of every writer, speech-to-text tools can facilitate your listening to prose, even when you don't—or can't—read it aloud. Journalist Michelle Woo points out that hearing your words read by another voice, even an artificial one, can overcome the problem of overexposure to your own writing. After having composed a piece of writing and then revised it and reread it multiple times, the effect of reading it aloud might be dulled. Instead, she argues, feed your text into a speech-to-text program, which can be a simple as a browser extension, or one of the many freely available ones. Hit Play, she explains, and then "simply be a listener. I like to print out my writing and make notes with a pen when I hear things that trip me up. You might prefer to make changes right there in the text. This is just a nice way to hear what your words sound like as an outsider. If you feel captivated and engaged, your readers will, too."*
>
> *Michelle Woo, "Why You Should Use a Text-to-Speech App to Read You Your Stories," Creators Hub, Medium, November 11, 2020, https://medium.com/creators-hub/why-you-should-use-a-text-to-speech-app-to-read-you-your-stories-36865c1ae635.

## STRATEGIES: MOVING, ADDING, CUTTING, LISTENING

- **MOVING.** The act of moving prose around typically occurs when you see the need for reorganization. What gets in the way of such reorganization is your sense of the words being fixed on the page or the screen. Consider one of three tools that will break that sense of fixity and free your mind to resee your parts in a new order: a movable table of contents, a scissors job, or digital platforms like Scrivener or Quoll Writer. Reviewing your transitions might help you spot places where reorganization might be needed. In addition to the usual transitional strategies we can use, consider experimenting with repetition and echo to link your paragraphs together.
- **ADDING.** Filling gaps in background knowledge will be one of the major reasons for you to add prose in the revision stage. But when you are reviewing a complete draft, you might look for three other pathways for additional writing: unfulfilled promises that you have made in your introduction or at the beginning of sections; opportunities to become better company; and places where you might enlighten the reader with new thought invitations.
- **CUTTING.** During the revision process, look out for the stories or paragraphs that stand out because you loved writing them or because you think they're *so good*. They might well be good, in which case pat yourself on the back and move on. But oftentimes we tell our favorite stories or include interesting things in our writing for our sake, not for the reader's. Highlight such questionable sections and ask the hard question: does it belong? Pay special attention to the places where you might divert your reader from your throughline. You don't have to murder everything you love in your prose, but reduce the number of distractions your reader will encounter as they follow your argument.
- **LISTENING.** Read your work aloud. Help your brain slow down and hear your prose as you speak it into the air. This simple act will help you notice when you are repeating your favorite words, making tired word choices, or using lots of words when a few will do.

The onerous task of proofreading your prose in search of basic mistakes will also be made much easier if you read your work aloud. Especially if you don't have access to early readers—such as when you are trying to turn around an op-ed quickly in response to a current event—reading your words aloud can do some of the work that might be normally done by a writing group or friends pressed into editing service for you.

## FINAL INJUNCTION

You probably have friends and colleagues with whom you discuss teaching. That discussion might occur in hallway conversation, in the moments before and after departmental committee meetings, or even on social media exchanges. Better still, you might attend events hosted by the teaching center on your campus, if you have one, or participate in conferences devoted to teaching. In these places we can discuss our achievements and obstacles, share good ideas with one another, and give and receive emotional support from people who know what we are going through.

Writers can also attend conferences and join regional communities devoted to writing, but the most essential community for a writer is formed on a smaller scale: the writers group.

Writers groups, which require you to gather with a small number of fellow writers and read and talk about writing, can facilitate every part of the writing and revision process. Writing group members are the early readers who scratch their heads while they are reading your first draft and say, "I'm not sure I understand what you're saying here." Cue new prose. Or, "I like this story, but I'm not sure you need it." Get out the scissors. I have been in two long-standing writers groups, and at this point in my life I would never undertake a larger writing project without the help of a writers group whose members ask questions about my topic and my writing, offer potential solutions to my problems, and sharpen my own editing skills by giving me the privilege of reading and editing their work in return.

Writers groups have various ways of working. In *Write No Matter*

*What: Advice for Academics*, Joli Jensen makes a distinction between two primary kinds of writers groups: support groups and content critique groups.[10] Support groups are essentially writing therapists. They invite members to share their frustrations and stumbling blocks in the writing process—and also the joys and triumphs—and offer ideas about how to keep writing. Support groups can also act as accountability tools. They set goals and deadlines and cheer on the writers who meet them. The members might gather once a month for writing time and then a meal, and just the awareness of that upcoming event might drive the members to be more productive.

Content critique groups, by contrast, give feedback on drafts. Jensen argues that support groups are what matter for academic writers, since any scholarly project will get feedback from early readers thorough the peer review process. When it comes to content critique groups for academic writing, Jensen doesn't mince words: "Do not join a content-critique writing group!"[11] She explains her reasoning this way: a mathematician shouldn't be giving a sociologist content feedback on her scholarly work. True enough. But since your ambitions include writing for a wider audience, this is *exactly* what you want: a mathematician giving feedback to a sociologist and vice versa. Two sociologists will share the same background information from the discipline, so they would never think to raise the questions posed by the mathematician. And the questions raised by a nonacademic writer in a content critique group might be even more important than ones raised by your disciplinary colleagues.

If you don't already belong to a writers group, and don't know how to get one off the ground, I will offer the advice I have always given to my children when they felt left out of things, or felt like there was nothing to do: everyone loves the organizer. Even when people turn you down because they're busy or already committed elsewhere, people are always grateful to be asked. Look around you for the writers on your campus, in your social circles, or even among social media connections. (As I was editing this chapter, I saw an academic issuing a request on LinkedIn for people to form a writers group, and she received multiple expressions of interest in the comments.) Make a list of people whose writing you admire, or whose subject areas interest you, or whom you know have writerly ambitions that they haven't achieved.

Reach out and propose a writers group to improve your revision process, submit more polished prose to your editors, and be happy to be in the company of people who care about words, ideas, and readers. Start the conversation and keep talking.

---

**CHAPTER SIX WRITING PROMPTS**

- If you have already done some drafting of your book, select a five-page sample and underline or boldface your transitions. Revise a few of them with "repetition and echo" transitions. If you haven't started drafting, review one of your previous publications and play around with the transition strategies presented in this chapter.
- Identify a dense section of your manuscript, such as a part in which you delineate a key theory or summarize a complicated piece of research. Point your writers group, especially the members who don't share your background knowledge, to those paragraphs and ask them what questions a novice reader might raise about that section. Revise them like a teacher.
- Select your longest chapter. Cut 5 percent of it. You can accomplish this task by chopping words here and there or singling out whole sentences or paragraphs for excision. If you have a chapter that's six thousand words long, at least three hundred words must be eliminated. As you complete this work, notice where you are finding excess words or a passage that could be cut. Take what you have learned and apply it to the rest of the manuscript.

# A FINAL WORD

The introduction to this book began with a scene in which I was browsing around the shelves of a used bookstore on Cape Cod and made a happenstance discovery of Edith Hamilton's work on ancient Greece. Although I had already begun thinking about the idea of *this* book before that February day in the winter of 2022, Edith Hamilton's work was the lightning strike that illuminated the places where I could visualize the connection between teaching and learning. But *The Greek Way* also rekindled a dormant passion in my life: learning languages. I had taken courses in Latin and ancient Greek in both high school and college, and I had loved them. Within a year after I had finished reading Hamilton's book, I began to relearn ancient Greek.

Recently, in the course of that study, I learned a new English word that has its roots in the ancient Greek language: *philomath*. You might know the word *polymath*, which refers to someone who knows many things in many fields. The word *philomath* might sound familiar, but it has a different meaning. Its roots are common ones: *philo*, which refers to love, and *math*, which relates to the Greek word for learning. A *polymath* is a person who has *acquired* much learning; a *philomath* is someone who loves the *process* of learning.

I love to know things, and I've made a good life out of knowing things. Publishers, readers, students—they all expect me to know things. But more than anything else, I love to learn new things. *Philomathy* has been the keyword of my life. I'm guessing that any educator reading this book will feel as I do. Whatever else might have drawn us into these pedagogical lives we have chosen, the pleasure and fulfillment we get from acts of learning continues to drive us forward.

The advice in this book is aimed at my fellow philomaths, with the hope that your love of learning will inspire you to move forward in your career both as a writer and as a teacher. Those of us who write and teach love learning for its own sake, but we also want to inspire it in others. We hope that our students will have such great learning experiences that they will take more courses in our fields; we hope that our readers will follow the tracks they find in our writing to new essays and books. Good philomaths ignite a passion for learning in their students and their readers.

In the wake of your reading of this book, I hope you will feel more committed than ever to the project of learning, both as a teacher and as a writer.

*(Our journey together can now conclude if you came here primarily for advice on developing your skills as a writer. But if your aspirations include writing a full-length book aimed at an audience outside your discipline, keep reading a little further. In the appendix that follows, I offer some guidance on how to undertake that task successfully.)*

## APPENDIX

# SUBMITTING, PUBLISHING, AND PROMOTING A BOOK

*A Syllabus*

---

**COURSE OVERVIEW**

Not all academics who have mastered the art of writing for wider audiences receive the publishing opportunities and readership they deserve. I have worked with many talented writers who labored to transform a complex idea into accessible prose, applied the kind of writing strategies I have recommended here, and found nothing but closed doors in the publishing world. At the same time, I can also point to multiple academic authors who—in my humble estimation—have found public audiences with depressingly mediocre writing. The quality of writing in a manuscript matters, but it doesn't tell the whole story.

    The final skills that audience-expanding authors must acquire are the ones that guide them successfully throughout the entire publication process, from the first contacts with an editor to the long-term promotion campaigns they must conduct on behalf of their published work. Academic writers sometimes bristle at the nature of this latter work, which seems antithetical to the deep thinking work we prize in higher education. But for your great ideas to educate the world, they must reach people. Your query or book proposal has to pop up on some busy editor's screen at the right moment. To survive the editorial and production gauntlet, your completed manuscript must be shepherded by a patient and responsive team. For audiences to fall in love with your book, it must first catch their attention somewhere: in a social media post or in the show notes of a podcast. Navigating through all the channels of the publishing ecosystem can prove daunting to academic authors.

In this appendix, which takes the form of a course syllabus, I will make the case that the skills needed to manage the publishing process resemble writing skills in an essential way: *they can be learned*. A basic awareness of the fundamentals of how books are acquired, produced, and sold arms aspiring authors with the knowledge they need to find and partner effectively with their editors. The writing skills that you have been developing will translate, with some modifications, into the unique genres of submission and book marketing: queries, proposals, and author questionnaires. To be sure, publishing systems—like humans and their fates—can be capricious and unfair. Bias exists in the publishing world, as it does everywhere. But if you commit yourself to learning this final set of skills, you give yourself the best possible chance, in the face of whatever barriers you will find, of seeing your work come to life in a traditional publishing outlet.

The remaining pages of this book are a syllabus, not the whole course. Plenty of editors and book coaches have taken deeper dives into the mechanics of publishing, the editorial process, and book promotion. I'll share their resources throughout the syllabus and encourage you to follow up with books, essays, and websites that offer wise counsel for academic authors. At the same time, I want to ensure that you have the basic information and guidance that will enable you to begin practicing your submitting, editing, and promoting skills. As a result, this syllabus will stretch a little longer than a typical college syllabus, with its bare outline of course topics and due dates and policies. It will include our **learning objectives**;

required and recommended **resources**, lightly annotated; a **course schedule**, which will describe the tasks of submitting, editing, and promoting your book in rough chronological order; and finally, the **assignments**. These assignments take the form of writing prompts that will be interspersed throughout the course schedule. Each prompt will be introduced with basic information about that stage of the process and basic advice for that specific writing task.

Read that material, try your hand at the prompts, consult the resources when needed, and become a knowledgeable steward of your book and its publishing fortunes.

**LEARNING OBJECTIVES**

By the end of this syllabus, you should have the knowledge and skills you need to submit your work to publishers, partner with them throughout the many months required to produce a book, and then become an assertive advocate for your published book. You will be able to:

- Identify relevant book publishers for your manuscript, and then craft materials that will convince acquisitions editors of its merits through queries and book proposals;
- Partner effectively with publishing staff, from editors and designers to marketing experts, throughout the process of your book's production; and
- Develop your community of readers after your book's publication through a website, social media postings, and ongoing work as a speaker and writer.

**REQUIRED READINGS**

The following three resources are essential reading for academic authors intending to publish for expanded audiences. (Full source citations for these books appear in the bibliography.)

William Germano, *Getting It Published: A Guide for Scholars and Anyone Else Serious about Serious Books* (2016)

> Bill Germano's career has included many years as an editor at several presses, including time as the editor-in-chief at Columbia University Press and vice president at Routledge. He also is a professor at the Cooper Union and the author of multiple works on writing and publishing. This overview covers much territory in very wise and readable prose.

Jane Friedman, *The Business of Being a Writer*, 2nd ed. (2025)

> A longtime editor at *Writer's Digest*, Friedman has extensive knowledge of the publishing industry and the key players in making a book successful. She shares advice about writing and publishing through her website, email newsletters, and essays in various publications. This book gathers her accumulated wisdom into one handy package, with an updated edition published in 2025.

Laura Portwood-Stacer, *The Book Proposal Book: A Guide for Scholarly Authors* (2021)

> Germano and Friedman offer broad guidance for writing and publishing a book, while Portwood-Stacer narrows her focus to the second-most-important document for a successful book (second only to the manuscript itself): the book proposal. Because book proposals are such foundational documents, the scope of Portwood-Stacer's guidance almost expands to the same level as Germano and Friedman's.

More specific resources—mostly shorter and available online—will be presented at the end of each of the three parts of the course.

## COURSE SCHEDULE AND ASSIGNMENTS

The schedule divides the publishing process into three parts: submission, editorial, and promotion. It follows a chronological order, but many of these events will overlap or occur in different sequences in your specific publishing journey. Each unit will be introduced with an overview, followed by a writing prompt. The three parts will also have their own introductory overviews.

## PART ONE: SUBMISSION

The most fundamental thing we know about learning any skill is that it requires repeated practice. You don't become a great tennis player unless you spend many hours swatting balls in the hot sun; you don't pump out gorgeous, knitted Christmas sweaters for your friends every year until you have spent a few winters making them plain rectangular scarves. For better or for worse, writers with long careers will get lots of practice at the tasks required for submitting books to publishers. Even when you are preparing your eighth book for submission, you will still be researching book publishers, writing queries and book proposals, and negotiating contracts. If writers ever reach the place where they can just send a terse note to an editor with an attached manuscript and receive a contract in an email reply, this author of seven books hasn't reached it yet.

It can seem disheartening to face down all the additional writing time needed for an effective submission—but it can also be enlightening. Every time you describe your project for a new editor or agent, you will discover new words, phrases, and even ideas that help you see it more clearly. Writing chapter summaries for a book proposal might reveal a running thread that you didn't know your project contained. Confronted with the prospect of distilling your project into a single paragraph in a query letter, you might luck into a gorgeous sentence that belongs in the manuscript itself. As you convince potential readers to buy your book, you will also be reminding yourself of why it matters. Bring a growth mindset into the process and allow it to educate you about the business of publishing books, writing for new audiences, and advocating for yourself and your writing.

Hewing to all the guidelines offered in this syllabus, and to all the advice proffered in the recommended resources, can be helpful but guarantees nothing. You will receive rejections. Follow the advice you give to your students when they have stumbled over the first block in your course: keep trying.

### Unit One: Laying the Groundwork

Long before you submit your book proposal to a publisher, you should establish as much of a track record as you can as an expert, writer, or public scholar. When I receive a book proposal from a potential author, I scan the overview and perhaps the chapter outline (more on these to come). But very early in my reading process, I will page through to the author biography or curriculum vitae (CV). As I peruse those documents, I am looking for two things:

- **PUBLICATIONS.** What has the author written already—books, journal articles, essays, blogs? A lot or little? Where exactly have they published? In addition to analyzing the publication record, I might even pause to hunt down an online essay to check the quality of their published writing.
- **PLATFORMS.** I will also quickly scan their online presence. Does the author have an existing platform that will enable them to promote a book to potential readers after it appears? If they haven't written much in traditional outlets, do they have a social media following? A website? A popular workshop series? A position in a relevant organization?

Hearing this might deflate readers who don't have strong credentials in these areas, or frustrate potential authors who want their book to be judged solely on its merits. But remember that publishers take a risk with every book they publish. They are wagering that the sales of your book, or its contributions to some greater good, outweigh the costs of its production. Moreover, each book they accept shoulders out other possibilities, since they can publish only a limited number of books each year. Examining your publications and platforms provides them with useful information about whether your book will be a good bet. Assuming similar quality in two proposed projects, it makes good sense for the publisher to accept the one that comes from the writer with an existing track record and the best opportunities to spread the word about their published book.

If you don't have a strong publication record, or have only a minimal presence in some relevant community or organization, start developing one now. Launch a website, open a social media account, start a newsletter, attend more conferences, submit op-eds to newspapers or other short-form publications. If you have recent research results that will lend themselves to publication in an academic journal, or an existing draft that has been waiting around for revision, speed them into publication as quickly as possible. Publication records and author platforms don't matter more than a great project, but they do matter.

> **WRITING ASSIGNMENT:** If your publication record or existing platform seems thin, complete one of the following prompts:
>
> - If you don't already have active social media accounts that are dedicated to the subject area of your book, start one and post at least once a week in the next month. See unit 10 for more ideas about what those posts might contain.
> - Search for local organizations that sponsor lectures from experts or authors: libraries, community centers, senior centers, nearby academic institutions. Send an email to the contact person at one of these places and offer to give a talk on your project area.
> - A deeper commitment to platform-building work might include developing a newsletter or blog on a platform such as Substack or Medium. If you were to imagine an ongoing series of essays (or podcasts or videos) on one of those platforms, what would be your focus? Just as a test of whether such a regular commitment would excite you, draft a title, a subtitle, and a post in the range of five hundred to one thousand words that would introduce your offerings to potential readers.

### Unit Two: Researching Publishers

You may know who publishes scholarly books in your field, but if you are hoping to expand your audience, you should reach beyond them. Possible publishers for your project might include larger commercial presses that feature works written by academic authors (such as Random House, Basic Books, or Norton); university publishers, both smaller ones that specialize in your field (in writing studies, for example, Utah State University Press) and larger ones that publish more general trade books (such as the University of Chicago Press, Harvard University Press, or Princeton University Press); and small and independent presses that might have both areas of specialization but also have general-interest lines (such as New Directions or Bellevue Literary Press). This section's prompt will ask you to create a short list of three to five publishers for your project. In preparation for that task, you will need to engage in some or all of the following research activities:

- **READ THEIR BOOKS.** Without an authentic engagement with the books produced by the publisher, you won't really know whether your manuscript will find a home there. Read (skim if you have to) a book or two from publishers on your short list. Does your manuscript read like their books? Would you be happy to be associated with those titles? (Bonus: As you read, you'll have more opportunities to observe the ways in which authors use or don't use the strategies recommended in *this* book.)
- **HANDLE THEIR BOOKS.** Get some representative books from each publisher into your hands. Are they functional carriers for ideas, or are they beautiful works of art in their own right—and do you care? Do you like the covers? The feel of the pages? How long are the books and how much text, in what size, has been fitted to the page? Both the reading and the handling stages of your research can be accomplished by whiling away a few hours on a weekend in a large bookstore or library.

- **CHECK THE BASICS.** The profile of the publisher might help you recognize your odds of getting published there. Check the size of its staff, the number of books published each year, years in business, the quality of their website. A smaller publisher will give your book more attention but won't have as many resources to throw behind it. A major press will offer prestige and more people working on your book's behalf—but they will be doing similar work for many other books and might not have the same level of commitment to you and your book. Would you prefer to swim in a Cape Cod kettle pond or a Great Lake?
- **READ SUBMISSION GUIDELINES.** Some of the basics of a book proposal will cross every publisher, such as an overview and a chapter outline. But many publishers will ask for specific documents not requested by others. See the next unit for more information on these documents. As you review submission guidelines for each publisher, determine whether they have any restrictions on simultaneous submissions. Most editors will prefer to have an exclusive look at any proposal or manuscript, instead of competing with a host of other editors. Some publishers have a stated policy that they will not consider simultaneous submissions, and authors should respect that policy. Even at the publishers that don't forbid simultaneous submissions, editors will look a little kindlier on exclusive ones, which suggest that their press is the prime object of your publishing dreams.
- **IDENTIFY THE CORRECT PERSON OR ADDRESS FOR YOUR SUBMISSION.** Books proposals are reviewed by acquisitions editors, each of whom will have areas of specialty. Most university presses and independent presses will have short profiles of the acquisitions editors on their staff, even if they are just short phrases that identify their areas of interest. But not all will. You might be submitting to a general e-mailbox. If you are submitting to a specific person, read those profiles and poke around online a little further; perhaps they have been featured on an institutional site or have given webinars. You might discover something that reveals insights into

what sort of titles they would welcome. If you have identified the right person, address them by name in your introductory email (i.e., not with the generic "Dear Editor").

- **CHECK FOR AGENT REQUIREMENTS.** For the larger commercial presses, you might need a literary agent. This should be stated clearly on the website. For most university and independent publishers, you do not need an agent. Literary agents have their role in the publishing ecosystem, but they are not mandatory. Some editors with whom I have worked have told me that they prefer to deal directly with authors, instead of working through an agent. If your dream press requires an agent, get one. They will have contacts at the publisher, negotiate a (better) deal, and speed up the process. But they will also take their 15 percent cut (a fair cut, to be sure, if they do their job well). All the research guidelines in this section, and in the sections on queries and proposals, will transfer directly into the submission process for agents.

---

**WRITING PROMPT:** Having visited bookstores and libraries, and done all the recommended internet sleuthing, draw up a list of your top three to five publishers. Each item on the list should include the following information:

- *Publisher name and two or three sentences on why they appeal to you.* Hit the points that matter most to you.
- *The submission guidelines.* This should include all materials listed by the publisher, perhaps boldfacing the ones that are unique to a specific publisher. I'm not a spreadsheet person, but I suspect that spreadsheets could be a useful tool to keep track of guidelines.
- *The person or address to which you will submit your work.* If applicable, note any relevant details of the acquisitions editor.
- *For your first choice, your submission date.* Give the editor at that dream press three to four weeks to respond. After that

> time, if you have received no response, send a polite follow-up. After another week with no response, assume that they are passing and submit the manuscript to your second choice, and any other presses that accept simultaneous submissions. Repeat as necessary.
>
> Create your list in whatever form appeals to you: text document, table, spreadsheet.

## Unit Three: Writing Book Proposals

With your list of potential publishers in hand, you can begin to develop your book proposal. This document plays an outsize role in the submission process and deserves as much attention as your manuscript itself. First-time authors might assume that they will send out their manuscript with a cover letter and then spend a few months in fear and trembling, waiting for the editor's response. But in most cases, the book proposal will determine whether an editor will even *read* your manuscript. A strong proposal makes the case for an editor to read and offer a contract on your book. A groundbreaking manuscript might never see the light of day because an author neglects this essential document, and assumes that their name, ideas, or writing will be enough to catch an editor's eye.

Put yourself in the position of an editor for a moment. An acquisitions editor will receive many book submissions over the course of a year, but reading submissions is just one part of their job. Once an acquisitions editor signs a book, they remain responsible for its fate throughout, and beyond, the publication process. They give feedback, line up reviewers, present it to internal audiences at the publisher, coordinate scheduling, and work with design and marketing staff. They will help champion your book after it has been published. Given the number of signed projects already on their plate, you shouldn't expect them to close their office door, cup of tea in hand, and devote an entire day to reading a submitted manuscript from an unknown author.

A book proposal presents them with a more manageable means of learning about your project, its ideas, and your writing. It summarizes your manuscript, describes how it unfolds, explains how it differs from existing books, and introduces you as an author. This section's prompt will ask you to develop the following components of your book proposal.

- **OVERVIEW.** A few pages long (three to four), this document covers the basics of your project. It describes your question or problem, the way you will answer it, your research base or methods, and anything else you believe is distinctive about your work. It should address your audience, the timeliness of your contribution, and your credentials. Although you will include a fuller author biography later in the document, the overview also includes a short introduction to the book's author. You might think of the overview as a précis of your complete proposal (you will sometimes see the word *précis* used for the overview, which helps distinguish it from the full proposal).
- **CHAPTER OUTLINE.** This might extend to five to ten pages. Each chapter should be covered in at least a full paragraph. Think about your throughline, discussed in chapter 2, as you are preparing this part of the document. Your chapter titles and descriptions will guide an editor along the pathway of your argument. The outline should highlight the new idea in each chapter, and perhaps the research base for each chapter's arguments or ideas.
- **COMPETITION.** Another page or two. This section identifies three to five titles that your book would compete with, most of which should have been published within the past few years (you can certainly include a foundational work or two for context). As you compose this part of the proposal, you can tap back into the skills you learned through compare-and-contrast assignments in primary or secondary school: here's where my book and this one overlap, but

here's how mine differs. Some authors will make the mistake of saying that their books are completely unique and have no competition. The fact that no similar books exist might make an editor nervous: the absence of other books like yours might suggest that nobody will be interested in it.

- **MARKETING, PROMOTION, OR AUDIENCE.** Not all publishers will want this section, and it might have any of these three titles or something similar. But what the editor wants to know is who will read your book, how the publisher would market it to that audience, and what role you will play in that process. If you have an existing or budding platform, highlight it here. If you have a social media following, an extensive speaking schedule, or a business or organization that would promote your book, this will be the section where you describe it. Detailing this information could be accomplished, again, in a few pages.

- **AUTHOR BIOGRAPHY.** A full page about you and your credentials, which should begin with the basics: academic position, education, publication, awards. You can describe the origin of your project in terms of your research or your passion. This section should be fuller and more specific than the generic biography you might provide on your website or for a conference. Highlight the parts of yourself that have made you *the* right person to write this specific book, and how you will make it successful (i.e., prior publishing and existing platform). For a university press, you can also include your CV. In my role as a series editor at a university press, I'm happy to receive a CV and I always review it—although I still want the standard author biography. But for non-university publishers, you should only include the CV if the submission guidelines mention it.

- **SPECIFICATIONS AND MANUSCRIPT STATUS.** Just a paragraph here at most. How long will your book be? Most nonfiction books clock in between seventy thousand and ninety thousand words, although everybody loves a nice compact book, so dipping below that range is fine. Note whether your book will contain images, graphics, or copyrighted material of any kind (for which you will need to obtain written permission to reproduce in your book). Finally, this paragraph should indicate the status of the manuscript and your timeline. How much of it have you written, and when do you expect to finish your first draft?

- **SAMPLE CHAPTER OR WRITING SAMPLE.** This document can range between ten and twenty-five pages, but the publisher's website should give you specific information on its requirement. The more substantive question about your sample has no clear answer: should you use your introduction or a body chapter? Whereas the introduction will give an editor an overview of your project, a sample chapter from the middle of the book will demonstrate whether you are capable of fulfilling your introduction's promises. (If your proposal has been requested, you can always ask what the editor prefers.) This sample reveals the quality of your writing, so work over this section of your manuscript thoroughly before including it.

> **WRITING ASSIGNMENT:** Write your first book proposal, directed to the publisher that tops your list. Once you have created that proposal, you should be able to replicate its core and add or subtract parts of it according to the specifications of the other publishers on your list.

### Unit Four: Queries and Introductions

The final document that will prepare the path for your manuscript to engage the attention of an editor might take one of two forms. A query will precede the submission of your proposal; an introductory letter will accompany it. Some publishers will invite authors to send a brief description of their project before they submit their proposal or manuscript, which enables the publisher to decide quickly whether it might be interested in learning more. This kind of brief description is called a *query*. Other publishers prefer to review the proposal as their first look at the material, in which case you will still precede the proposal with a short letter of introduction to yourself and the project. In both cases, the work of this document can be accomplished in a single page. The submission guidelines of the publisher will inform you about which document it prefers: a query before submitting your proposal, or an introductory letter accompanying your proposal. (If the publisher doesn't specify, submit your proposal with the letter of introduction.)

Queries and letters of introduction have the same purpose: enticing an editor to read your proposal. Fight the temptation to compose the equivalent of an academic job letter, which can run several pages long in an effort to give a complete vision of you. As you write this document, focus on hitting the following marks, presented roughly in the order in which they might appear in a well-organized letter.

- **OPENING: MAKE THE EDITOR CURIOUS.** Introduce the fascinating question or problem that drove your project's development, as recommended in chapter 1. This (short) paragraph deserves all of your writerly attention.
- **MIDDLE: PREVIEW YOUR ARGUMENT.** Include a *very* short statement of your argument and perhaps a word or two about the book's structure or research base. You have probably heard of the "elevator pitch": How could you summarize your idea during the thirty seconds you might spend in an elevator ride with an editor?
- **CLOSE: GIVE CREDENTIALS.** Usually the final paragraph of an essay will summarize your academic positions, your publications, or other relevant experiences. Prior publications and current platforms deserve a special place in this paragraph.

*The following two components could appear in brief paragraphs before or after the main content.*

- **STATE YOUR INTEREST IN THE PUBLISHER.** Just as in the academic job application process, you can send the same letter to every

institution, but the best letters will explain why you want a job on their specific campus. If the books of the publisher you're writing to have been valuable to you in some way, mention that.
- **SPECIFY WHAT YOU ARE OFFERING.** Include whatever the editor will find in your attached documents. For a query, note somewhere what you have available to send if they are interested. For either a query or an introductory letter, note the state of the manuscript: beginning stages, partially written, or complete.

Hitting all of these marks in a one-page document, composed of three or four modest paragraphs, will seem intimidating. To give you a little assistance on how it can be accomplished, I have included a query letter that I thought did an excellent job of hitting four of them. The missing piece was the author's credentials, but that could have been easily corrected with revision. This query was sent to me by the author, who was proposing a book for the book series I edited at West Virginia University Press. I have reproduced it here with her permission.

> Dear Professor Lang,
>
> I am writing to share with you the attached proposal for a book on the online retention crisis in higher education. Today, over 30% of all college students take at least some of their course work online. Yet, students in online classes fail and drop out at significantly higher rates than students in face-to-face classes.
>
> In the book I propose, Building Rapport in Online Higher Education, I argue that the heart of the retention problem is the lack of human connection in online classes. Using data I have collected from both long-term and short-term teaching experiments over the past 10 years, I demonstrate that when faculty build rapport with the students in their online classes, they can erase the retention gap.
>
> The full proposal, including an annotated table of contents, is attached here for your review, and my cv is as well. I think the

> *Teaching and Learning in Higher Education series would be a great fit for this book, which is accessible, yet grounded in research. Small Teaching is a book I return to often as a teacher and a writer. I would love the opportunity to talk with you further about this proposal.*
>
> *Thank you for your consideration and happy new year!*
>
> *All the best,*
> *Rebecca Glazier*

Short, sweet, and successful. I was immediately interested. In the end, the press decided it had too many similar books in its pipeline and did not make an offer. But the query eventually paid off, and Rebecca's excellent book was published by Johns Hopkins University Press.

> **FINAL WRITING PROMPT FOR PART ONE:** Compose the document that would precede your book proposal for the press at the top of your list. It should fit onto a single page of print.

## Part One Bonus Unit: Book Contracts

After your introduction and book proposal arrive at the publisher, it might pass through several stages of review. If the acquisitions editor likes it, they could ask you for some additional thinking or revision. They could also subject it to internal review or send it out for peer review. Many university presses will use outside peer review for both proposals and finished manuscripts. When it comes back from peer review, or even just from an internal review at the publisher, at least three outcomes are possible:

- **A PASS.** They might or might not give you a reason for this decision not to pursue your project. If you receive any feedback on

your proposal, it's likely to be short and vague. They will have moved on to the next author, and you should move along to the next publisher.
- **AN INVITATION.** They will request to review the completed manuscript. If you have already completed it, you can submit it immediately; if not, you will submit it when complete. Such an invitation to continue the process does *not* constitute any kind of promise or implied contract to publish the book.
- **A BOOK CONTRACT OFFER.** Best case: they offer you a contract to publish your book. If this offer comes in response to a proposal, it will be an *advance contract*, which will be contingent upon your completion of the book according to the specifications spelled out in your contract.

In the second scenario, the invitation, the following outcomes can occur, which will be familiar to anyone who has submitted their work to an academic journal:

- **REJECTION.** Unhappily, you may or may not receive detailed reasons for the rejection. Manuscripts can be dismissed without sending them out for peer review. The acquisitions editor or an in-house editorial board might deem the project unsuitable or unsound. If it passes through the in-house review, it still might be rejected as a consequence of concerns raised by the peer reviewers.
- **REVISE, RESPOND, OR BOTH.** If the editor or editorial team has initial concerns about your manuscript, they might require revisions before they send it out for peer review. If peer reviews are supportive but concerned, you will have to write a response, just as you would with an academic journal, detailing your revision plans. If that response, and the subsequent revisions, pass muster, the publisher will extend a contract offer.
- **CONTRACT.** Your manuscript is accepted and you are offered a book contract. Look at you! Have a craft beer or cup of fancy tea. Or both.

Whether or not you have completed your manuscript when you receive your offer, your contract will likely specify that you are promising to deliver a manuscript that fulfills its requirements and will thus be subject to a final review. At a university press, for example, the final approval will come from the press's board. So signing the contract itself is not the final hurdle—but it's the highest one.

The contract will also lay out all of the legal and financial details. Book contracts will contain many clauses and subclauses, many of which will be boilerplate and not really up for negotiation. Especially if you are writing your first book or working with a university or independent press, you won't find much room for negotiation even on the nominally negotiable things, such as royalty rates. Consider whether fighting for a half-percent increase in your royalties is worth potentially spoiling your relationship with your new editor and making that person wary when you come calling with your next book proposal. If you would like to gain a better understanding of book contracts, and how authors should manage them, check out the additional resources in this unit.

Otherwise, promptly, and joyfully, complete the following writing prompt.

> **BONUS WRITING PROMPT:** Sign your book contract.

## ADDITIONAL RESOURCES FOR PART ONE

Jane Friedman, "How to Write a Query Letter: Nonfiction and Memoir," JaneFriedman.com (2023)
> In this essay on her website, Friedman packages the parts of the query in a slightly different format than I describe here; compare and make your choices.[1]

"What's a Book Proposal?" Kate McKean, *Agents and Books*, Substack (2019)
> A literary agent and author of the popular Substack newsletter *Agents and*

*Books*, McKean boils the book proposal down to its essentials: what to include and what you don't need.[2]

"Advance Contracts, Explained," Laura Portwood-Stacer, *The Manuscript Works* (2022)

I included Portwood-Stacer's book on book proposals as one of the required readings for the course, but this blog essay outlines the nature of advance contracts, how they transform into regular contracts, and why you should or should not hope for one.[3]

"Model Trade Book Contract," Authors Guild (2020)

This organization has represented the interests of published writers for more than a century. It has developed a model trade contract that it believes offers a fair deal for both writers and publishers. This multipage resource presents every clause in a standard contract, along with helpful commentary on each piece. Note: The Authors Guild is an advocacy organization, and you'll see that stance reflected in the commentary, which can be critical of conventional publishing practices.[4]

Publisher and Agent Submission Guideline Pages

Many publishers and literary agents offer helpful advice on crafting the documents that will appeal to them, and you might find helpful perspectives on the guideline pages from publishers beyond the ones to which you intend to submit.

---

PART TWO: EDITORIAL AND BOOK PRODUCTION PROCESSES

For a book to become successful, a small community has to gather around it. The community would not exist without you—but neither would it exist in final form without publishers, editors, editorial assistants, designers, marketers, rights specialists, and other publishing professionals. The written text you produce comes cloaked in the handiwork of all of these people. As your book wends its way through the publication process, they will all contribute to its ultimate form—and to various degrees, to its ultimate fate.

Good authors value and respect the contributions of every

member of their publishing community. Academics, in particular, might lose sight of the expertise that a cover designer or marketing copy specialist brings to the table. You might disagree with some of the decisions made about your manuscript, its title and subtitle, book cover, jacket copy, and other aspects of its presentation. But whenever you receive feedback, are presented with suggestions, or are shown materials that the publisher has created on your behalf, keep these four principles always in mind:

1. Most editors and publishing staff will have more experience publishing books than you do. You possess your expertise, as do they. View them as partners and collaborators.
2. Everyone at the publisher wants your book to succeed as much as you do. Their livelihoods depend on producing great books. They would love to see your book crack the bestseller list.
3. Express your opinions throughout the publishing process, and stand behind them if they are essential to your vision. If you don't understand a manuscript constraint or decision, offer suggestions or alternatives.
4. Nobody wants the author to be unhappy, which means they will accommodate you until they see a firm obstacle to the book's success—at which point they might make a final decision you don't like. Don't fight every battle. When you encounter a hard no, respect that decision and concentrate your energies elsewhere.

A good teacher treats the members of a classroom learning community with respect, empathy, and goodwill. The teacher produces and guards the vision of the course but invites everyone to contribute to that vision. Bring those qualities to the publishing community that forms around your book.

**Unit Five: Editing**

When your manuscript receives final approval, it will be sent into production. An editorial assistant or production manager at the press will send you a timeline that will specify the major steps in the process, along with the deadlines for your contributions to that process. Once the production threshold has been crossed, you will no longer have opportunities for substantive revision. Your final contributions to the manuscript itself will consist of lighter acts of shaping: copyediting, proofreading, and (potentially) creating the index.

- **COPYEDITING.** A copy editor will review the entire manuscript; you will receive a marked-up copy showing their work and be asked to approve their suggested changes and answer any clarifying questions they have posed, in addition to making any final edits yourself. Authors tend to think about copyediting as fixing words here and there, catching basic mistakes, and identifying missing references. Copy editors do all this, but it's more complicated when it comes to books. You might have told a funny story in your introduction and inadvertently repeated it in chapter 9; the copy editor will catch that for you. Copy editors eliminate redundancies and point out gaps. Most academic authors will find their complex sentences tightened up. Note that the copy editor's changes are submitted for your approval; you don't have to accept all their suggestions. But if a copy editor flags wording or other problems in your prose, they did so because it made them stumble as a reader, so take their concerns and recommendations seriously.

- **PROOFREADING.** The page proofs, which will arrive next, will display your manuscript exactly as it will appear on the printed or digital page. At this point you will read the book again—you will be heartily sick of reading it by this point—to check for mistakes, typos, and even formatting issues. But you will not be able to make extensive wording changes at this point. If for some reason you feel like you need to change something substantial, you will have to pay out of pocket for the book's reformatting. As long as you have given your full attention to revising and copyediting, this problem shouldn't arise. With respect to the errors, which you can correct at this stage, remember the advice in chapter 6: if you worry about missing some, read it aloud.

- **INDEXING.** Your contract will specify whether you are responsible for your index. Some presses will handle this work, but more likely you will either be asked to create your own index or will need to pay for someone to do it for you. This cost can be significant. Most indexers charge per page, and at the time of this writing, $5 per page (or higher) was the standard rate. Your compact manuscript of two hundred pages will cost you $1,000 to index. If you do the indexing yourself, you will find plenty of online resources to guide you through this complex task. Creating a good index requires a lot of time and work, so allot the space in your schedule for it. It can be worth your time. Because you know your book better than anyone else, you will likely produce the best index for it. Before we all went all digital in our lives, indexers in the days of yore would use index cards for this task (that's why they're called *index* cards, aha!)—and that option remains available even today.

For all these tasks, the editorial schedule will give you two key dates: the date when you will receive these materials, and the date when they are due back. Your window might be as short as two weeks or as long as six weeks. *Meeting these deadlines is essential.* A delay of even a few weeks in meeting one of them could push your book's publication date back three or six months, since publication dates are tied to seasonal catalogs (e.g., Spring 2025, Fall 2025), and those appear on schedules determined far in advance.

After these three tasks of copyediting, proofreading, and indexing are completed, you won't see the manuscript again before it reappears as a review copy or finished book, which might not be for several months.

---

**WRITING PROMPT:** Given the likelihood that you will be producing your own index, this prompt will prepare you for that task. Page through the indexes of two or more books in your area of specialty and note the categories of items you find there:

> concepts, people, places. Start a new document and write ten to twenty index items for your book. Don't worry about tracking down page numbers. Just get a little practice thinking like an indexer. Wherever you are in the composition or editorial process, return to this document after every writing session and add potential new terms to your evolving index.

## Unit Six: Author Questionnaires

Every author has two great hopes: to complete their book and to have people read it. To achieve the first of these two hopes, follow the advice of writing books like this one. To achieve the second one, complete your author questionnaire with diligence and creativity.

You will be sent this document relatively early in the production process and given a deadline to complete it. *Your work on this document will be more important than anything else you do to support the marketing of your book.* Answering its many questions will require many hours and even days of work. Take your time with it and spread your attention to it over the course of multiple writing and thinking sessions. Craft responses to its questions, think about them further, and then come back to them and add new information and ideas as they occur to you. Use its questions to inspire you to think creatively about strategies for getting your work into readers' hands.

Based on these comments, you can probably surmise that the author questionnaire is not like the questionnaire you get at the doctor's office that you can fill out in the waiting room. It will begin innocuously, with questions about your address, your positions, awards you have won. Then it will intensify by asking you to describe your book in multiple ways, in shorter and longer versions: maybe a few paragraphs, a short paragraph, a single sentence. Then it will finish with a series of questions designed to help the marketing team get your book in front of as many influential people and places as possible. Your author questionnaire will ask you to provide the following:

- Your credentials: your academic positions, your research, other relevant experience
- Places where you have lived, places where you might have done extensive work, or travel plans you might have around the time of the book's publication
- Bookstores that you frequent, or where you might know the owners or employees
- Publications that are local to you, such as a hometown newspaper or cultural magazine, or that are local to places that appear in your book
- Any contacts you might have in the media in their many forms
- Parts of your book that might be good for serialization in magazines or on websites
- Prizes for which your book might be eligible
- College courses that might feature your book
- Conferences in your field where you might speak or attend
- Your website and social media accounts and your activity on all of them
- The names of "big mouths" in your field—in other words, influential people who have an outsize voice through their social media platforms
- People who could write blurbs for your book
- A one- or two-sentence description of your book, and a three-hundred-word description of your book (which might be culled for book jacket copy)
- A description of what makes your book unique
- Languages you speak or other countries where you have contacts
- Any other creative ideas you might have to promote your work generally or to specific audiences

When you realize the extent of the work you will have to put into this document, you might feel a mite of frustration. Why can't the marketing people hunt down some of this information for themselves, or come up with their own ideas for the podcasts or journals they should send review copies to? Isn't that their job? To be sure, and the publisher will indeed send out advance review copies to media outlets, journals, and influential people in your field. The publisher will develop this list based on its research on your book and its topic and the publisher's previous relationships with review outlets and reviewers.

But remember that the marketing folks are creating plans for books in many fields, and nobody has the same grasp of your book and its potential readership as you do. They don't read the specialized publications in your field, listen to the podcasts you listen to, or know the big names who would be interested in your ideas. You are the foremost expert on the subject of your book *as a book*.

The more information and ideas you provide on the author questionnaire, the more successful the marketing team will be in their work on your behalf. The questions that draw out this information might look different from publisher to publisher, and you might find ones not covered here and others you aren't asked. In every case, err on the side of giving more information whenever you can. Any piece of information might seem irrelevant to you, but your marketing person might know or find a way to make use of it to reach new audiences.

---

**WRITING PROMPT:** Begin work on your questionnaire as soon as it arrives, and then return to it in several more sessions, to give your brain time to develop new ideas to fill out your responses. Challenge yourself to make three specific marketing recommendations in response to the final, open-ended question in which you are asked to offer your own ideas.

**Unit Seven: Book Covers, Book Jackets, Catalogs, and Press Releases**

Good news and bad news: you will not be asked to design your book's cover or to write the copy for the book jacket, the publisher's catalog, or press releases sent to media outlets. Design and marketing teams will draw from your author questionnaire responses to develop these materials. While you should welcome the contributions of these people, you might have a strong vision for any or all of those pieces and wish you could create or draft them yourself. Instead, an editor might inquire about your general preferences about cover colors or themes, or examples of book covers that you like. A designer or design team will then get to work, and later you will be shown a proposed book cover or a choice between two possibilities, and asked for your preference or feedback. For jacket or catalog copy, the publisher will request your responses or edits on already drafted written materials. When you see these materials, you might love them or you might be unhappy. Perhaps, in the latter case, you believe they reduce the complexity of your argument or draw too much attention to the most controversial of your three major arguments.

Remember this, then. Book covers, book jackets, catalogs, and press releases are marketing tools. They have been developed to capture the attention of a reader browsing in a bookstore, skimming an email, or surfing the internet. They don't purport to represent your ideas in all their glorious complexity. They entice the reader to open the book and *then* encounter your groundbreaking ideas within its pages. While you absolutely should provide suggestions and feedback on the materials that are created and drafted on your book's behalf, remain deferential throughout this process. Design and marketing professionals own the expertise here, in the way you own the expertise on your topic.

Book covers can sometimes prove a special challenge for publisher-author relationships. Here as well you must understand that book cover design walks a fine line between art and commerce.

And as with any genre, it evolves. The book covers you loved in your formative scholarly years might have fallen out of favor in terms of their reader appeal. The proposed book cover that you will eventually be shown should reflect any preferences you articulated, such as preferred colors or styles. But be aware that by that time, much thought and work has already been completed. This will not be the right time to say: "I don't like any of these options—but here's a better cover design that I created with an AI tool / was created by my artistic friend / is based on a childhood photo of mine!" Such a sentiment will not elicit the enthusiastic response you are hoping for.

At the same time, the publisher wants you to be happy with your book, and in general the staff will welcome your ideas if those ideas are presented with a little self-awareness. This unit's writing prompt is thus optional. If you are happy to let the professionals ply their trades and offer feedback as requested, you may move on to the final unit of this part of the course.

> **WRITING PROMPT:** If you have ideas for your book's cover design, summarize them into a single paragraph. As soon as the final manuscript has been transmitted into production, include that paragraph in a brief email to your editor. Clarify that your ideas are offered in the spirit of collaboration, not as demands or instructions for how your book should be designed. Expect a noncommittal response like this one: "Thanks. I've forwarded your message to the team."

## Unit Eight: Title and Subtitle

Once you have reconciled yourself to the limited control you have over the design features of your book, you will have to carry that thinking into your book's title and subtitle. Those words and phrases might feel sacred to you, intimately tied to your conception of the book. They came to you in a fit of inspiration, or you spent time crafting them over days or weeks, and they capture the spirit of your book perfectly. I have felt this way about every single one of my book titles and subtitles. And every one of them was revised in response to requests from the publisher. I could have fought harder for my proposed titles, I suppose, but in some of these cases I got the sense that their requests were not negotiable. Nobody imposed titles on me, but they pointed out flaws in my titles and subtitles and indicated that they were fatal. Subsequently, we brainstormed possible alternatives together and found workable solutions.

Just as with book covers, titles and subtitles do important work for the design and marketing of your book. The heavier weight of that work will fall onto the subtitle, which publishers prefer to be explanatory and heavy on searchable keywords. Many great nonfiction books have single-word or short-phrase titles that reflect the creativity of the author, but most of these are paired with a much more prosaic subtitle. If you do a little searching in popular nonfiction books, you'll notice some patterns in the subtitles. If you have written a book telling people to do something in the right way, the publisher might want the word *guide* or *advice* in your subtitle. If you are arguing that we need to change our thinking about some familiar topic, the publisher might suggest words like *new* or *revolutionary* or *radical*. Publishers also like question-starter words like *how* and *why* and *when*. All these strategies are designed to catch the reader who has come looking for help or information or ideas, does a keyword search, and finds your title in the results.

The final writing prompt of this unit encourages you to use the same brain to think like a writer *and* marketer. It also recognizes that whatever you come up with, the publisher might ask you to revise. Before you undertake it, flip through the nonfiction in your nearest bookshelf and see if you can glean principles that might help you.

> **WRITING PROMPT:** Write down three possible titles for your book. Exercise your creativity here, playing with single words or very short phrases. Then write three explanatory subtitles, each

> of them paired with one of the titles. Make sure the subtitles include at least one or two searchable keywords. Once you have created your own possibilities, feed them into generative AI and let its results expand your vision. Don't get attached to anything. Remain playful and open to revision.

**Bonus Unit: Expressing Gratitude**

Lots of people labored to turn your words into a finished product. Express gratitude along the way in your email correspondence, but also thank those publishing partners in the acknowledgments of your book.

> **BONUS WRITING PROMPT:** If you haven't done so already, revise your acknowledgments section to mention the names of the editors and other publishing staff who helped create your book.

## ADDITIONAL RESOURCES FOR PART TWO

Carol Fisher Saller, *The Subversive Copy Editor: Advice from Chicago (or, How to Negotiate Good Relationships with Your Writers, Your Colleagues, and Yourself)*, 2nd ed. (2016)
> You might not be ready for a full deep dive into the art of copyediting, but this brief and witty book illuminates the essence and significance of the work from the perspective of a longtime copy editor.[5]

Rachel Toor, "The Reality of a Writing a Good Book Proposal," *Chronicle of Higher Education* (2013)
> In this essay, Toor makes an interesting argument that authors should search

online for examples of author questionnaires (not difficult to find) and respond to the questions as a way of writing their book proposals.[6]

Debbie Berne, *The Design of Books: An Explainer for Authors, Editors, Agents, and Other Curious Readers* (2024)
> This short book offers a quick education on the art and craft of producing books, not only the covers and jackets but all the other visual features of a book, including fonts and pages.[7]

Jody Rein and Michael Larsen, "Secrets to Developing the Best Title for Your Nonfiction Book," in *How to Write a Good Book Proposal*, 5th ed., Writer's Digest Books (2017)
> This excerpt can be found on Jane Friedman's website. It offers plentiful examples of effective titles and subtitles for nonfiction books as well as principles for creating your own.[8]

Marion Winik, "Writing a Book Is the Easy Part: On Titles and Subtitles," *Kirkus Reviews* (2019)
> Babies get their names from the get-go, Winik writes in this humorous and helpful essay, as opposed to books, where "the title often comes last, with difficulty and dissent, sometimes with the author on the sidelines."[9]

---

### PART THREE: PROMOTING YOUR BOOK

The notion of promoting your book can spur an oppositional reflex from academic writers. Self-promotion seems anathema to the life of the mind, not fit for a true researcher and thinker. Most academics also carry around mental backpacks full of imposter syndrome, which prevent them for promoting their work too vigorously. You might wonder why you need to promote your book anyway, because don't publishers have marketing teams to handle that stuff? You wrote the book, after all; they should promote it, right? You would prefer to return to your lab or office and wait for the royalty checks to arrive.

If you have won a Nobel Prize, you can rest easy on this assumption. For the rest of us, book promotion will depend heavily on the engagement of the author. The publisher will do its share, but it expects authors to do their full share as well. In my work as an editor, I have seen time and again that the fate of a book depends *almost entirely* on the level of commitment made by the author to promote their book to others. This will be especially true for first-time authors and those who are publishing with smaller presses.

Part 3 of our course will thus prepare you to create the promotional strategies and materials you will need to support your newly published book.

### Unit Nine: Websites

All of your promotional strategies should have a digital landing site from which they can emerge and return, which means you need a website. You already might have a basic one within your institutional pages or one that you have created as a repository for your publications and general interests. But professional author web pages reflect your commitment to your identity as a writer. You don't necessarily have to hire a professional web designer to establish that commitment; enough website-building tools exist to guide you through the process if you choose that route. But if you plan to do it yourself, first engage in some learning: take a short course, read a book, watch tutorials. You can find some of those in the additional resources section for part 3. Many authors (including this one), though, hire a professional to build their pages. This might cost you several thousand dollars, but the quality will almost certainly be higher—and will preserve more of your time for your other responsibilities.

Whatever else your website will do, it should convey one essential message: you hope to continue your relationship with your readers (and potential readers) beyond the confines of your printed book. Great teachers inspire their students to keep learning; some students will be so inspired by a great teacher that they take multiple courses with the same professor. An author website makes it easy for readers to identify the best pathways to continue their learning journey with you: buying your next book, inviting you to speak on their campus, following you on social media. While book marketing does have the ultimate goal of getting your book into the hands of more readers, writers achieve that goal when they form communities and build relationships with people who share the same interests and passions that brought you to your writing desk.

To that end, I pass along one piece of advice from my own web designer, who helped me see my website as a site of *connectivity*, not just as a tool for self-promotion: Build a website that displays your full range of expertise as an educator, instead of focusing on a single book. Of course you will want your website to feature and promote the book you have finished, but remember that readers visiting your website are looking to connect with you, and not just be sold a book. In addition to learning about your book, make sure that visitors discover more about you as a writer, see the scope of your research, and learn how they can connect with you. Pay attention to the tabs that lead visitors to your profile, your openness to speaking and interviewing, your other published work or media appearances, and your social media accounts and contact information.

---

**WRITING PROMPT:** Visit the web pages of three to five authors whose work you admire. Make a list of components that you find on their home page. These might include the author's biography, their current books, news and events, or endorsements of their work. With those possibilities in mind, sketch out the basic layout of your web page, specifying what you will name the tabs leading to the subpages, and what each one will contain. Once you have made these decisions, begin building your own site or use them to start a conversation with a professional designer.

## Unit Ten: Social Media

Whatever conflicted feelings that academic authors might have about self-promotion might intensify at the prospect of promoting their book on social media. To be fair, those shared spaces on the internet *can* be sinkholes of self-promotion—and promotion more generally—by influencers and advertisers. But they can also serve as powerful engines for authors to connect with readers. When I finish a great book and want to keep learning from that author, I hop online and see whether the author has social media pages where my learning journey might continue.

When I do discover a new author on social media, the one thing I *don't* want to see is an account in which the author only posts links to buy their book, advertisements for speaking services, or glowing reviews or media coverage. My academic revulsion to self-promotion will kick in, and I won't hit the Follow button. Instead, I hope to find a well-rounded human being, the person I enjoyed spending time with while reading their book. I'm curious to know how the subject area of their book continues to evolve, the authors they read and like, glimpses of their life as a teacher and a writer, and the places where they might be speaking in person or online.

For this reason—but *please* do your own research, and ask your editor and marketing team for their advice—I recommend that academic authors limit the amount of space they allot to promote their book(s) on social media accounts. I counsel authors in my book series to have no more than 20 percent of their social media posts directly promoting their publications or paid events. The rest of their posts should stem from their identities as teachers, readers, scholars, and humans. Here are some handy verbs to summarize how authors can expand the scope of their social media posts:

- **AMPLIFY.** Shine light on voices, institutions, programs, and resources that you believe deserve wider recognition. If you are committed to promoting the work of diverse academics and writers—as we all should be—share links to their work and their social media accounts.

- **ADMIRE.** You are a reader as well as a writer. If you have discovered a terrific new book or essay, let your followers know about it. Post a link or an image of the cover. Say something about what you admired about the writing.
- **INFORM.** After you have finished your book, you can continue to educate readers about your subject through your social media feeds. Apart from pointing them to specific resources, let followers know about new discoveries or controversies in your field.
- **HUMANIZE.** In chapter 5, I presented an argument for humanizing yourself as an author, in the same way that we allow students in the classroom to catch glimpses of our full personalities. On social media as in our writing, a little goes a long way. Offer the occasional snapshot of yourself as a teacher, writer, family member, or curious learner.

As a final point in favor of embracing the possibilities of social media, the amplification possibilities it creates can work in both directions. The readers you connect with on social media might be able to extend the influence of your work. A scholar in your field might discover your book through LinkedIn and offer to review it for a popular media outlet. A journalist searching for experts to consult for a feature article might discover you on X (formerly Twitter) and reach out to you for a quote and mention your book in the article. An organization might follow your social media profile to your website, where they discover that you are available for lectures and workshops and offer you an honorarium to speak at their annual conference. These acts of amplification will be more likely to happen if you have established a solid presence in the social media sphere.

The writing prompt that follows does not assume that you use any particular social media platforms. Elon Musk's takeover of Twitter in 2023 further fractured an already fractured social media landscape, and platforms will continue to arise, have their moment, and fall into oblivion. Nobody should feel compelled to appear on all of them, or even a handful of them. Pick the one or two that appeal to your sensibilities and commit yourself to six months or a year's worth of posting a few times per week after your book has been published.

> **WRITING PROMPT:** In response to the list of short prompts that follows, script four social media posts for the week of your book's publication (after the first week, you can reduce the number of weekly posts to one or two). A few of these are self-promotional, but it's publication week, so you should lean a little harder on that angle.
>
> - **DAY ONE.** Announce your book's publication on the morning of its official publication day. Most books are officially published on Tuesdays. Include a link or note about one upcoming event featuring the book.
> - **DAY TWO.** Write a short post focused on the experience of writing a book: an image of your writing space, a friend's word of encouragement, a note of gratitude toward your family.
> - **DAY THREE.** Select one source that informed your project and encourage readers to engage with it, follow the author on social media, or attend one of their upcoming events.
> - **DAY FOUR.** Tell your followers/connections about the last great book you read, whether or not it relates to the subject of your book. Explain why it captivated you.
>
> As your social media presence grows, and you receive responses to your posts, you should not feel compelled to respond to them all. But respond to everyone who interacts with these four posts, even if that only means hitting the Like button on their comment and following them back.

## Unit Eleven: Making Yourself Available

An author's website and social media accounts can drive a third powerful engine for promoting your published book: speaking engagements, interviews, podcasts, and other activities. At one time, authors longed to have their books reviewed in the publications they admire, from the *New York Times* to the flagship journal in their field. But with the proliferation of media outlets in the world, book reviews have lost their prominence as *the* vehicle for driving book sales. Instead, many readers learn about new books when authors give lectures or workshops based on their book, are profiled in the local newspaper, or appear on a podcast. To ensure that such opportunities come their way, authors must advertise their availability—and even their enthusiasm—for engaging in them.

Your website provides the perfect vehicle to accomplish this. One tab or subpage of your site should focus on your work as a speaker or interviewee. Express your enthusiasm about sharing your research with new audiences and provide your contact details. Give an overview of your research and background, and point to your relevant publications. Describe how you would interact with a book club. For invited speaking engagements, help potential hosts envision an event that features your work. Develop titles and abstracts, and then note that you are not limited to these talks and are willing to meet the needs of specific events.

After a successful speaking engagement or interview or podcast, draw from the experience to fill out the relevant page of your website. If you know that you gave a good speech or helped an organization through consulting, reach out to your host and ask if you can get a blurb from them for your website. I have found that hosts who seem genuinely pleased by your work are very happy to do this. (If I'm not sure they are pleased, or if I feel that I wasn't at my best, I don't ask!) Ask for photos from these events or take them yourself. A good web designer will find a creative way to incorporate endorsements and photos into your web page. In addition to the blurbs, list places where you have spoken or consulted in the past.

Even a simple list of locations and events will demonstrate that you are regularly engaged in this work. The availability page of a website thus can be a work in progress that starts before publication and continues as you engage in all these activities.

Your social media accounts should affirm your commitment to sharing your ideas postpublication. The 10 percent to 20 percent of your social media posts dedicated to self-promotion can include announcements of upcoming events and expressions of celebration or gratitude for recently finished ones. Saying thanks to people, institutions, and event organizers should form a regular part of your social media (and probably life) practice.

> **WRITING PROMPT:** Write the text section of your web page on your availability, including abstracts for two or three lectures or workshops you could offer based on your expertise and your book, and one image of you in educating mode: teaching, speaking, interviewing.

### Unit Twelve: Publish Essays Based on Your Book's Subject

Publishers will expect and encourage you to publish essays based on your book. Based on conversations with my own editors, they prefer that you start this process no sooner than your publication day. If a reader discovers your essay in a media outlet and finds it intriguing enough to buy your book, they should be able to find it through a quick search, click the Purchase button, and have it in hand within a few days. If you begin publishing essays based on your book a few months in advance of publication day, a reader might make a resolution to buy your book—but we (OK, I) make a lot of resolutions, and we (I) forget about most of them. At the very least, you should have one essay planned for the days and weeks after the book's official release date.

Most of the recommendations that this book offers about

nonfiction writing translate easily into the kinds of essays you might write for popular and intellectual media outlets, from opinion pieces in your hometown newspaper to historically prestigious magazines like the *Atlantic* and the *New Yorker*. Just as in your book, build these essays from intriguing questions and problems, step beyond the evidentiary traditions of your discipline, keep the reader's attention in mind, and be good company for your reader. For media outlets, you must work a little harder to find an angle that connects to the present moment. In the months leading up to publication, keep an eye out for events and trends about which you—or your book—might have something useful and unique to say. When you spot one, send a query to the editor with your pitch (which won't differ much from the sample query discussed earlier in the course).

Be realistic about your expectations. Writers flock to places they recognize and value as readers, and by all means you should send your pitches their way. But don't neglect the broader universe of publications that feature writing by academic authors, and maybe start by targeting a slightly less aspirational publication. Consider the following publications that welcome essays from academic authors of newly published books:

- **LOCAL NEWSPAPERS.** Most traditional newspapers have opinion and editorial pages (op-ed) that feature essays and arguments from local authors. Seek out a local angle for your book's topic, and send a pitch to the editor of those pages (you can find their email address on the site).
- **CAMPUS PUBLICATIONS.** All three of my alma maters produce quarterly magazines that they send to alumni, and all of them at least occasionally publish an essay by an alumni or faculty author. Target both your alumni institutions and the campus where you work now.
- **CHRONICLE OF HIGHER EDUCATION AND INSIDE HIGHER ED.** Both of these daily publications feature multiple essays by guest authors every week. While they both have dedicated sections about

academic life (including teaching, researching, administrating), they also welcome general-interest essays based on new research, new ideas, and new books from academics.
- **THE CONVERSATION.** This nonprofit organization publishes newsworthy essays by academic experts. It takes pride in filling that specific niche. It can serve as a great starting point for building your résumé of published pieces in diverse media outlets.

For these outlets, and every other publication you target, familiarize yourself with the kinds of essays that they publish and ensure that your proposed or submitted essay fits easily with what you find there. You can submit a fifteen-hundred-word essay for a newspaper editorial, but such essays typically run to no more than eight hundred words. Don't make it easy for an editor to reject your submission simply because you didn't check the submission guidelines.

If you don't find a publisher for your essays, and even if you do find one, you can become the publisher of your own short-form work through platforms like Substack and Medium. As social media has become a fraught enterprise for many academics, these newsletter-style platforms have gained in popularity. They work on a subscription basis. Building up subscribers can be a challenge, but many academics have found surprising new audiences for their writing through them. I continue to publish essays in traditional media outlets, but I launched a newsletter of mine while working on this book, and I enjoy the less formal nature of the writing that I do there (although I miss the careful eyes and helpful suggestions of an editor). See the additional resources section for part 3 for some articles that can guide you through the process of creating a successful newsletter.

> **WRITING PROMPT:** Ideal-case scenario, the op-ed editor of your local newspaper has heard from one of your colleagues—they

> have kids in day care together—that you have a new book coming out. She invites you to write an essay, to be printed on your publication day, connected to the topic of your book. The essay must fall between 750 and 900 words (with zero wiggle room in either direction), and she would prefer if you can make a connection to a local or current issue—or both. Write that essay for her.

## Bonus Unit: Signing Copies of Your Book

One clause in a book contract might pass unnoticed by first-time authors, but it connects to a final strategy for book promotion: making strategic use of your author copies—and, when those have flown out the door, copies of your book purchased using your author discount. These are standard features of a book contract, and the numbers might vary. But typically you will be sent ten to twenty advance review copies (ARCs) of your book before its official publication date, and then you will have access to buy additional copies at a deep discount, usually in the 40 percent to 50 percent range.

At most presses, dozens of ARCs will be sent to media outlets, influential people in your field, and others you specified in your author questionnaire. Those books, and their mailing costs, will not cost you anything. But you will have the extra copies that the press has sent to you, or that you have purchased, and they can serve a variety of purposes. Of course you can give copies to your closest loved ones (I always send one to my dad, although I'm pretty sure he doesn't get beyond reading the first few pages). Pack along a copy or two when you attend conferences for serendipitous encounters with people who might appreciate your work.

But your author copies can also serve as tokens of thanks for people who have helped you promote the book: event organizers, podcast hosts, and interviewers. These folks might already own a copy; if so, sign another one and ask them to give it to a friend or colleague. At a speaking event, offer to sign one that the organizers can raffle off at the end of your talk. If you keynote an event attended by people from many organizations or institutions, and someone approaches you to inquire about your availability for future events, hand them a copy.

For all of these occasions, you will elevate the experience slightly by signing the book. Most authors append something extra to their bare signature: a word, a phrase of inspiration, a doodle. You definitely don't want to be caught off guard the first time you have to sign a book for a stranger and have to think of something to write on the spot.

I hope you will enjoy this final writing prompt, and celebrate it as your happiest promotional work as a newly published book author.

> **BONUS WRITING PROMPT:** Compose or draw whatever will appear above or below your signature in a signed copy of your book.

## ADDITIONAL RESOURCES FOR PART THREE

Derek Krissoff, "Book Marketing as Collaboration," *Book Work* (2024)
> If the notion of promoting yourself and your book is anathema to you, start your reading with this enlightening and inspiring interview between editor Derek Krissoff and author Neema Avisha, who published a highly successful university press book on growing up queer in Appalachia. Key quote: "I don't think you sell books by building a one-dimensional platform whose purpose is to sell books. I think that community and relationships sell books, and I think that social media can be a vehicle by which community and relationships get built."[10]

Jane Friedman, "A Step-by-Step Guide to Build Your Author Website," *Writer's Digest* (2021)

This piece offers exactly what the title promises, including considerations of when you might elect to seek professional help for this essential task and links to free tools for do-it-yourselfers.[11]

Allison K. Williams, "Writers, Stop Using Social Media (Like That)," Jane Friedman (2023)

This essay published on Jane Friedman's website parallels my perspective on social media: engage with it, but temper your expectations and let it foster conversations between you and readers.[12]

The OpEd Project

This organization, which was founded in 2008 to help "under-represented experts" reach new audiences through writing opinion and editorial pieces, houses terrific resources on its website (https://www.theopedproject.org/). It has an admirable and intense commitment to championing diverse voices and perspectives.

Devoney Looser, "Writing a Book or Article? Now's the Time to Create Your 'Author Platform,'" *Chronicle of Higher Education* (2018)

Looser is a Jane Austen scholar who smartly capitalized on modern-day cultural Austen-mania in a couple of crossover books. While some of the specific ideas in this column have become dated, its roll-up-your-sleeves attitude toward platform building remains current.[13]

# ACKNOWLEDGMENTS

In the prologue, I gave you a brief version of the medical ordeal that accompanied the initial creation of this book: an attack of myocarditis, months spent in the intensive care unit (ICU), and a heart transplant. I left out one important detail: during the transplant surgery, a blood clot was loosened from somewhere in my chest and traveled to my brain, causing a stroke. When I woke up from anesthesia, I had complete expressive aphasia. I had to learn to speak again from scratch, recovering and rehearsing words that I had learned fifty years ago.

This was a slow and exhausting process. The nurses drilled me on the names of the objects in my hospital room; after I came home, my wife ran flash cards with me every day. A speech therapist came to the house for a few months, giving me tests, tasks, and encouragement. The words returned, first in speech and then in writing. I remember the day that I showed something I had written to my speech therapist, like a toddler handing his stick-figure drawing to a proud parent. After I began writing again, I could feel my new heart beat with a little more energy. The demands of writing and editing the book encouraged my damaged brain to rewire itself. I can track the progress of my healing in parallel lines to its creation.

The acknowledgments for this book are thus far-reaching, extending to everyone who first saved my life and then supported me as I wrote this book. I start with the folks who kept me alive in the hospital: the cardiac team at Tufts Medical Center, especially Drs. Amanda Vest and Michael Kernahan, the overseers of my cardiac care, and Dr. Masashi Kawabori, who put a new heart into my body. At a low estimate, another fifty doctors, physician assistants, nurse practitioners, and nurses came in and out of my hospital room during my months in the ICU. They all deserve my gratitude, as do the staff members who drew blood for my labs, X-rayed and scanned me, made me food, washed my gowns, cleaned my room, and more. I thank the social workers who comforted my family and the priests and ministers who prayed over me.

After I came home from the hospital, a physical therapist and a speech therapist came to my house on a regular basis for a few months. In addition to helping me regain my lost capacities, these two women gave me hope. If you know people in these fields, thank them for their work. They are miracle workers. Thank you, Stacey and Jen.

After I was able to start writing again, what a pleasure it was to re-form my writers group and revise these chapters with the insights of Sarah Cavanagh and Mike Land. May you be blessed with such great readers and writers in your writers groups.

My agent Jessica Papin put this book into the hands of University of Chicago Press executive editor Elizabeth Branch Dyson, and working with both of them has been pleasant and productive. I'm especially grateful to Elizabeth for her comments on my many drafts, our meetings in Chicago, and her willingness to meet online when I needed help or consolation. She has had saintly patience with me. I was glad to have Lori Meek Schuldt as my sharp-eyed copy editor. Members of the editorial, production, and marketing teams at the press read parts of the manuscript to further my education about the editing, production, and marketing of a book. Much gratitude to all of them.

## ACKNOWLEDGMENTS

Many people in my community helped me and my family over the last two years, but the most important two communities in my life did the yeoman's work: my siblings (Tom, Tony, Peggy, and Bill) and my children (Katie, Madeleine, Jillian, Lucie, and Jack). Special thanks as always to my brother Tony, fellow academic and author, for running interference for me with editors and event hosts when I was in the hospital, and for launching the reading philosophy group with me when my brain woke up.

My wife Anne came to my hospital room *every day* for three months and sat with me from noon until dinnertime. I'll say again what I said before they wheeled me into my first surgery, when they advised us to say goodbye to each other in case I didn't survive: You've always been the one.

These acknowledgments must conclude with a person I have never met but who has enabled me to keep living: the anonymous donor of my heart. I will give thanks for you, and pray for your family, every day of my life.

And a plea to my readers: Donate your organs.

# NOTES

*Note: For shortened citations of books in the notes, refer to the bibliography for the full citation.*

## PROLOGUE

1. Shout-out to Parnassus Books in Yarmouth Port, Massachusetts, where I remain a frequent customer.
2. Hamilton, *Greek Way*.
3. Readers can find a full account of Hamilton's fascinating life in a recently published biography by Victoria Houseman, *American Classicist*.

## INTRODUCTION

1. In the wake of the financial troubles at the University of West Virginia, that series was closed down in 2023 and restarted in a new guise at the University of Oklahoma Press, where I now coedit it with Michelle Miller from Northern Arizona University. Derek Krissoff, with whom I cofounded the original series when he was the director of West Virginia University Press, remains with us as an editor-at-large for the new series.
2. Germano, *Getting It Published*, 234.
3. Karin Larsen, "UBC Forestry Prof Name-Dropped on Ted Lasso Says She Might Have to Start Watching Show," CBC, October 9, 2021, https://www.cbc.ca/news/canada/british-columbia/ubc-forestry-professor-ted-lasso-1.6205259.

4. You can see the scope of her labor around the book at her website: https://suzannesimard.com/.
5. Robin Bernstein, "Can You Reverse a Defeatist Habit That Sabotages Your Writing?" *Chronicle of Higher Education*, October 11, 2021, https://www.chronicle.com/article/can-you-reverse-a-defeatist-habit-that-sabotages-your-writing?
6. Bernstein, "Can You Reverse a Defeatist Habit?"

## CHAPTER ONE

1. I can't remember the details of that workshop, but I am 99 percent certain that it was conducted by my longtime mentor Ken Bain, whom you will meet in chapter 5.
2. This course overview appeared in the University of Iowa's undergraduate course catalog, accessed online July 30, 2024, https://myui.uiowa.edu/my-ui/courses/details.page?ci=146686&id=1019148.
3. For Egan's full course overview and syllabi, see BrownX, "Fantastic Places, Unhuman Humans: Exploring Humanity through Literature; ENGL102x," EdX, Brown University, accessed July 3, 2024, https://courses.edx.org/courses/course-v1:BrownX+ENGL102x+1T2018/de6ac30fb2ae41fca987a68eb42d589e/.
4. Beverly Daniel Tatum, "Why All the Black Kids Are (Still) Sitting Together in the Cafeteria (Q&A)," *Education Week*, November 1, 2017, https://www.edweek.org/leadership/opinion-why-all-the-black-kids-are-still-sitting-together-in-the-cafeteria-q-a/2017/11.
5. Hari, *Stolen Focus*, 170.
6. Jensen, *Write No Matter What*, 88.
7. Kristine Nolin, "What Makes Smoky, Charred Barbecue Taste So Good? The Chemistry of Cooking over an Open Flame," Conversation newsletter, June 3, 2022, https://theconversation.com/what-makes-smoky-charred-barbecue-taste-so-good-the-chemistry-of-cooking-over-an-open-flame-184206.
8. James M. Lang, "News Flash . . . Harvard Students Cheat, Too," *Time*, September 11, 2013, https://ideas.time.com/2013/09/11/news-flash-harvard-students-cheat-too/.
9. Benjamin Markovits, "Lord Byron Was Hard to Pin Down: That's What Makes Him Great," *New York Times*, April 19, 2024, https://www.nytimes.com/2024/04/19/books/review/lord-byron-200-years-death.html.
10. Michael S. Roth, "Happy Birthday, Kant! The Great Philosopher Was Also a Great Theorist of Education," *Chronicle of Higher Education*, April 24, 2024, https://www.chronicle.com/article/happy-birthday-kant.
11. Annoyingly, a small slice of the Stoicism community has distorted the philosophy to promote silly ideas about masculinity; one hopes that they will

eventually move on and find other ways to tell us all what it means to be a *real* man these days (eye roll).

## CHAPTER TWO

1. Roberts, *Pueblo Revolt*, 8.
2. Sword, *Air and Light and Time and Space*, 14.
3. Laufer, *Dreaming in Turtle*, 3.
4. Ehrenreich, *Nickel and Dimed*, 1.
5. Kevin Bourque, "Mapping the Literature Survey: Locating London in British Literature I," in *Teaching the Literature Survey Course: New Strategies for College Faculty* (Morgantown: West Virginia University Press, 2018), 11–30.
6. Willingham, *Outsmart Your Brain*, 6.
7. Brittany K. Robertson, "Black Women Navigating the Workplace: A Few Strategies," *Inside Higher Ed*, April 28, 2022, https://www.insidehighered.com/advice/2022/04/29/career-strategies-black-women-staff-members-higher-ed-opinion.
8. William McComas, "12 Leadership Lessons Based on 25 Years of Being Led," *Chronicle of Higher Education*, May 23, 2022, https://www.chronicle.com/article/12-leadership-lessons-based-on-25-years-of-being-led.
9. I make this criticism lightly and with all empathy, because—as you will learn at the end of this book—I understand the challenges of writing a book in the wake of a stroke.
10. Coven, *Writing on the Job*, 14.
11. Coven, *Writing on the Job*. See also PlainLanguage.gov, *Federal Plain Language Guidelines*, US General Services Administration, March 2011, https://www.plainlanguage.gov/media/FederalPLGuidelines.pdf.
12. Sword, *Stylish Academic Writing*, 133.
13. See Laymon, *Heavy*, for thought-provoking example of letters to a writer's mother.

## CHAPTER THREE

1. Olga Khazan, "The Myth of 'Learning Styles,'" *Atlantic*, April 11, 2018, https://www.theatlantic.com/science/archive/2018/04/the-myth-of-learning-styles/557687/.
2. See Silberman, *NeuroTribes*.
3. Ewing, *Ghosts in the Schoolyard*, 3.
4. Ewing, *Ghosts in the Schoolyard*, 7.
5. This story is in the public domain, and you can find free versions online.
6. Michelle Miller, *Michelle Miller's R3 Newsletter*, Substack, https://michellemillerphd.substack.com/.

7. The Learning Scientists, *The Learning Scientists* (blog), https://www.learningscientists.org/blog.
8. Kathryn Linder and Chrysanthemum Mattison Hayes, *High-Impact Practices in Online Education: Research and Best Practices* (London: Routledge, 2018), 1.
9. Martha B. Coven, "Writing about Numbers," *Inside Higher Ed*, February 22, 2023, https://www.insidehighered.com/advice/2023/02/23/tips-academics-writing-effectively-about-numbers-opinion.
10. Althea Need Kaminske, "The Benefits of Reducing Smartphone Use," *The Learning Scientists* (blog), April 21, 2023, https://www.learningscientists.org/blog/2022/4/20-1.
11. I describe this experience in more detail in James M. Lang, "Yinka Shonibare's Earth Kid (Boy) and Classroom Participation," *A General Education*, Substack, July 30, 2024, https://jamesmlang.substack.com/p/yinka-shonibares-earth-kid-boy-on.
12. Elizabeth Bruenig, "Dead Man Living," *Atlantic*, October 2, 2022, https://www.theatlantic.com/ideas/archive/2022/10/alabama-inmate-execution-alan-miller/671620/.
13. Michael Grunwald, "Why the Florida Fantasy Withstands Reality," *Atlantic*, October 1, 2022, https://www.theatlantic.com/ideas/archive/2022/10/hurricane-ian-florida-real-estate/671629/.

## CHAPTER FOUR

1. Lang, *Distracted*. See especially chapter 2, on the history of distraction and education.
2. Banjerlee and Duflo, *Poor Economics*, 1.
3. Cavanagh, *Spark of Learning*, 1.
4. Slingerland, *Drunk*, 3.
5. Ionita quoted in Matthew Reisz, "How to Write a Successful Trade Book," *Times Higher Education*, December 22, 2022, https://www.timeshighereducation.com/depth/how-write-successful-trade-book.
6. The notion of directed attention fatigue has been developed most fully by Stephen Kaplan, whose research focuses on the role that the natural world plays in restoring it. See Stephen Kaplan, "The Restorative Benefits of Nature: Toward an Integrative Framework," *Journal of Environmental Psychology* 15, no. 3 (September 1995): 169–82.
7. Michelle Faverio and Andrew Perrin, "Three-in-Ten Americans Now Read E-books," Pew Research Center, January 6, 2022, https://www.pewresearch.org/short-reads/2022/01/06/three-in-ten-americans-now-read-e-books/.
8. Gazzaly and Rosen, *Distracted Mind*, 5.
9. Gazzaly and Rosen, *Distracted Mind*, 13.
10. Kimmerer, *Braiding Sweetgrass*, 43.

11. Vanderbilt, *Beginners*, 261.
12. Laufer, *Dreaming in Turtle*, 261.
13. Hamilton, *Greek Way*, 256.
14. Ionita quoted in Reisz, "How to Write a Successful Trade Book."
15. Citton, *Ecology of Attention*, 84; italics mine.

## CHAPTER FIVE

1. Felten and Lambert, *Relationship-Rich Education*, 20. The authors attribute this phrase to David Scobey.
2. Kahneman, *Thinking, Fast and Slow*, 3.
3. Sherman Alexie, "Superman and Me," in *Writing about Writing: A College Reader*, 2nd ed., ed. Elizabeth Wardle and Douglas Downs (Boston: Bedford/St. Martin's, 2014), 129–30.
4. Kreiner, *Wandering Mind: What Medieval Monks Tell Us*, 21.
5. The following prompt produced these sentences on ChatGPT in April 2024: "Write me a three-sentence paragraph, in academic language, on why tech fasts don't improve our attention in the long term."
6. Turel Ofir, Alexander Serenko, and Nick Bontis, "Family and Work-Related Consequences of Addiction to Organizational Pervasive Technologies," *Information and Management* 48, no. 2 (2011): 88.
7. Hayot, *Elements of Academic Style*, 49.
8. Puett and Gross-Los, *Path*, 28.
9. M. Miller, *Remembering and Forgetting*; Zull, *Art of Changing the Brain*; Oakley et al., *Uncommon Sense Teaching*.
10. M. Miller, *Remembering and Forgetting*, 133–35.
11. Lowry, *Landscaping Ideas of Jays*, 121.
12. M. Miller, *Remembering and Forgetting*, 46–47.
13. Corballis, *Wandering Mind: What the Brain Does*, 15–16.
14. Kreiner, *Wandering Mind: What Medieval Monks Tell Us*, 99.
15. Kreiner, *Wandering Mind: What Medieval Monks Tell Us*, 111.

## CHAPTER SIX

1. Germano, *On Revision*, 74.
2. Percy Bysshe Shelley, "Mutability," Poetry Foundation, accessed August 5, 2024, https://www.poetryfoundation.org/poems/54563/mutability-we-are-as-clouds-that-veil-the-midnight-moon.
3. This phenomenon has been studied, for example, with preservice teachers in Mitchell J. Nathan and Anthony Petrosino, "Expert Blind Spot among Preservice Teachers," *American Educational Research Journal* 40, no. 4 (2003): 905–28.

4. Seneca, *Letters from a Stoic*, 210.
5. Forrest Wickman, "Who Really Said You Should 'Kill Your Darlings'?" *Slate*, October 18, 2013, https://slate.com/culture/2013/10/kill-your-darlings-writing-advice-what-writer-really-said-to-murder-your-babies.html.
6. King, *On Writing*, 197.
7. Germano, *On Revision*, 3.
8. Nancy Gaines Bober, "Working with a Narrator for Your Audio Book," webinar, Cape Cod Writers Center, January 2, 2023. The webinar's recording is only available to members of the center, but you can visit her website: NGB Voice, https://ngbvoice.com/.
9. Cindy Nebel, "When Revising, Read Out Loud," *The Learning Scientists* (blog), October 20, 2023, https://www.learningscientists.org/blog/2022/10/20-1.
10. Jensen, *Write No Matter What*, 137–41.
11. Jensen, *Write No Matter What*, 137.

---

## APPENDIX

1. Jane Friedman, "How to Write a Query Letter: Nonfiction and Memoir," Jane Friedman (website), January 14, 2024, https://janefriedman.com/query-letters-nonfiction-memoir/.
2. Kate McKean, "What's a Book Proposal?" *Agents and Books*, Substack, June 25, 2019, https://katemckean.substack.com/p/whats-a-book-proposal.
3. Laura Portwood-Stacer, "Advance Contracts, Explained," *Manuscript Works* (blog), May 11, 2022, https://manuscriptworks.com/blog/advance-contracts-explained.
4. "Model Trade Book Contract," Authors Guild, March 12, 2020, https://authorsguild.org/resource/model-trade-book-contract/.
5. Saller, *Subversive Copy Editor*. (See full listing in bibliography.)
6. Rachel Toor, "The Reality of Writing a Good Book Proposal," *Chronicle of Higher Education*, February 11, 2013, https://www.chronicle.com/article/the-reality-of-writing-a-good-book-proposal/.
7. Berne, *Design of Books*. (See full listing in bibliography.)
8. Jody Rein and Michael Larsen, "Secrets to Developing the Best Title for Your Nonfiction Book," Jane Friedman (website), updated July 19, 2023, https://janefriedman.com/how-to-title-your-nonfiction-book/. Originally published in Jody Rein and Michael Larsen, *How to Write a Good Book Proposal*, 5th ed. (Cincinnati: Writer's Digest Books, 2017).
9. Marion Winik, "Writing a Book Is the Easy Part: On Titles and Subtitles," *Kirkus Reviews*, October 27, 2019, https://www.kirkusreviews.com/news-and-features/articles/writing-book-easy-part-titles-and-subtitles/.
10. Derek Krissoff, "Book Marketing as Collaboration," *Book Work*, Substack,

April 22, 2024, https://derekkrissoff.substack.com/p/book-marketing-as-collaboration.

11. Jane Friedman, "A Step-by-Step Guide to Build Your Author Website," *Writer's Digest*, updated February 12, 2021, https://www.writersdigest.com/getting-published/step-step-guide-build-author-website.

12. Allison K. Williams, "Writers, Stop Using Social Media (Like That)," Jane Friedman (website), updated May 5, 2024, https://janefriedman.com/writers-stop-using-social-media-like-that/.

13. Devoney Looser, "Writing a Book or Article? Now's the Time to Create Your 'Author Platform,'" *Chronicle of Higher Education*, July 16, 2018, https://www.chronicle.com/article/writing-a-book-or-article-nows-the-time-to-create-your-author-platform/.

# BIBLIOGRAPHY

Note: This bibliography includes books from which citations were drawn and ones that were mentioned as examples of particular writing techniques. For all other citations, full bibliographic information appears in the notes.

Abraham, Laurie Kaye. *Mama Might Be Better Off Dead: The Failure of Health Care in Urban America*. Chicago: University of Chicago Press, 2019.

Baggini, Julian. *The Great Guide: What David Hume Can Teach Us about Being Human and Living Well*. Princeton, NJ: Princeton University Press, 2023.

Bain, Ken. *What the Best College Teachers Do*. Cambridge, MA: Harvard University Press, 2004.

Banerjee, Abhijit V., and Esther Duflo. *Poor Economics: A Radical Rethinking of the Way to Fight Global Poverty*. New York: Public Affairs, 2011.

Baron, Naomi S. *How We Read Now: Strategic Choices for Print, Screen, and Audio*. New York: Oxford University Press, 2021.

Bernstein, Robin. *Racial Innocence: Performing American Childhood from Slavery to Civil Rights*. New York: NYU Press, 2011.

Berne, Debbie. *The Design of Books: An Explainer for Authors, Editors, Agents, and Other Curious Readers*. Chicago: University of Chicago Press, 2024.

Bolte, Jill Taylor. *My Stroke of Insight: A Brain Scientist's Personal Journey*. New York: Penguin, 2006.

Bryson, Bill. *One Summer: America, 1927*. New York: Doubleday, 2013.

Carson, Rachel. *Silent Spring*. New York: Mariner Books, 2022.

Cavanagh, Sarah. *The Spark of Learning: Energizing the College Classroom with the Science of Emotion*. Morgantown: West Virginia University Press, 2016.

Citton, Yves. *The Ecology of Attention*. Translated by Barbary Norman. Cambridge: Polity, 2017.

Corballis, Michael. *The Wandering Mind: What the Brain Does When You're Not Looking*. Chicago: University of Chicago Press, 2015.

Coven, Martha. *Writing on the Job: Best Practices for Communicating in the Digital Age*. Princeton, NJ: Princeton University Press, 2022.

Davis, Kenneth C. *Great Short Books: A Year of Reading—Briefly*. New York: Scribner, 2022.

Ehrenreich, Barbara. *Nickel and Dimed: On (Not) Getting By in America*. New York: Henry Holt, 2001.

Ewing, Eve. *Ghosts in the Schoolyard: Racism and School Closings on Chicago's South Side*. Chicago: University of Chicago Press, 2018.

Felten, Peter, and Leo M. Lambert. *Relationship-Rich Education: How Human Connections Drive Success in College*. Baltimore: Johns Hopkins University Press, 2020.

Fogg, BJ. *Tiny Habits: The Small Changes that Change Everything*. Boston: Houghton Mifflin Harcourt, 2020.

Friedman, Jane. *The Business of Being a Writer*. 2nd ed. Chicago: University of Chicago Press, 2025.

Gazzaly, Adam, and Larry Rosen. *The Distracted Mind: Ancient Brains in a High-Tech World*. Cambridge, MA: MIT Press, 2017.

Germano, William. *Getting It Published*. Chicago: University of Chicago Press, 2016.

Germano, William. *On Revision: The Only Writing That Counts*. Chicago: University of Chicago Press, 2021.

Gessner, David. *Leave It as It Is: A Journey through Theodore Roosevelt's American Wilderness*. New York: Simon and Schuster, 2020.

Hamilton, Edith. *The Greek Way*. New York: W. W. Norton, 1964.

Hari, Johann. *Stolen Focus: Why You Can't Pay Attention—And How to Think Deeply Again*. New York: Crown, 2023.

Hayot, Eric. *The Elements of Academic Style: Writing for the Humanities*. New York: Columbia University Press, 2014.

Houseman, Victoria. *American Classicist: The Life and Loves of Edith Hamilton*. Princeton, NJ: Princeton University Press, 2023.

Jensen, Joli. *Write No Matter What*. Chicago: University of Chicago Press, 2017.

Kahneman, Daniel. *Thinking, Fast and Slow*. New York: Farrar, Strauss and Giroux, 2011.

Kimmerer, Robin Wall. *Braiding Sweetgrass: Indigenous Wisdom, Scientific Knowledge, and the Teaching of Plants*. Minneapolis: Milkweed Editions, 2013.

King, Stephen. *On Writing: A Memoir of the Craft*. New York: Scribner, 2000.

Kreiner, Jamie. *The Wandering Mind: What Medieval Monks Tell Us about Distraction*. New York: Liveright, 2023.

Lang, James M. *Cheating Lessons: Learning from Academic Dishonesty*. Cambridge, MA: Harvard University Press, 2013.

Lang, James M. *Distracted: Why Students Can't Focus and What We Can Do about It*. New York: Basic Books, 2020.

Lang, James M. *Small Teaching: Everyday Lessons from the Science of Learning*. 2nd ed. San Francisco: Jossey-Bass, 2021.

Larson, Erik. *The Devil in the White City: Murder, Magic, and Madness at the Fair that Changed America*. New York: Vintage, 2004.

Laufer, Peter. *Dreaming in Turtle: A Journey through the Passion, Profit, and Peril of Our Most Coveted Prehistoric Creatures*. New York: St. Martin's Press, 2018.

Laymon, Kiese. *Heavy: An American Memoir*. London: Bloomsbury, 2018.

Lowry, Judith Larner. *The Landscaping Ideas of Jays: A Natural History of the Backyard Restoration Garden*. Berkeley: University of California Press, 2007.

Lukacs, John. *Five Days in London, May 1940*. New Haven, CT: Yale University Press, 2001.

Miller, Lulu. *Why Fish Don't Exist: A Story of Loss, Love, and the Hidden Order of Life*. New York: Simon and Schuster, 2020.

Miller, Michelle. *Remembering and Forgetting in the Age of Technology: Teaching, Learning, and the Science of Memory in a Wired World*. Morgantown: West Virginia University Press, 2022.

Nathan, Rebekah. *My Freshman Year: What a Professor Learned by Becoming a Student*. New York: Penguin, 2005.

Oakley, Barbara, Beth Rogowsky, and Terrence Sejnowski. *Uncommon Sense Teaching: Practical Insights in Brain Science to Help Students Learn*. New York: TarcherPerigee, 2021.

Portwood-Stacer, Laura. *The Book Proposal Book: A Guide for Scholarly Authors*. Princeton, NJ: Princeton University Press, 2021.

Puett, Michael, and Christine Gross-Loh. *The Path: What Chinese Philosophers Can Teach Us about the Good Life*. New York: Simon and Schuster, 2016.

Roberts, David. *The Pueblo Revolt: The Secret Rebellion that Drove the Spaniards Out of the Southwest*. New York: Simon and Schuster, 2005.

Saller, Carol Fisher. *The Subversive Copy Editor: Advice from Chicago (or, How to Negotiate Good Relationships with Your Writers, Your Colleagues, and Yourself)*. 2nd ed. Chicago: University of Chicago Press, 2016.

Sapolsky, Robert M. *Why Zebras Don't Get Ulcers: A Guide to Stress, Stress-Related Diseases, and Coping*. New York: W. H. Freeman, 1995.

Schumacher, Julie. *Dear Committee Members: A Novel*. New York: Vintage, 2015.

Seneca. *Letters from a Stoic*. Translated by Robin Campbell. London: Penguin, 2004.

Silberman, Steve. *NeuroTribes: The Legacy of Autism and the Future of Neurodiversity*. New York: Avery, 2015.

Simard, Suzanne. *Finding the Mother Tree: Discovering the Wisdom of the Forest*. New York: Penguin, 2021.

Singh, Simon. *Fermat's Last Theorem*. New York: HarperCollins, 2012.

Slingerland, Edward. *Drunk: How We Sipped, Danced, and Stumbled Our Way to Civilization*. New York: Little, Brown Spark, 2021.

Sword, Helen. *Air and Light and Time and Space: How Successful Academics Write*. Cambridge, MA: Harvard University Press, 2017.

Sword, Helen. *Stylish Academic Writing*. Cambridge, MA: Harvard University Press, 2012.

Tatum, Beverly Daniel. *Why Are All the Black Kids Sitting Together in the Cafeteria? And Other Conversations about Race*. 20th anniversary ed. New York: Basic Books, 2017.

Vanderbilt, Tom. *Beginners: The Joy and Transformative Power of Lifelong Learning*. New York: Knopf, 2021.

Wadham, Jemma. *Ice Rivers: A Story of Glaciers, Wilderness, and Humanity*. Princeton, NJ: Princeton University Press, 2021.

Willingham, Daniel. *Outsmart Your Brain: Why Learning Is Hard and How You Can Make It Easy*. New York: Gallery Books, 2023.

Zull, James. *The Art of Changing the Brain*. 2003. Reprint, New York: Routledge, 2023.

# INDEX

Abraham, Laurie Kaye, 34
academic writing, 5–7, 173–74, 206; expert blind spots, 155, 158; jargon, 121; paragraphs, 125–26; transitions, neglect of, 155
accessible writing style, 117
adding, 157, 160; background knowledge, filling gaps in, 158–59, 167; better company, 159, 167; blind spots, 158–59; invitation to think, 159–60, 167; missing parts, 158
advance review copies (ARCs), 213
*Aeon* (magazine), 22–23
*Agents and Books* (McKean), 191–92
aha moment, 37
*Air and Light and Time and Space: How Successful Academics Write* (Sword), 44
Alexie, Sherman, 127
allusions, 134–35, 146, 159
Amazon, 86–87
Aristotle, xi, 47
*Aristotle's Way: How Ancient Wisdom Can Change Your Life* (Hall), 45

artificial intelligence (AI), 13, 33, 147; AI Callouts, 166. *See also* generative artificial intelligence (AI)
assignments, 175
*Atlantic* (magazine), 22–23, 81, 211
attention, 112; attention tools, 113; closing, 113–14; cognitive breaks, 90; distraction, 89; joint attention, 114–15; supporting, 90–91; text divisions and breaks, 113; writer's tools of, 91
Aurelius, Marcus, 34, 47–48
Austen, Jane, 215

backlist, 36
*Bad Feminist* (Gay), 156
Baggini, Julian, 106
Bain, Ken, 116, 222n1
Banjerlee, Abhijit V., 92–93
Banksy, 135
Baron, Naomi, 21
Basic Books, 180
Beckett, Samuel, 96–97

*Beginners: The Joy and Transformative Power of Lifelong Learning* (Vanderbilt), 110
Bellevue Literary Press, 180
Berne, Debbie, 203
Bernstein, Robin, 14
Berry, Wendell, 66
Big Ideas, 18, 23–24, 27–28, 32, 58
"Black Women Navigating the Workplace: A Few Strategies" (Robertson), 51
blind spots, 155, 158–59
blogs, 7, 75, 78
Bober, Nancy Gaines, 164–65
"Book Marketing as Collaboration" (Krissoff), 214
*Book Proposal Book, The: A Guide for Scholarly Authors* (Portwood-Stacer), 176
book topics: celebrations and anniversaries, 33; change your audience, 19; consider purpose, 35–36; creating better ideas, 23–25, 27; current events, 32; dialogue with other answers, 18; disciplinary discoveries, 33; identifying questions, 18–24, 35–38; making new connections, 35; present moment, 19, 32, 34–35; seasons and cycles, 33; subtitles, 20–21; timeliness, 32–34, 36, 38; topical, 34
*Boston Globe* (newspaper), 159
Bourque, Kevin, 48
*Braiding Sweetgrass: Indigenous Wisdom, Scientific Knowledge, and the Teaching of Plants* (Kimmerer), 104–5
Bruenig, Elizabeth, 81–82
Bryson, Bill, 46
*Business of Being a Writer, The* (Friedman), 176

BuzzFeed, 48–49
Byron, Lord, 33

Cape Cod Writers Community, 164
Carson, Rachel, 47
Cavanagh, Sarah, 92–94
Center for Teaching Excellence, 4
*Cheating Lessons* (Lang), 32
Chicago (Illinois), 69, 77; Bronzeville, 68
*Chronicle of Higher Education* (magazine), 24, 33, 98–99, 211–12; "Advice" section, 51
Churchill, Winston, 46
*Cigar Aficionado* (magazine), 145
Citton, Yves, 114
classrooms: physical space of, 39–40; time, 40
closings: asking or prompting questions, 110–11; call for action, 110; closing the loop, 111–12; final story, 109
confidence, 15
Confucius, 132
connectivity, 205
Conversation (online news source), 31
Corballis, Michael, 140
course description, 16–18
Coven, Martha, 59, 77
COVID-19 pandemic, 25, 46, 162
crossover books, 215
curation, 51
cutting, 160, 163; "kill your darlings," 161–62; throughline, detouring from, 162, 167

data, 67–68. *See also* evidence
Davis, Kenneth C., 46
*Dear Committee Members* (Schumacher), 63

*Design of Books, The: An Explainer for Authors, Editors, Agents, and Other Curious Readers* (Berne), 203
*Devil in the White City, The* (Larson), 63
Dickinson, Emily: as lover of the dash, 103
directed attention fatigue, 96, 224n6
*Distracted: Why Students Can't Focus and What We Can Do about It* (Lang), 86–87
*Distracted Mind, The* (Gazzaly and Rosen), 101
*Dreaming in Turtle: A Journey Through the Passion, Profit, and Peril of Our Most Coveted Prehistoric Creatures* (Laufer), 44, 110
*Drunk: How We Sipped, Danced, and Stumbled Our Way to Civilization* (Slingerland), 92
Duflo, Esther, 92–93

*Ecology of Attention, The* (Citton), 114
editorial and book production processes, 192; acknowledgments, 202; author questionnaire, 196–98; book covers, 199–200; copyediting, 194; editing, 193–94; indexing, 195; proofreading, 194; title and subtitle, 200–201
Egan, James, 17–18
Ehrenreich, Barbara, 44
*Elements of Academic Style, The* (Hayot), 130
English composition, 39
Epictetus, 34
evidence, 66; contextualizing, 67, 75–81, 85–86, 88; Gen AI, 71–72; high context, 79; how much, 67; linking back to main idea, 80; list of, 70; low context, 78; medium context, 78–79; stories as evidence, 67, 75, 81–88; streamlining, 72–75, 85; telling great stories, 81–86; varying, 67–70, 85, 87–88. *See also* data
Ewing, Eve, 68–69, 77
expanding readership, 5, 8, 12, 14, 66–67, 75, 139, 173; awareness of audience, 7; good company, 139; particular audiences, tuning and retuning of, 6; writing, tailoring of, 7

Faulkner, William, 160–61
Felton, Peter, 147
Fermat, Pierre de, 63
*Fermat's Last Theorem* (Singh), 63
*Finding the Mother Tree: Discovering the Wisdom of the Forest* (Simard), 9–10
first drafts, 149–50
*Five Days in London* (Lukacs), 46
Fleming, Michael, 92
Fogg, BJ, 28
Friedman, Jane, 176, 191, 203, 214–15

Gay, Roxanne, 156–57
Gazzaly, Adam. 101
generative artificial intelligence (AI), 146, 148; ChatGPT, 12–13, 26–27, 71, 225n5; Copilot, 12–13; Claude, 12–13; GenAI Callouts, 13, 26–27, 52–53, 71–72, 98–99, 147, 166; section breaks and section headings, 98–99. *See also* artificial intelligence (AI)
Germano, William, 8, 151–52, 164, 176
Gessner, David, 109
*Getting It Published: A Guide for Scholars and Anyone Else Serious about Serious Books* (Germano), 8, 176

*Ghosts in the Schoolyard: Racism and School Closings on Chicago's South Side* (Ewing), 68–69
gift of learning, 14
good ideas, 24–25
Goodreads, 86–87
Google alerts, 33
*Great Guide, The: What David Hume Can Teach Us about Being Human and Living Well* (Baggini), 106
great ideas, 25, 29
*Great Short Books: A Year of Reading—Briefly* (Davis), 46
*Greek Way, The* (Hamilton), x–xi, 171
Grunwald, Michael, 82–83
*Guardians of the Galaxy* (film), 136

Hall, Edith, 45
Hamilton, Edith, x–xiii, 4, 110–11, 171
Hari, Johann, 29
*Harper's* (magazine), 81
Harvard University, 32
Harvard University Press, 180
Hay Literary Festival, 10
Hayot, Eric, 130
Hemingway, Ernest, 33
Hitler, Adolf, 46
Homer, x, 134–35
hooks, bell, 111
"How Much Land Does a Man Need?" (Tolstoy), 72
"How to Write a Query Letter: Nonfiction and Memoir" (Friedman), 191
*How We Read Now: Strategic Choices for Print, Screen, and Audio* (Baron), 21
Hume, David, 106
*Hunger* (Gay), 156

*Ice Rivers: A Story of Glaciers, Wilderness, and Humanity* (Wadham), 34
idea breeding, 27
idea hybridity, 24
*Inside Higher Ed* (magazine), 211–12; "Career Advice" section, 51
invitational language, 117; learning tools of, 118; managing vocabulary, 121–22; paragraphs, 125–29; simplifying sentences, 123–25
invitational prose, 120, 122, 127–28, 142, 145, 159; generative AI, 146–47
invitations to think, 118, 130, 159–60; allusions, 134–35, 146; attending to readers in the room, 119; being good company, 137–42, 146; everyday examples, 131–32, 135; metaphors, 132–34, 146; prompts and questions, 136–37; readers in room, 142–46; thought experiments, 135–36; writer as good company, 119
Ionita, Casiana, 92–93, 112

*Jane Eyre* (Brontë), 45
jargon, 121
Jensen, Joli, 30, 60, 168–69
joint attention, 114–15
Jordan, David Starr, 139
*Journal of Applied Research in Memory and Cognition* (journal), 165–66

Kahneman, Daniel, 121–22
Kant, Immanuel, 33
Kaplan, Stephen, 224n6
Keats, John, 134
"kill your darlings," 160–62
Kimmerer, Robin Wall, 104–5
King, Stephen, 161

Kreiner, Jamie, 108, 127–28, 141
Krissoff, Derek, 214, 221n1

Lambert, Leo, 147
*Landscaping Ideas of Jays, The: A Natural History of the Backyard Restoration Garden* (Lowry), 134
Lang Evidence Ratio, 73
Larsen, Michael, 203
Larson, Erik, 63
Laufer, Peter, 44, 110
learning objectives, 16, 30–32, 38, 117, 174–75
learning process, 120, 147
Learning Scientists, 74–75, 78
learning styles, 65; kinesthetic, 66; visual, 66
*Leave It as It Is: A Journey through Theodore Roosevelt's American Wilderness* (Gessner), 109
life stories, 63
LinkedIn, 169–70
listening, 163, 166; common or tired words, relying on, 165, 167; favorite words, relying on, 165; identifying mistakes, 165; overextending phrases and sentences, 165; proofreading, 168; reading out loud, 164–65, 167–68
lists, 54–55, 60, 62; categories, 50; complexity, 50; hierarchy, 50; knowledge, understanding, and inspiration, 50; mix and match, 51–52; organizing principles, 49–50, 52; revision and experimentation, 50
literature reviews, 75–76
Looser, Devoney, 215
*Lord of the Rings, The* (Tolkien), 45
Lowry, Judith Larner, 134
Lukacs, John, 46

Macmillan, 19
*Mama Might Be Better Off Dead: The Failure of Health Care in Urban America* (Abraham), 34
*Manuscript Works, The* (Portwood-Stacer), 192
*Mass Audubon Society* (magazine), 144
McComas, William, 51
McKean, Kate, 191
Medium, 179, 212
metaphors, 132–34, 144, 146
Miller, Lulu, 139–40
Miller, Michelle, 74, 133, 136, 221n1
mission statements, 30, 60
"Model Trade Book Contract" (Authors Guild), 192
Mollick, Ethan, 26
moving, 151; digital writing programs, 154, 167; internal logic, 152; movable table of contents, 152–53, 167; reorganizational tools, 152; scissors, 153–54, 167
Musk, Elon, 207–8
*My Freshman Year: What a Professor Learned by Becoming a Student* (Nathan), 46
*My Stroke of Insight: A Brain Scientist's Personal Journey* (Taylor), 52

narratives, 42, 45, 60, 62; braided, 63; chronological, 46–48, 52; geographical mapping, 48; *in medias res*, 47; nonchronological, 47; pacing, 54
Nathan, Rebekah, 46
New Directions, 180
*New Yorker* (magazine), 81, 98, 211
*New York Times* (newspaper), 144, 156–57

*Nickel and Dimed: On (Not) Getting By in America* (Ehrenreich), 44
Nolin, Kristine, 31
nonfiction reading: element of surprise, 12
Norton, 180

Obama, Barack, 59
*Odyssey* (Homer), x, 134–35
Oliver, Mary, 66
*One Summer: America, 1927* (Bryson), 46
"On First Looking into Chapman's Homer" (Keats), 134–35
OpEd Project, 215
opening sentences: intriguing facts, 94; provocative statements, 95; quotations, 94–95; shocking statistics, 94; stories, 94
*On Revision: The Only Writing That Counts* (Germano), 151–52, 164
*On Writing* (King), 161
Orwell, George, 44
outlines: reverse, 61; sentence, 60
*Outsmart Your Brain: Why Learning Is Hard and How You Can Make It Easy* (Willingham), 49

pacing, 42, 53, 55, 61–62, 64; interludes, 56; moments of surprise, 54; narratives, 54; quests, 54
Parnassus Books, 221n1
*Path, The: What Chinese Philosophers Can Teach Us about the Good Life* (Puett and Gross-Loh), 132
peer review: book contract offer, 190; contract, 190–91; invitation, 190; pass, 189–90; rejection, 190; revise, respond, or both, 190
philomath, 171–72
platform building, 10–11, 179, 215
Plato, xi, 135–36

*Poetics* (Aristotle), 47
polymath, 171
*Poor Economics: A Radical Rethinking of the Way to Fight Global Poverty* (Banjerlee and Duflo), 92
Portwood-Stacer, Laura, 176, 192
Princeton University Press, 180
promotion, 203; author websites, 204–5, 209–10; publishing essays based on book's subject, 210–12; signing copies, 213–14; social media, 206–8, 210
publishing process: editorial, 176; promotion, 176; submission, 176–91
*Pueblo Revolt, The: The Secret Rebellion That Drove the Spaniards Out of the Southwest* (Roberts), 43
"purple prose," 83–84
Pythagoras, 63

queries, 186–89
quests, 42–45, 60, 62; pacing, 54
Quiller-Couch, Arthur, 161
Quoll Writer, 154, 167

*Racial Innocence: Performing American Childhood from Slavery to Civil Rights* (Bernstein), 14
Random House, 180
reader attention: intriguing facts, 94; openings, 91–95; provocative statements, 95; quotations, 94–95; shocking statistics, 94; stories, 94; text breaks, 98, 113; text divisions, 95–98; titled sections and subsections, 98. *See also* small attention tools
reader comments, 86–87
reading experience: as learning experience, 91
"Read Sample" features, 22

"Reality of a Writing of a Good Book Proposal, The" (Toor), 202–3
recycling file, 163
Rein, Jody, 203
*Relationship-Rich Education* (Felten and Lambert), 147
*Remembering and Forgetting* (Miller), 136
*Republic* (Plato): as extended thought experiment, 135
required readings, 175–76
revision: adding, 150, 157–58, 167; background knowledge, 158–59; better company, 159; cutting, 150, 160–63, 167; digital writing programs, 154; listening, 151, 163–68; major acts of, 150; missing parts, 158; movable table of contents, 152–53; moving, 150–52, 167; reorganizational tools, 152–54; scissors, 153–54; transitions, 154–57; writers groups, 168
Roberts, David, 43
Robertson, Brittany K., 51
Robertson, Donald, 47–48
Roosevelt, Theodore, 109
Rosen, Larry, 101
runoff file, 162

Saller, Carol Fisher, 202
Sapolsky, Robert, 19, 35
Schumacher, Julie, 63
Scrivener, 154, 167
"Secrets to Developing the Best Title for Your Nonfiction Book" (Rein and Larsen), 203
Seneca, 34, 159–60
Shelley, Percy Bysshe, 152
*Silent Spring* (Carson), 47
Simard, Suzanne, 8–10
similes, 132
Singh, Simon, 63

Slingerland, Edward, 92–93
small attention tools: boldface, 100–102, 106; bullets and lists, 105–6; closings, 108–14; exclamation points, 104; graphs and tables, 107–8; italics, 100–102; paragraph length, 104–5; punctuation, 103; Venn diagrams, 107. *See also* reader attention
*Small Teaching* (Lang), 49–50
social media, 7, 10, 86, 206–8, 210
Socrates, 135
*Spark of Learning, The: Energizing the College Classroom with the Science of Emotion* (Cavanagh), 92
"Step-by-Step Guide to Build Your Author Website, A" (Friedman), 214–15
Stoicism, 35, 47–48, 222–23n11
*Stolen Focus: Why You Can't Pay Attention—And How to Think Deeply Again* (Hari), 29
structures, 40, 64; braided narratives, 63; choices, 41–43; guided tours, 62; life stories, 63; lists, 42–52, 54–55, 62; narratives, 42, 45–48, 60, 62; pacing, 42; quests, 42–45, 60, 62; throughlines, 42, 56–61
submission, 177; agent requirements, 182; author questionnaires, 174; guidelines, 181; laying groundwork, 178–79; platforms, 178–79; proposals, 174; publications, 178–79; queries, 174, 186–89; researching publishers, 180–83; writing book proposals, 183–86
Substack, 71, 75, 179, 212
*Subversive Copy Editor, The: Advice from Chicago (or, How to Negotiate Good Relationships with Your Writers, Your Colleagues, and Yourself)* (Saller), 202

"Superman and Me" (Alexie), 127
survey courses, 48
Swift, Taylor, 135
Sword, Helen, 44, 61, 163
syllabus, 11, 16, 30, 137, 174–75, 177

Tatum, Beverly Daniel, 20, 35
Taylor, Jill Bolte, 52, 55
teaching online, 25
*Teaching to Transgress* (hooks), 111
teaching workshops, 16
*Ted Lasso* (television series), 9
text divisions, 95–97; text breaks, 98; titled sections and subsections, 98
*Thinking, Fast and Slow* (Kahneman), 121
throughlines, 42, 62, 64; cramming, be wary of, 58; creative headings, 59–60; losing of, 57; maintaining of, 56–61; outlines, 60–61; question headings, 59–60; reminders of, 59–60; reverse outlines, 61; running outline, 60; sentence outlines, 60; statement headings, 59–60; strategies of, 58–61; topic headings, 59–60
*Time* (magazine), 32
timeliness, 32–34, 36, 38
*Tiny Habits: The Small Changes That Change Everything* (Fogg), 28
Tolstoy, Leo, 67, 72
Toor, Rachel, 202–3
transitions, 151–52, 154, 160; expert blind spots, 155; repetition and echo, 156–57; subtitles and headings, 155–56; words of order and relationship, 156
Tulley, Christine, 153
"12 Leadership Lessons Based on 25 Years of Being Led" (McComas), 51
Twitter, 207–8

United Kingdom, 23–24
University of Chicago Press, 180
University of Iowa, 222n2
University of Oklahoma Press, 221n1
Utah State University Press, 180

Vanderbilt, Tom, 110

Wadham, Jemma, 34
*Wall Street Journal* (newspaper), 144
*Wandering Mind, The: What the Brain Does When You're Not Looking* (Corballis), 140–41
*Wandering Mind, The: What Medieval Monks Tells Us about Distraction* (Kreiner), 108, 127–29, 141
Welty, Eudora, 160–61
West Virginia University Press, 4–5, 25, 221n1
*What the Best Teachers Do* (Bain), 116
"'Why Are All the Black Kids Sitting Together in the Cafeteria?' And Other Conversations about Race" (Tatum), 20
*Why Fish Don't Exist: A Story of Loss, Love, and the Hidden Order of Life* (Miller), 139
Wilde, Oscar, 160–61
Wiles, Andrew, 63
Williams, Allison K., 215
Willingham, Daniel, 49, 55
Winik, Marion, 203
Woo, Michelle, 166
words, sentences, paragraphs, 119–20, 128–30, 145–46; active voice, 125; loss of focus, 126; managing vocabulary, 121–23; object-verb-subject, 124; passive voice, 124–25; purpose of, 127; simplifying sentences, 123–25; subject-verb-object, 124; topic sentences, 126–27; transition sentences, 126;

using active verbs, 124; volume reduction, 126

*Write No Matter What: Advice for Academics* (Jensen), 30, 168–69

"Writers, Stop Using Media (Like That)" (Williams), 215

writers groups: LinkedIn, 169–70; revision process, 168; support groups and content critique groups, distinction between, 168–69

writer's tools of attention: capturing, 91; closing strategies, 91; openings, 91–94; small attention tools, 91; text divisions, 91, 95–98

writing: teaching, connection between, xii–xiii, 1–3

writing assignments, 179, 186

"Writing a Book Is the Easy Part: On Titles and Subtitles" (Winik), 203

"Writing a Book or Article? Now's the Time to Create Your Author Platform" (Looser), 215

writing book proposals: author biography, 185; chapter outlines, 184; competition, 184–85; marketing, promotion, or audience, 185; overview, 184; samples, 186; specifications and manuscript status, 185–86

writing for the public, 7–11, 14–15, 30

writing habits to break: overextending phrases and sentences, 165; relying on common or tired words, 165; relying on favorite words, 165

*Writing on the Job: Best Practices for Communicating in the Digital Age* (Coven): heading types, taxonomy of, 59–60

writing prompts, 12, 30, 38, 56, 64, 88, 115, 137, 148, 170, 175, 182–83, 195–96, 198, 200–202, 205, 208, 210, 212–14

writing strategies, 6–7, 13, 30, 91, 118, 151, 173

writing styles: accessible, 117; book publishers, 145; good company, 139; political leanings, 144; publication, specific focus, 143–44; regional focus, 144; targeted audience, 143

writing techniques, 4, 146

X, 207. *See also* Twitter